ABOUT THE BOOK

The current failure of so many religious institutions, along with the spiritual emptiness pervading late-modern industrial societies, can't be blamed just on "secularization." So many sincere people thirst for spiritual meaning, yet they don't find it in failing religious institutions. At the same time, so many sincere people are spiritually despairing over the refusal by hyper-masculine global elites of Modern Industrial Civilization to turn away from their profitable but anti-ecological systems, which are so rapidly devastating the creative communion of life across our loving Creator's beloved planet Earth.

In this ground-breaking book, eco-philosopher and Catholic theologian Joe Holland links those two challenges. Principal author of the widely read text *Social Analysis: Linking Faith and Justice* and ghostwriter for two highly praised *Appalachian Pastoral Letters*, he insightfully explores the late-modern breakdowns of both civilization and spirituality. He correlates the social and ecological breakdown of Modern Industrial Civilization with its deeper cultural breakdown of Modern Psychological Spirituality, which is found in both Catholic and Protestant forms, as well as in other religious forms. At the same time, he explores the emergence, albeit still only seminal, of Postmodern Ecological Spirituality, which is already planting regenerative seeds for a future Postmodern Ecological Civilization.

This challenging book provides essential background for: 1) understanding at the deep level the interwoven late-modern global devastation of ecological, societal, and spiritual life; and 2) seeking at the deep level the holistic postmodern global regeneration of ecological, social, and spiritual life, which Pope Francis has called "integral ecology."

ABOUT THE AUTHOR

 JOE" HOLLAND is an eco-philosopher and Catholic-Christian theologian exploring the global transition to Postmodern Ecological Civilization..

Joe completed his Ph.D. from the University of Chicago in the field of Ethics & Society, an interdisciplinary dialogue of Theology with Philosophy and Social Science. At Chicago, he studied Theology with David Tracy, Philosophy with Paul Ricoeur, and Social Science with Gibson Winter. He was also a Fulbright Scholar in Philosophy at the Universidad Católica in Santiago, Chile during the last year of the democratic-socialist government of Salvador Allende, which was overthrown by the murderous dictatorship of General Augusto Pinochet.

Joe is Emeritus Professor of Philosophy & Religion at Saint Thomas University in Miami Gardens, Florida and Adjunct Professor in its School of Law; Permanent Visiting Professor at the Universidad Nacional del Altiplano in Puno, Peru; President of Pax Romana / Catholic Movement for Intellectual & Cultural Affairs - USA and Editor of its Pacem in Terris Press, with both based in Washington DC; Vice-Chair of Catholic Scholars for Worker Justice, with offices in in Boston, Massachusetts and at Georgetown University in Washington DC; and a member of the International Association for Catholic Social Thought, based at the Catholic University of Leuven in Belgium.

Earlier, Joe served for 15 years as Research Associate at the Washington DC Center of Concern, created jointly by the international Jesuits and the US Catholic Bishops to work with the United Nations on global issues. Later, he taught at New York Theological Seminary in New York City, at the Theological School of Drew University in Madison, New Jersey, and at the Florida Center for Theological Studies in Miami, Florida. For both the Center of Concern and Pax Romana, he served as NGO Representative to the Economic and Social Council of the United Nations in New York City.

Joe also served as Research Coordinator for the 1976 Theology in the Americas Conference. In addition, he co-founded the American Catholic Lay Network, the National Conference on Religion & Labor (co-sponsored by the AFL-CIO), and Catholic Scholars for Worker Justice. Plus, he was founding Director of the Pallottine Institute for Lay Leadership & Research at Seton Hall University.

Joe has published 15 other books and many articles. His book with Peter Henriot, *Social Analysis: Linking Faith and Justice*, has more than 100,000 copies in print, including 2 US editions, 5 foreign-language editions, and 2 foreign English editions. He was also writer for the 1975 document *This Land is Home to Me* (A Pastoral Letter on Powerlessness in Appalachia by the Catholic Bishops of the Region), and for its 1995 sequel document *At Home in the Web of Life* (A Pastoral Message from the Catholic Bishops of Appalachia on Sustainable Communities).

In the United States, Joe has lectured at Georgetown, Harvard, Notre Dame, Princeton, and many other universities. Internationally, he has lectured at Institut Catholique in Paris, France; Sophia University in Tokyo, Japan; Pontifical Catholic University in São Paulo, Brazil; Pontifical Catholic University in Porto Alegre, Brazil; Universidad Mayor de San Andres in La Paz, Bolivia; and Universidad Nacional del Altiplano in Puno, Peru.

In 1986, Joe received the Boston Paulist Center's Isaac Hecker Award for Social Justice; in 2002, the Athena Medal of Excellence from the Universidad Nacional del Altiplano in Puno, Peru; and in 2013 the Irish Echo's Labor Award for contribution to the US labor movement. Joe is married to Paquita Biascoechea Holland, a native of Puerto Rico, and they have two wonderful grown children and four wonderful young grandchildren. His too infrequent hobby is sailing, especially in the beautiful green waters of the Caribbean Sea.

POSTMODERN ECOLOGICAL SPIRITUALITY

Catholic-Christian Hope
for the Dawn of a Postmodern Ecological Civilization
Rising from within the Spiritual Dark Night
of Modern Industrial Civilization

JOE HOLLAND

www.joe-holland.net

PACEM IN TERRIS PRESS

Devoted to the global vision of Saint John XXIII,
prophetic founder of Postmodern Catholic Social Teaching,
and in support of the search for a Postmodern Ecological Civilization,
which will seek to learn from the rich spiritual wisdom-traditions
of Christianity and of our entire global human family.

www.paceminterrispress.com

ISBN-13: 978-0692503225
ISBN-10: 0692503226

Published preliminary form 20187-07-01
Final form with corrections 2017-08-01

Pacem in Terris Press publishes scholarly books directly or indirectly related to
Catholic Social Teaching and its commitment to justice, peace, ecology,
and spirituality, and on behalf of the search for a Postmodern Ecological Civilization.

In addition, in order to support ecumenical and interfaith dialogue, as well as dialogue
with other spiritual seekers, Pacem in Terris Press publishes scholarly books from other
Christian perspectives, from other religious perspectives, and from perspectives
of other spiritual seekers that promote justice, peace, ecology,
and spirituality for our global human family.

Opinions or claims expressed in publications from Pacem in Terris Press
represent the opinions and claims of the authors and do not necessarily represent
the official position of Pacem in Terris Press, the Pacem in Terris Ecological Initiative,
Pax Romana / Catholic Movement for Intellectual & Cultural Affairs - USA
or its officers, directors, members, and staff.

PACEM IN TERRIS PRESS
is the publishing service of

PAX ROMANA
Catholic Movement for Intellectual & Cultural Affairs
USA
1025 Connecticut Avenue NW, Suite 1000,
Washington DC 20036
www.paceminterris.net

This book is dedicated
to my visionary and inspiring friend Mabel Gil.
She grew up linked to the Catholic Worker movement,
along with her childhood playmate, the late Tamar Hennessy,
who was the daughter of Servant of God Dorothy Day.
Peter Maurin, co-founder of the movement with Dorothy Day
tutored both Mabel and Tamar in his prophetic vision.
Now in her nineties, Mabel is still speaking out
with the powerful voice of prophetic love.

This book is also dedicated
to my many and dear friends in the Maryknoll family
of brothers, lay members, priests, and sisters,
for their heroic and holy dedication to the Gospel of Jesus the Christ,
in service of global mercy, justice, peace, ecology, truth, and love;

And to the memory of Sister Margaret Clare Dreckman (1917-2006),
past leader of the Sisters of Saint Francis of Dubuque, Iowa,
long filled with the charismatic power of the Holy Spirit,
wise spiritual counselor to me and to so many others,
and dear friend;

And also to the memory of Venerable Solanus Casey (1870-1957),
member of the Capuchin branch of the followers of St. Francis of Assisi,
lover of the poor and the sick,
and Spirit-filled instrument of God's healing power.

Yours are the heavens, and yours is the earth:
the world and its fullness you have founded ...

PSALM 89: 12

Those who live on the land can hardly fail to appreciate the
nobility of the work they are called upon to do.
They are living in close harmony with Nature – the majestic temple of Creation.
Their work has to do with the life of plants and animals,
a life that is inexhaustible in its expression,
inflexible in its laws, rich in allusions to
God the Creator and Provider.

SAINT JOHN XXIII
MATER ET MAGISTRA

An ecological spirituality ... can motivate us to
a more passionate concern for the protection of our world ...
The ecological crisis is also a summons to profound interior conversion ...
What [we] need is an "ecological conversion"...
a loving awareness that we are not disconnected from the rest of creatures,
but joined in a splendid universal communion ...
[with] awareness that each creature reflects something of God
and has a message to convey to us.

FRANCIS OF ROME
CARE FOR OUR COMMON HOME

TABLE OF CONTENTS

PREFACE

In 2013, when beginning to work on this project, I did not yet know that Pope Francis (elected as Bishop of Rome in that same year) would issue his great 2015 ecological encyclical, LAUDATO SI' - ON CARE FOR OUR COMMON HOME.[1] Nor did I know that, in his prophetic document, he would explicitly call for "ecological spirituality."[2] When Francis' great document did appear, I was already well advanced into the manuscript for this book. The timing was certainly coincidental, and I hope also providential.

Francis' great ecological encyclical addresses what he calls "integral ecology," which means holistic ecology. With that concept, Francis integrates concern for natural ecology with concern for human ecology, and especially in relation to humans who are poor or in any way vulnerable. At the same time, he links his integrated concepts of human ecology and natural ecology with his call for "ecological spirituality," which we might also describe as mystical-prophetic "spiritual ecology."

---

[1] For the Vatican's official English text of this encyclical letter, see:
http://w2.vatican.va/content/francesco/en/encyclicals/documents/papa-francesco_20150524_enciclica-laudato-si.html. (Accessed 2015-07-15.)

[2] See the encyclical's "Chapter Six: Ecological Education and Spirituality," Par. 216.

In this book, I propose further integrating Francis' concept of "integral ecology" – again, including natural ecology and human ecology – with the rephrasing of his concept of "ecological spirituality" as "spiritual ecology." I propose integrating those three concepts into a single comprehensive framework that I call the "*evolving creative communion of life's integral ecology*," or more simply "ecological co-creativity."[3]

Within this comprehensive framework, I also propose that we understand all of cosmic creation, which we now know is evolving, as analogously alive. This proposed comprehensive framework understands all of cosmic creation as both holistic and evolving, and as embracing *the interwoven natural, human, and spiritual fabric of life's integral ecology,* across our loving Creator's beloved garden-planet Earth.

First of Three Interrelated Books

In its relation to the papal encyclical tradition, this book has had a curious genesis. It unexpectedly turned out to be the third in a series of three interrelated manuscripts, yet the first of the three to be published.

The first manuscript, long ago largely completed, investigates the prophetic social teachings of Saint John XXIII, who was Bishop of Rome ("pope") from 1958-1963. That manuscript is tentatively titled THE PROPHETIC GLOBAL VISION OF SAINT JOHN XXIII: RADICAL-TRADITIONAL FOUNDER OF POSTMODERN CATHOLIC SOCIAL TEACHING.

While working on that manuscript about John, a haunting voice told me that, before publishing it, I should write and publish a second manuscript. That manuscript, the voice said, should address the late modern breakdown of what I call here (in perhaps a too complex phrasing) "Modern Western Industrial-Colonial Civilization," or more simply "*Modern Industrial Civilization*."

---

[3] For an initial exploration of the creative communion of life, see my earlier book, CREATIVE COMMUNION: TOWARD A SPIRITUALITY OF WORK (Paulist Press, 1989).

2

That second manuscript is tentatively titled SOCIAL ANALYSIS II – END OF THE MODERN WORLD: TOWARD A REGENERATIVE POSTMODERN GLOBAL ECOLOGICAL CIVILIZATION. It builds on my earlier book with Peter Henriot SJ, SOCIAL ANALYSIS: LINKING FAITH AND JUSTICE.[4] Hence, the first part of the tentative title as SOCIAL ANALYSIS II.

In the second part of that tentative title, the phrase "The End of the Modern World" is taken from the English translation of the title of a landmark 1950 book by the distinguished Italian-German and Catholic-Christian philosopher, Romano Guardini.[5] As the first manuscript will explore, Guardini's book appears to have influenced the social teaching of Saint John XXIII. In addition, Pope Francis, while still a young Jesuit, began a doctoral dissertation about Guardini's thought. Much later in LAUDATO SI', he cited Guardini's book eight times!

While I was working on that second manuscript, the same voice once more began to haunt me. This time it said that, before publishing either of the two manuscripts mentioned above, I should first write, and then publish beforehand, yet a third book on ecological spirituality (this current book). The reason why, according to the haunting voice, was that only an ecological spirituality would give us adequate vision and courage to deal with the confusing, turbulent, and even dangerous breakdown that Guardini had defined as "The End of the Modern World."

The Term "Postmodern"

At the "End of the Modern World," the only adjective that we have so far to name what follows is "postmodern." In this book, as noted earlier, the term "postmodern" is not used in the common and even nihilist sense of what may be called "Deconstructive Postmodernism." From the viewpoint of my analysis, Deconstructive Postmodernism is not

---

[4] Revised and Enlarged Edition (Orbis Books), 1983.

[5] See Romano Guardini, DAS ENDE DER NEUZEIT, 9TH edition (Würzburg, 1965). For an English translation, see THE END OF THE MODERN WORLD (ISI Books, 1998).

3

truly postmodern but only *late modern*.[6] By contrast, the word "post-modern," as used here, refers to what I have named (again, in perhaps too complex a phrasing) the seminally emerging "Postmodern Global Electronic-Ecological Civilization." A simpler name is "*Postmodern Ecological Civilization*."

I see this seminally emerging Postmodern Ecological Civilization as called to be grounded philosophically and scientifically in what I have described as the emerging "Postmodern Holistic Evolutionary-Ecological Cosmology," or in simpler terms the "*Postmodern Ecological Cosmology*." That emerging Cosmology is now beginning to displace what I call the receding "Modern Western Atomistic-Mechanistic-Materialist Cosmology," or more simply the "*Modern Mechanical Cosmology*."

Like the second manuscript, this book sees the Postmodern Ecological Civilization as rising out of the integral-ecological breakdown of Modern Industrial Civilization, which Guardini called "The End of the Modern World." Since that modern form of Western Civilization has now become globalized, its late modern integral-ecological breakdown constitutes a global experience.

In rounded centuries, this book dates Modern Industrial Civilization as running from 1500 to 2000 CE (beginning before the standard dating for the modern Industrial Revolution, as will be explained later in the SOCIAL ANALYSIS II book). It dates the emerging Postmodern Ecological Civilization as beginning in 2000 CE, although only seminally.

All of this will be explained somewhat in this book, but more fully in the SOCIAL ANALYSIS II book. Meanwhile, this book primarily explores how the underlying postmodern ecological transformation of Cosmol-

---

[6] For a critical analysis of "Deconstructive Postmodernism," see the rich study by Fredrick Jameson, POSTMODERNISM, OR, THE CULTURAL LOGIC OF LATE CAPITALISM (Durham, North Carolina: Duke University Press, 1991)." On the origins of "Deconstructive Postmodernism" as a poetic movement in Peru, and on its subsequent development and spread across the Western world, see Perry Anderson, THE ORIGINS OF POSTMODERNITY (London: New Left Books, 1998).

4

ogy is providing the philosophical-scientific foundation for *correlative ecological transformations in civilization and spirituality.*

As we will soon see, the correlative transformation in spirituality is the passage from what I call the "Modern Dualistic-Psychological Spirituality of Interiority," or more simply *"Modern Psychological Spirituality,"* toward what I call the "Postmodern Holistic-Ecological Spirituality of Co-Creativity," or more simply *"Postmodern Ecological Spirituality."* It is the passage from the modern form of the spirituality of interiority to the emerging postmodern integral-ecological spirituality of the evolving creative communion of life (or co-creativity).

CORRELATIVE POSTMODERN TRANSFORMATIONS

ERA:	MODERN	POSTMODERN
COSMOLOGY:	MODERN WESTERN ATOMISTIC-MECHANICAL MATERIALIST COSMOLOGY	POSTMODERN GLOBAL EVOLUTIONARY-ECOLOGICAL HOLISTIC COSMOLOGY
CIVILIZATION:	MODERN WESTERN INDUSTRIAL-COLONIAL CIVILIZATION	POSTMODERN GLOBAL ELECTRONIC-ECOLOGICAL CIVILIZATION
SPIRITUALITY:	MODERN WESTERN DUALISTIC-PSYCHOLOGICAL SPIRITUALITY OF INTERIORITY	POSTMODERN GLOBAL HOLISTIC-ECOLOGICAL SPIRITUALITY OF CO-CREATIVITY

Four Deep Eras of Human Culture

The second manuscript in this series of three (again tentatively titled SOCIAL ANALYSIS II) will explore more fully the postmodern transformation within the widest human historical context. It will do so by proposing an ideal-type framework of *four deep eras* in the long evolutionary journey of our human family. While that book will provide a detailed analysis of these four ideal types, the following chart (with dating rounded off to thousands of years) gives a brief overview.[7]

FOUR DEEP ERAS OF HUMAN CULTURAL EVOLUTION

(Ideal Types & Concentric Circles)

HISTORICAL ERA	SOCIETAL FORM	UNDERLYING COSMOLOGY	GROUNDING SPIRITUALITY	SYMBOLIC-MYTHIC FOUNDATION
PRIMAL SPEECH ERA: *(Beginning before 100,000 BCE?)*	**LOCAL TRIBE**	**CYCLICAL-ORGANIC HOLISM** *(Webs & Cycles of Spirit-filled Universe)*	**ORGANIC IMMANENCE** *(Animist Religion)*	**EGALITARIAN MATRIFOCAL COMMUNITY** *(Female Revolution)*
CLASSICAL WRITING ERA: *(Beginning c. 5,000 BCE?)*	**CITY-STATE & AGRICULTURAL EMPIRE**	**HIERARCHICAL SPIRIT-MATTER DUALISM** *(Spirit Above & Matter Below)*	**HIERARCHICAL TRANSCENDENCE** *(Priestly Religion)*	**ARISTOCRATIC PATRIARCHAL HIERARCHY** *(Male Revolution Part 1)*
MODERN PRINT ERA: *(Beginning c. 1,500 CE)*	**NATION-STATE & INDUSTRIAL EMPIRE**	**ATOMISTIC MECHANICAL MATERIALISM** *(Anti-spiritual Reductionism)*	**PSYCHOLOGICAL INTERIORITY** *(Devotional Religion)*	**BOURGEOIS HYPER-MASCULINE FREEDOM** *(Male Revolution Part 2)*
POSTMODERN ELECTRONIC ERA: *(Beginning c. 2,000 CE)*	**GLOBAL ECOLOGICAL CIVILIZATION** *(Projected)*	**CO-CREATIVE ECOLOGICAL EVOLUTION** *(Holism of Matter/Spirit)*	**ECOLOGICAL CO-CREATIVITY** *(Panentheistic Religion[8])*	**CO-CREATIVE ECOLOGICAL PARTNERSHIP** *(Female-Male Mutuality)*

These four deep historical eras are not understood as linear, as if each new era replaced the prior era. That is the erroneous modern Western understanding of time – expressed, for example, in commercial "throw-

---

[7] The dating of these eras is broadly rounded in centuries or half centuries. Technologically, the Postmodern Electronic Era begins in 1945 with the ENIAC computer.

[8] See the discussion of Panentheism later in this book.

away" manufacturing as "planned obsolescence." Rather, these four deep eras are analogous to the rings of a living tree, for which growth is organic and for which older rings still lives in the present.

Such an organic yet also evolutionary understanding of time is holistically both conservative and progressive. Hence, though we are now at the end of the long Western and now globalized Modern Era, the authentic contributions of Modernity, along with authentic contributions from the earlier Classical and Primal Eras, need to be conserved as life-giving gifts to the emerging postmodern future.

Within the framework of these four deep historical eras, the seminally emerging and global Postmodern Ecological Civilization, like all past eras, is not a utopian project. Each deep era has its own strengths and weaknesses, as well as its own seeds of initial generation and later degeneration.

Also, the emerging new era carries its own powerful temptations, against which Christians and all humans will have to struggle. Indeed, while this book proposes a positive vision for Postmodern Ecological Civilization, the threat of dystopian alternatives remains strong. Such dystopian threats will be explored in the SOCIAL ANALYSIS II book.

In addition, as noted, the SOCIAL ANALYSIS II book will elaborate on the ideal types of these four deep eras. It will also explore various scenarios for the breakdown of the modern industrial-colonial form of Western Civilization. That breakdown could be gradual or sudden, and the transformation could be positive or negative. Further, the transformation could even lead to the collapse of Western Civilization.

More likely, however, Western Civilization, as one of the ancient and great civilizations of the human family, could overcome the breakdown of its modern industrial-colonial form, by tapping back into regenerative roots still alive within its ancient traditions. It could then make a resilient transition to a postmodern ecological form.

Even though we do not know what the future holds, we may be certain that the postmodern transition will be turbulent, confusing, and dangerous. Indeed, we are already living within that turbulence, confusion, and danger. For that reason, as we journey through the difficult transition seeking a future Postmodern Ecological Civilization, *we need a mystical-prophetic ecological spirituality to inspire us and to guide us*.

The Phrase "Catholic-Christian"

The title of this book also uses the phrase "Catholic-Christian." The adjective "Christian" is added to the adjective "Catholic" for three reasons.

- *All Catholic Churches.* First, the phrase "Catholic-Christian" – with a broader meaning than "Roman Catholic" – includes all twenty-four Catholic Churches in communion with the Catholic Bishop of Rome, whom Catholics understand as carrying a special Petrine Ministry. Each of these twenty-four Catholic churches stands as autonomous ("*sui-juris*" in the Western Catholic Church's Canon Law), with its own rich historical, theological, and spiritual traditions. The Roman Church, though the largest Catholic Church because of its long alliance with Western colonialism,[9] nonetheless remains only one of the twenty-four.

- *Catholic as Christian.* Second, this book uses the phrase "Catholic-Christian," because some Evangelical Christians say to Catholics: "I am Christian, not Catholic." Apparently, in their minds, the adjectives "Christian" and "Catholic" have nothing to do with each other. By contrast, the phrase "Catholic-Christian" makes clear that all twenty-four Catholic Churches across planet Earth are indeed Christian, and carry ancient Christian roots.

---

[9] The Western or Roman Church constantly received as prizes vast new territories invaded and conquered by Western Imperialism – from the time of Charlemagne through to early modern Western mercantile colonialism and up to modern industrial colonialism.

8

- ***The Global Christian Family.*** Third, I offer this book as a dialogical gift to all Christians. Hence, the phrase "Catholic-Christian" places Catholic Christianity within the larger global Christian family, and it seeks a postmodern Catholic-Christian future in partnership with the full Christian family across our garden-planet Earth.

Hope & Prayer

In conclusion, I hope and pray that this book, now additionally inspired by Francis' prophetic encyclical LAUDATO SI', may prove of some small service in promoting the ecological spirituality that both Saint Francis of Assisi and Francis of Rome have called for. I further hope and pray that this book may advance Francis of Rome's prophetic postmodern global call for the integral-ecological regeneration of life across our loving Creator's beloved garden-planet Earth.

1

INTRODUCTION

CANTICLE OF THE CREATURES

Most high, all powerful, all good Lord!
All praise is Yours, all glory, all honor, and all blessing.

To You, alone, Most High, do they belong.
No mortal lips are worthy to pronounce Your name.

Be praised, my Lord, through all Your creatures,
especially through my lord Brother Sun,
who brings the day; and You give light through him.
And he is beautiful and radiant in all his splendor!
Of You, Most High, he bears the likeness.

Be praised, my Lord, through Sister Moon and the stars;
in the heavens You have made them bright, precious, and beautiful.

Be praised, my Lord, through Brothers Wind and Air,
and clouds and storms, and all the weather,
through which You give Your creatures sustenance.

Be praised, my Lord, through Sister Water;
she is very useful, and humble, and precious, and pure.

Be praised, my Lord, through Brother Fire,
through whom You brighten the night.
He is beautiful and cheerful, and powerful and strong.

Be praised, my Lord, through our sister Mother Earth,
who feeds us and rules us,
and produces various fruits with colored flowers and herbs.

Be praised, my Lord, through those who forgive for love of You;
through those who endure sickness and trial.

Happy those who endure in peace,
for by You, Most High, they will be crowned.

Be praised, my Lord, through our sister Bodily Death,
from whose embrace no living person can escape.

Woe to those who die in mortal sin!

Happy those she finds doing Your most holy will.
The second death can do no harm to them.

Praise and bless my Lord, and give thanks,
and serve Him with great humility.

SAINT FRANCIS
OF ASSISI

BROTHER SUN & SISTER MOON

I n announcing the postmodern spiritual transformation,[1] the subtitle of this book refers to the "Dark Night" of Modern Industrial Civilization and to the "Dawn" of Postmodern Ecological Civilization. It uses those words from Earth's solar cycle, rather than the chronological words "beginning" and "ending," for two important reasons.

Journeying Through the "Dark Night"
of Modern Industrial Civilization

First, when Saint Francis of Assisi's "Brother Sun" descends down the horizon and seems to disappear from us into the "Dark Night," Brother Sun's work for our garden-planet Earth is not ending but only receding from our view. After twilight, Brother Sun, though hidden from us, continues his life-giving work of nourishing our garden-planet Earth.

So too is it with the "Dark Night" of Modern Industrial Civilization. At the end of the Modern Western Era, signaled by the global breakdown of the integral ecology of life across its interwoven natural, human, and spiritual fabric, Modern Psychological Spirituality is receding.[2]

Yet the important work of the ancient spirituality of interiority is not ending, only its modern form. In the seminally emerging Postmodern Ecological Civilization, the ancient spirituality of interiority will continue to nourish our inner spirits, but in a different and holistically postmodern ecological manner.

---

[1] Again, as noted in the Preface, the term "postmodern refers here to the new historical period inaugurated by the emerging Postmodern Ecological Cosmology, made feasible by the postmodern Electronic Revolution. That "New Cosmology" then provides the philosophical-scientific foundation for both civilization and spirituality.

[2] The word "psychological" comes from two ancient Greek words, namely *psyche* and *logos*, with the first word meaning "soul" and the second (at least in this context) meaning "logic." Hence, from its ancient Greek roots, "psychology" means the "logic of the soul."

The "spirituality of interiority" refers to consciousness of the Divine presence experienced within the *inner-subjective psychological self* – often spontaneously, aided by meditation, and intensified in mysticism. To be healthy, Catholic-Christian inner-subjective consciousness of the Divine presence needs to function in communion with its correlative outer-objective consciousness of the Divine presence, revealed within the evolving webs and cycles of Nature, and within the evolving story of human history (itself nested within the evolving story of Nature).

The famous 1577 masterpiece by the great Spanish mystic, Saint Theresa of Ávila, THE INTERIOR CASTLE, is a healthy early modern expression of the abiding Catholic-Christian tradition of the ancient spirituality of interiority.[3] The even more famous early modern Catholic-Christian guide, THE SPIRITUAL EXERCISES OF SAINT IGNATIUS, is also a healthy early modern example of that ancient spirituality.[4] The EXERCISES were composed between 1522 and 1524 by the great Basque spiritual visionary, Saint Ignatius of Loyola. Those early modern Catholic-Christian classics, while heightening spiritual interiority, did not lose spiritual consciousness of the Divine presence revealed within the exteriority of Nature and human history.

With the later modern Western form of the psychological spirituality of interiority, however, consciousness of the inner-subjective Divine presence became forgetful of the outer-objective Divine presence. With that narcissistic forgetfulness, the reduction of spirituality only to its interior psychological dimension implicitly supported secularization of the outer-objective world by treating it as purely materialist.

Still worse, there have been recent philosophical-scientific attempts to eliminate even inner-subjective spirituality, by trying to explain human consciousness entirely through the modern philosophical doctrine of

---

[3] Dover Thrift Edition, 2007. The original Spanish title is EL CASTILLO INTERIOR / LAS MORADAS (The Interior Castle / The Dwelling Places).

[4] For an English translation (among other editions), see the Image reprint edition, 1964.

Scientific Materialism.[5] In that reductionist doctrine, human consciousness is claimed to be the meaningless, atomistic-mechanical, and purely materialist product of what is claimed to be the human body's own meaningless and atomistic-mechanical Materialism, which in turn is claimed to be part of the meaningless and atomistic-mechanical Materialism of the entire Universe.[6]

Seeking the "Dawn" of a
Postmodern Ecological Civilization

Second, returning to the "Dark Night" and "Dawn" of the solar cycle, recall that "Dawn" does not immediately follow Brother Sun's twilight. Similarly, the historical twilight of Modern Industrial Civilization does not lead immediately to the "Dawn" of Postmodern Ecological Civilization. First, there comes the long "Dark Night."

The late modern secularized forms of economic, cultural, and political institutions, including secularized universities, are now blocking out spiritual meaning. In the place of spiritual meaning, they are now proclaiming intellectual triumph for the anti-spiritual doctrine of Scientific Materialism, as well as what will soon be explained as Nietzschean voluntarist Nihilism. All this signifies that Modern Industrial Civilization has now entered its "Dark Night" of *spiritual emptiness.*

In the sixteenth century, the profound spiritual poem and treatise written between 1577 and 1585 by the renowned Catholic-Christian mystic, Saint John of the Cross, was given the name DARK NIGHT OF THE SOUL.[7]

---

[5] The phrase "Scientific Materialism" was introduced by the distinguished British mathematician and philosopher, Alfred North Whitehead (1861-1947). We will return shortly to explain Whitehead's phrase.

[6] See, for example, Daniel C. Dennett, CONSCIOUSNESS EXPLAINED (Little, Brown & Co, 1991), as well as Nicholas Humphrey, A HISTORY OF THE MIND: EVOLUTION AND THE BIRTH OF CONSCIOUSNESS (Simon & Schuster, 1992).

[7] See Saint John of the Cross, DARK NIGHT OF THE SOUL (Dover Thrift Editions, 2003), with the original Spanish title being LA NOCHE OSCURA DEL ALMA. I am indebted to my

While John used the "Dark Night" imagery in the mode of Christian Neo-Platonic mysticism, the phrase has also been used in Western Catholic Christianity to describe a depressing spiritual crisis, where the Divine presence seems to disappear entirely from consciousness.

It is in this second sense that the term "Dark Night" is used here. For so many major secular institutions of the 'advanced' center-countries of Modern Industrial Civilization, awareness of the Divine presence has disappeared from public consciousness. Today, so many 'educated' elite Western persons, and especially so many 'educated' elite leaders of Western institutions, have accepted the intellectual triumph of Scientific Materialism.

Further, in the second half of the twentieth century, the hegemonic intellectual power of Scientific Materialism became compounded with the rise of a voluntarist form of philosophical Nihilism. That Nihilism is rooted in the radically voluntarist thought of the nineteenth-century German philologist Friedrich Nietzsche (1844-1900).[8] In addition, as the second book SOCIAL ANALYSIS II will explore, Nietzschean Nihilism is promoted by late modern Neoliberal Capitalism's anti-ecological culture of limitless commodification and ceaseless consumerism.

In addition, as the SOCIAL ANALYSIS II book will also explore, late modern Scientific Materialism and Nietzschean Nihilism are implicitly promoted by neoliberal global financial institutions, by neoliberal global culture industries, and even by neoliberal globalized university networks.

---

colleague and friend Dr. Cristobal Serrán-Pagán, for his valuable research on Saint John of the Cross and Saint Teresa of Avila.

[8] As should be apparent, I do not agree with the widely held benevolent reading of Friedrich Nietzsche, initiated by Walter Kaufmann in his influential 1950 book, NIETZSCHE: PHILOSOPHER, PSYCHOLOGIST, ANTICHRIST, reprint edition (Princeton University Press, 2013). For a critique of Kaufmann's benevolent interpretation of Nietzsche, see Conor Cruise O'Brien's now classic essay "The Gentle Nietzscheans," NEW YORK REVIEW OF BOOKS, November 5, 1970, available at:

http://www.nybooks.com/articles/1970/11/05/the-gentle-nietzscheans (accessed 2017-04-12).

Again, the resulting spiritual emptiness – increasingly typical of 'educated' elites within the 'advanced' industrialized regions – represents a spiritual "Dark Night" for the entire society. For that reason, in such intellectually 'advanced' regions, contemporary Catholic-Christian ecological prophets like Pope Francis are few. By and large, the 'advanced' institutions of Modern Industrial Civilization have become devoid of Spirit-inspired leaders.

Late Modern Global Assaults
on Life's Integral Ecology

The growing late modern cultural triumph of Scientific Materialism and Nietzschean Nihilism is not simply an intellectual-spiritual problem. It is also an ecological-societal problem. The reason is that those doctrines claim to strip all creatures across planet Earth (including humans), and throughout the Cosmos, of spiritual meaning. They then undermine ethical guidance by eliminating traditional intellectual-spiritual restraints on economic, political, and cultural power.

As a result, we now watch, and so often in helpless fashion, as endless numbers of our loving Creator's beloved creatures – including within our loving Creator's beloved human family – suffer devastating late modern assaults. Those assaults include:

- *Global economic plundering* of our planetary ecosystem, for the competitive accumulation of money, power, and fame;

- *Global political violence* from international campaigns of crime, terrorism, and endless war, as well as international campaigns for abortion and euthanasia that foreshadow a revival of eugenics;

- *Global cultural degradation* from competitive international commercial consumerism and entertainment media, as well as from lucrative international criminal networks of drugs, pornography, and human trafficking.

Further, so great are the late modern global assaults on natural ecology that they have already begun to inflict *"the sixth great extinction of life"* on our loving Creator's beloved garden-planet Earth.[9]

Yet, although we may feel lost within the late modern "Dark Night," we have not been spiritually abandoned. For, within this "Dark Night," there is a small spiritual light akin to what Saint Francis of Assisi called "Sister Moon." In this small spiritual light, we discover a haunting and symbolically feminine spiritual presence, whose name is *Holy Spirit*.[10]

As we seek healing paths toward a regenerative postmodern global ecological future, the Holy Spirit's warm spiritual light seeks to guide us toward integral-ecological regeneration. Yet, like our physical Sister Moon, her guiding light waxes and wanes, and in the present moment of that passage her light does not yet shine full.

---

[9] See Elisabeth Kolbert, THE SIXTH EXTINCTION: AN UNNATURAL HISTORY, Reprint Edition (Picador, 2015).

[10] In the second volume of his magisterial three-volume series on the history of the Holy Spirit in Christian Theology, Stanley M. Burgess has pointed out that early Syrian Christian writers (until the fourth century, when the Imperial Church emerged) referred to the Holy Spirit as *feminine*, and even described the Sacred Trinity as Father, *Mother*, and Son. See his THE HOLY SPIRIT: EASTERN CHRISTIAN TRADITIONS (Baker Academic, 1989), especially p. 6. Prof. Burgess also notes that, while the role of the Holy Spirit has often been diminished in Western Theology, "pneumatology always has been at the very heart of Eastern Theology" (p. 1). He further notes that, while many Western theologians have dismissed the Eastern emphasis on the Spirit as "pneumacentrism," many Eastern theologians have "charged the West" with "Christocentrism" (p.1).

In the Semitic languages of Hebrew, Aramaic (which Jesus spoke), and ancient Syrian (related to Aramaic), the word "spirit" is feminine. It is also helpful to recall, as the ACTS OF THE APOSTLES tells us, that it was in Antioch of Syria that the early followers of Jesus were first called "Christians" (11:26). Thus, the ancient Christian tradition of Syria, including its symbolically feminine understanding of the Holy Spirit, stands close to the very origins of Christianity.

For more on the Holy Spirit as "Mother," see Msgr. Seely J. Beggiani, EARLY SYRIAC THEOLOGY WITH SPECIAL REFERENCE TO THE MARONITE TRADITION (University of America Press, 1983); Joan Schaupp, WOMAN: IMAGE OF THE HOLY SPIRIT (Dimension Books, 1975); and Donald Gelpi SJ. THE DIVINE MOTHER, (University of America Press, 1984).

Such is our current Western spiritual situation. We have entered into the spiritual "Dark Night" of Modern Industrial Civilization. To guide us through its spiritual darkness, the Holy Spirit as our spiritual "Sister Moon" is only beginning to illumine the way toward a regenerative postmodern integral-ecological future. Yet we may be confident that, when her warm and guiding light does shine full, she will clearly show us the fullness of her regenerative path. But, before that happens, she is calling us to plant seeds of regeneration for life's integral ecology.

Generations ago, the great English Jesuit poet Gerard Manley Hopkins, in his famous 1877 mystical poem GOD'S GRANDEUR, foresaw the Holy Spirit's light-bearing appearance within the "Dark Night" of Modern Industrial Civilization. Thus, Hopkins wrote:

> *The world is charged with the grandeur of God.*
> *It will flame out, like shining from shook foil;*
> *It gathers to a greatness, like the ooze of oil*
> *Crushed. Why do men then now not reck his rod?*
> *Generations have trod, have trod, have trod;*
> *And all is seared with trade; Bleared, smeared with toil;*
> *And wears man's smudge and shares man's smell: the soil*
> *Is bare now, nor can foot feel, being shod.*
>
> *And for all this, Nature is never spent;*
> *There lives the dearest freshness deep down things;*
> *And though the last lights off the black West went,*
> *Oh, morning, at the brown brink eastward, springs —*
> *Because the Holy Ghost over the bent World*
> *broods with warm breast and with ah! bright wings.*[11]

---

[11] GERARD MANLEY HOPKINS: POEMS AND PROSE (Penguin Classics, 1985).

This book is exploratory. It explores the proposal that the global Catholic-Christian family – as well as the ecumenically wider global Christian family and even the entire global human family – are all called to embrace the emergence of Postmodern Ecological Spirituality.

In its exploration, this book historically contextualizes this postmodern Catholic-Christian spiritual emergence as *following five earlier long waves of Catholic-Christian spirituality*, with the last form being Modern Psychological Spirituality. This book sees that modern form of spirituality as now having entered its historical breakdown, in correlation with the current historical breakdown of Modern Industrial Civilization. Within that breakdown, the book makes special reference to the decline of the *modern "apostolic" form of Catholic-Christian "religious life,"* which has been grounded in Modern Psychological Spirituality, and to the emergence of Catholic-Christian *new lay movements*, which the book sees as called to seek grounding in Postmodern Ecological Spirituality.

In addition, within the emerging Catholic-Christian lay spiritual framework, this book calls for *an ecological lay "New Monasticism,"* which in a humble and prayerful manner would try to provide spiritual leadership for our turbulent, confusing, and even dangerous journey toward Postmodern Ecological Civilization.[12]

Catholic-Christian Spirituality
& Human Spirituality

The book contextualizes the emerging postmodern Catholic-Christian ecological spirituality, which it sees as lay in character, within the wid-

---

[12] An earlier use of the phrase "New Monasticism" has a different though complementary focus from the ecological mission proposed here. On that earlier and different focus, see: *https://en.wikipedia.org/wiki/New_Monasticism* (accessed 2016-11-15). In addition, see Rory McEntee & Adam Bucko, THE NEW MONASTICISM: AN INTERSPIRITUAL MANIFESTO FOR CONTEMPORARY LIVING (Orbis Books, 2015).

er movement of natural human spirituality. Such a contextualization of Catholic-Christian spirituality in relation to the grounding spirituality of humanity has long been the Catholic-Christian way.

As Saint Thomas Aquinas (1225-1274) taught us more than seven centuries ago, *"Gratia non tollit naturam, sed perfecit."*[13] Translators typically render that statement as "Grace does not destroy Nature, but perfects it." In a more illuminative manner, Saint John Paul II once translated the statement as "Grace does not destroy Nature, but fulfills its potential."[14]

Thus, authentic Catholic-Christian spirituality understands Divine grace as seeking to heal, and to perfect, the wounded but still gifted potential of our natural spirituality. Healing that wounded but still gifted potential becomes more important than ever, since we now live within the historical breakdown that Romano Guardini named "The End of the Modern World."

Late Modern Breakdown of Civilization, Spirituality, & Evangelization

Though it will not be developed here, the book implies that, within the 'advanced' West, *the late modern crisis of Catholic-Christian evangelization* is in major part the result of the historical collapse of Modern Psychological Spirituality, which then causes the spiritual "Dark Night" of Modern Industrial Civilization. The modern form of the psychological spirituality of interiority is being undermined by the late modern psychological narcissism of capitalist consumerism, and by the late modern philosophical secularization of society and even of the inner psychological self.

---

[13] SUMMA THEOLOGIAE, I. I. 8 ad 2.

[14] MESSAGE ON CHRISTIAN HUMANISM IN THE THIRD MILLENNIUM, 2003, available at *https://w2.vatican.va/content/john-paul-ii/en/speeches/2003/september/documents/hf_jp-ii_spe_20030929_congresso-tomista.html.*

CATEGORY	RECEDING	EMERGING
GROUNDING COSMOLOGY:	MODERN WESTERN ATOMIST-MECHANICAL MATERIALIST COSMOLOGY	POSTMODERN GLOBAL ECOLOGICAL-EVOLUTIONARY HOLISTIC COSMOLOGY
CONTEXTUAL CIVILIZATION:	MODERN WESTERN INDUSTRIAL-COLONIAL CIVILIZATION	POSTMODERN GLOBAL ELECTRONIC-ECOLOGICAL CIVILIZATION
CORRELATIVE EVANGELIZATION:	MODERN WESTERN INDUSTRIAL-COLONIAL EVANGELIZATION	POSTMODERN GLOBAL ELECTRONIC-ECOLOGICAL EVANGELIZATION
CORRELATIVE SPIRITUALITY:	MODERN WESTERN DUALIST-PSYCHOLOGICAL SPIRITUALITY OF INTERIORITY	POSTMODERN GLOBAL HOLISTIC-ECOLOGICAL SPIRITUALITY OF CO-CREATIVITY
CATHOLIC-CHRISTIAN INSTITUTIONAL SPIRITUAL WAVE:	MODERN WESTERN APOSTOLIC RELIGIOUS COMMUNITIES	POSTMODERN GLOBAL REGENERATIVE LAY MOVEMENTS *(Including Proposed Lay Ecological New Monasticism)*

Looking to the present, this book analyzes the late modern Western Catholic-Christian crisis of evangelization as part of the correlative breakdowns of Modern Industrial Civilization and of Modern Psychological Spirituality. Looking to the future, the book points toward the regenerative breakthrough of a Postmodern Ecological Civilization, as well as of a Postmodern Ecological Spirituality and a Postmodern Ecological Evangelization.[15]

Note also that, in its social analysis, this book sometimes links the term "industrial" with the term "colonial" – thus, the more complex name of "Modern Western Industrial-Colonial Civilization." The adjective "colonial" is included because *the global colonization of Earth and peoples has been essential to Modernity's industrialization,* and in both its capitalist and socialist forms. Further, the industrial colonization of Earth and people has been for the most part uncritically accepted, and still worse sometimes supported, by ecclesial elites of the modern Western Catholic-Christian and Protestant-Christian evangelizations.

Further, and as noted, Modern Industrial Civilization includes both of Western Modernity's two dominant ideological forms, namely, Liberal Capitalism and Scientific Socialism. Both of these modern ideologies of Materialism, despite functioning as antagonistic forms of Modern Industrial Civilization, have largely supported the modern global colonization and devastation of life's integral ecology.[16]

The industrial-colonial linkage has been central to Modern Industrial Civilization's ever expanding, yet ultimately unsustainable, extraction of "natural resources" (an anthropocentric utilitarian concept that despiritualizes Nature) for human "utility" (another utilitarian concept). It has also been central to modern industrialism's search for "cheap labor" (yet another utilitarian concept that commodifies human beings). Together these anti-ecological utilitarian projects – one natural and the other human – constitute the industrial colonization and devastation of Earth's family of creatures, including of so many humans.

---

[15] As we will see later in this book, and as the second book in this series of three will explore more fully, society's shift from an *industrial* to an *electronic* foundation constitutes the technological basis for the postmodern transformation.

[16] Some socialist governments have pursued important though insufficient ecological policies, especially in the Scandinavian region. In addition, some capitalist governments have also taken important yet insufficient steps toward ecological sustainability.

On another negative note, our human family is now also facing the possibility that development of Artificial Intelligence (AI) and robotics, guided primarily by corporate and military funding and criteria, could soon marginalize wide ranges of human labor.[17] That process could end much of the search for "cheap labor." But it would do so by eliminating significant amounts of global employment, which would then precipitate vast global human suffering.

Cultural-Spiritual
Explorations of Thomas Berry

The Catholic-Christian exploration of Postmodern Ecological Spirituality, as proposed in this book, draws in great part for inspiration on the intellectual-spiritual explorations in evolutionary ecology by the late Catholic-Christian cultural historian Thomas Berry (1914-2009).

Thomas Berry's visionary explorations stand as foundational contributions pointing beyond what will later be explained as first Platonic and later Cartesian and Kantian dualisms, and as pointing toward a holistic Postmodern Ecological Spirituality with both broadly human and specifically Christian forms.[18]

Sister Kathleen Deignan, C.N.D, Ph.D. – Professor of Religious Studies at Iona College, Director of its Spirituality Institute, and a leading intellectual-spiritual leader promoting Thomas Berry's thought – has helpfully highlighted his teaching about ecological spirituality, which he sometimes called "Earth spirituality." In that teaching, as Sister Kathleen

---

[17] On the vigorous debate over Artificial Intelligence, see John Markoff, MACHINES OF LOVING GRACE: THE QUEST FOR COMMON GROUND BETWEEN HUMANS AND ROBOTS (Harper Collins, 2015).

[18] On Thomas Berry's Catholic contribution to ecological spirituality, see Thomas Berry & Mary Evelyn Tucker, THE SACRED UNIVERSE: EARTH SPIRITUALITY AND RELIGION IN THE TWENTY-FIRST CENTURY (Columbia University Press, 2009). See also Thomas Berry's early book, THE DREAM OF THE EARTH (Sierra Club, 1988), and one of his last books, THE GREAT WORK: OUR WAY INTO THE FUTURE (Bell Tower Random House, 1999). For more information on this prophetic figure, see http://thomasberry.org (accessed 2016-06-24).

Deignan emphasizes, Earth spirituality does not begin with human consciousness, but has its roots in the spiritual nature of Earth itself. Thus, in a recent essay, she shares the following quote from Thomas Berry's article, "The Spirituality of the Earth."

> *The spirituality of the Earth refers to a quality of the Earth itself, not to a human spirituality with special reference to the planet Earth. Earth is the maternal principle out of which we are born and from which we derive all that we are and all that we have. We come into being in and through the Earth. Simply put, we are Earthlings.*[19]

She then blends her own moving reflections with this important teaching of Thomas Berry:

> *He reminds us that the whole burden of modern Earth spirituality is to narrate the story of the birth of the human from our Mother the Earth, and how significant the title "Mother Earth" is for its intimacy, sense of relationality, and mutual care. Thomas tenderly tells us, "our long motherless period is coming to a close," and hopefully with it the violation of Earth ... Then, in a startling proposal for its deep traditionalism, Thomas elects Mary, the mother of Jesus, the archetypal "Madonna" of Western Civilization, to carry the embryonic burden of the new Christic humanity, and indeed to bear the personification of Earth herself.*[20]

Within the range of Christian theological traditions, Professor Willis Jenkins, of the University of Virginia, has given a specific location to the work of Thomas Berry. As background to that location, he has con-

---

[19] Thomas Berry, "The Spirituality of the Earth," in Thomas Berry & Mary Evelyn Tucker, Editor, THE SACRED UNIVERSE: EARTH, SPIRITUALITY, AND RELIGION IN THE TWENTY-FIRST CENTURY, (New York: Columbia University, 2009), p. 69; cited in Kathleen Deignan, "The Spirituality of the Earth: Reflections on an Essay by Thomas Berry," in Mary Evelyn Tucker & John Grim, Editors, LIVING COSMOLOGY: CHRISTIAN RESPONSES TO THE JOURNEY OF THE UNIVERSE (Orbis Books, 2016), p. 115.

[20] Kathleen Deignan, "Spirituality of the Earth," p. 121, with quotes from Thomas Berry's essay, pp 76-77.

trasted three distinct strategies adopted by contemporary Christian Practical Theology in relation to ecology and grace. He has described these three strategies as:

- Ecojustice (sanctification)
- Christian Stewardship (redemption)
- Ecological Spirituality (deification)

Professor Jenkins sees the first and second strategies as having roots in Western Christianity, with the first linked to Western Roman Catholicism and the second linked to Western Evangelical Protestantism. He sees the third strategy of Ecological Spirituality as rooted in the Eastern Christian Churches.[21]

Yet, breaking with his own geographical-denominational map, Professor Jenkins identifies the Western Catholic-Christian contribution of Thomas Berry as *Ecological Spirituality*. Thus, Thomas Berry as a Catholic-Christian thinker appears out of the Western box.[22]

---

[21] See Willis Jenkins' insightful book, ECOLOGIES OF GRACE: ENVIRONMENTAL ETHICS AND CHRISTIAN THEOLOGY (Oxford University Press, 2008). In his typology, *Thomas Aquinas* stands out as a foundational theologian for the first strategy of "Ecojustice," since in his hierarchical dualism "supernatural" grace perfects Nature ("sanctifying" it). For Willis Jenkin's account of the strategy of "Christian Stewardship," *Karl Barth* stands out as a foundational theologian, since for him grace triumphs over Nature ("redeeming" it). For his account of the third strategy of "Ecological Spirituality," the outstanding foundational theologian becomes the Syrian patristic 'father' *Maximus the Confessor*, whose thought is further developed by the twentieth-century Russian Orthodox theologian *Sergei Bulgakov*. In the Eastern traditions, Willis Jenkins notes, there is no separation between Nature and grace, since it sees grace as "deifying" Nature ("*theosis*").

[22] It is presumably not coincidental that Thomas Berry was also a scholar of Eastern religions. He continued and deepened the pioneering explorations of the spiritual meaning of evolution by the Jesuit scientist and mystic Pierre Teilhard de Chardin (1881-1955), who also had deep interest in the Eastern religions as well as in the Eastern churches.

Again, in response to the interrelated breakdowns of the modern Western forms of civilization, spirituality, and evangelization, this book proposes that we need to awaken to the Holy Spirit's call to begin the prophetic journey toward the "Dawn" of regenerative Postmodern Ecological Civilization. We also need to be nourished by the emerging and regenerative Postmodern Ecological Spirituality, which can inspire and guide us toward the emerging Postmodern Ecological Evangelization and toward the emerging Postmodern Ecological Church.

In this awakening to which the Holy Spirit now calls us, we need to reflect analytically on the paths to be pursued and the hurdles to be overcome, for both church and society. To do that, we need to employ ever deepening levels of social analysis. Only then will we be able adequately to understand the full depth of the postmodern transformation. And only then will we be able to seek regenerative pathways fully commensurate with the full depth of that transformation.

While the second book (again, SOCIAL ANALYSIS II) in this series of three will more fully explore these deepening levels of analysis, let us identify and briefly explain them here as:

- Level 1 – Issues, Policies, & Institutions
- Level 2 – Integrating Systemic-Societal Ideologies
- Level 3 – Underlying Philosophical-Scientific Cosmology
- Level 4 – Deep Symbolic-Mythic Foundations

Level 1
Issues, Policies, & Institutions

The first level analyzes the "End of the "Modern World" at its surface. It addresses issues, policies, and institutions of the modern social systems – again, named by Guardini the "Modern World" and named here "Modern Industrial Civilization." This is the level at which journalism operates. It provides the essential social-analytical starting point of information, with an initial analysis of that information. The overwhelming number of issues, policies, and institutions involved in the postmodern transition are, however, too many to list here. For that reason, we can only note this level as the beginning of social analysis.

Level 2
Integrating Systemic-Societal Ideologies

This second and deeper level of social analysis examines the *integrating modern systemic-societal ideologies* guiding the dominant interpretations of issues, policies, and institutions. We can trace the intellectual origin of this ideological level to the Modern European Enlightenment, which took place especially in the eighteenth century but also continued into the nineteenth century.

That intellectual movement applied to society what was then called the "Mechanical Philosophy" (the Modern Mechanical Cosmology) grounding Europe's seventeenth-century's "New Science." That application then generated what became the Social Sciences, or more broadly the Human Sciences (including Psychology). As we will see later, both the Natural Sciences grounded in the modern "Mechanical Philosophy," and their derivative Social or Human Sciences, all carry ancient roots in the atomistic-mechanical Materialism of Epicurean Philosophy.

The "Mechanical Philosophy" claimed that the Universe and everything within it is atomistic-mechanical and materialist. The Modern European Enlightenment applied that Cosmology's atomistic-mechanical and materialist interpretation of reality to the interpretation of both human societies and the human person. That largely happened in two successive and opposed ideological waves: first, during the eighteenth century as the *liberal-capitalist* wave and, next, in more radical form during the nineteenth century as the *scientific-socialist* wave.

- *Liberal Capitalism.* During the eighteenth century, the first wave of the Modern European Enlightenment produced the ideology later called Liberal Capitalism. Early on named the "Liberal Political Economy," or simply "Liberalism," its best-known foundational thinker was the Scottish philosopher Adam Smith (1723-1790).

- *Scientific Socialism.* During the nineteenth century, the Enlightenment's second wave produced its opposite ideological cousin of "Scientific Socialism," also known as "Marxism." Its best-known foundational thinker was the German philosopher Karl Marx (1818-1883).

Although mutually opposed, those two modern Western ideologies shared the common philosophical-scientific ground of the Modern Mechanical Cosmology, which Whitehead named "Scientific Materialism." Yet they differed on how best to organize society in light of that modern cosmological paradigm.

The first wave of Liberalism developed an *individualist and voluntarist* understanding of society, while the second wave of Marxism developed a *collectivist and rationalist* (though only instrumentally rationalist) understanding of society. While there are a range of differing tendencies within these two ideological waves, the following ideal-type summary may be useful for a broad understanding of their distinct logics.

- *The liberal-capitalist wing* has prioritized a substantively empty concept of *freedom* (or liberty) for supposedly deracinated and disconnected *autonomous individuals*, supposedly guided primarily by *self-interest*. Promoting liberal freedom as voluntarist-individual *choice*, Modernity's liberal wing has promoted autonomous individualism across economic, political, and cultural life. And it has canonized the dangerous fantasy that the *voluntarist 'Free Market,'* rather than human persons embedded within ecologically-rooted organic communities, should function as the foundational structure for modern society.

- *The scientific-socialist wing,* by contrast, has prioritized a materialist understanding of *social justice,* drawn from Marx's secularization of Jewish and Christian messianic teachings. Marxian social justice is to be achieved through *revolutionary mass movements of the working-class* ("mass" being a term from Newtonian Physics), with the working class to be guided 'scientifically' by the ideology's instrumental rationality. Although it also views individual members of the working class as deracinated and atomized, Marxism nonetheless has sought through organizing to massify them for class conflict.[23] Promoting rationalist collectivism across society, it has canonized the dangerous fantasy that the *'Rationalist State,'* rather than human persons embedded within ecologically-rooted organic communities, should function as the foundational structure for modern society.

Through their fundamental differences, both modern ideological traditions have promoted opposite, incomplete, and sometimes distorted (although in another sense complementary) understandings of democracy. On one side, what has been called "Democratic Capitalism" has emphasized the individual autonomy of the human person and voluntarist entrepreneurship.[24] On the other side, what has been called "Democratic Socialism" (or "Social Democracy") has emphasized the social relationships of the human person and rationalist solidarity.[25]

---

[23] Again, in the scientific-socialist case, human persons are also viewed as individual "atoms" within society, but they are to be organized into a mass force for revolutionary purposes. Yet, according to Marx, their collectivization for revolution, and their subsequent guidance by the collectivizing 'Rational State,' are only *temporary,* since Marx projected that his ideological system would in the end produce "Pure Communism," which he saw as an 'emancipated' libertarian society of deracinated and autonomous individuals. Thus, Marx was ultimately a libertarian.

[24] See Michael Novak, THE SPIRIT OF DEMOCRATIC CAPITALISM, Revised Edition (Madison, 1990).

[25] See Michael Harrington, SOCIALISM: PAST AND FUTURE (Arcade Publishers, 2011).

Yet, as noted, both sides have grounded democracy in the reductionism of scientific-materialist interpretations of the human person and of human society. As a result, both ideologies have faced totalitarian temptations. Scientific Socialism has been threatened by its totalitarian temptation of Dictatorial Communism, and Liberal Capitalism has been threatened by its totalitarian temptation of Dictatorial Fascism.

Further, the underlying Scientific Materialism of both modern Western ideologies has led their adherents to promote *modern secularization,* but again in different ways. Proponents of the Marxian ideology have tried to use the 'Rationalist State' – sometimes even forcibly – to marginalize religion, or even to eliminate it. At the same time, proponents of the liberal ideology have tried to promote a 'Free-Market' toleration for religion, but also to pressure for its psychological privatization, and thus to undermine religion's public influence and to replace it with a dominant culture of Scientific Materialism.

It is important to point out, however, that the problem is not with the persons who promote or follow these ideologies – they are all the Creator's beloved creatures – but rather with the philosophical errors that the ideologies contain. Certainly, for both ideologies, there are evil promoters and followers. But most promoters and followers of both ideologies are presumably good and noble persons.

Ecologically concerned Christians need, therefore, not to reject promoters and followers of either of the ideological sides. Rather, ecologically concerned Christians need to dialogue with promoters and followers of both ideologies, in the hope of humbly and respectfully helping them to overcome the philosophical errors of their ideologies, and yet also to continue and even to expand the valid contributions of their ideologies. If that were to happen, we could all work together toward regeneration of integral ecology.

Level 3
Philosophical-Scientific Cosmology

So far in this review of levels of social analysis, we have seen that, because it is not sufficient to end social analysis at the surface or journalistic level of issues, policies, and institutions, we need to look deeper at the guiding ideological systematization of that surface level. But ideology alone also is not sufficient to explain the late modern breakdown of life's integral ecology, since modern materialistic ideologies constitute philosophical-scientific applications to society of their shared and underlying Modern Mechanical Cosmology (again, what Whitehead called "Scientific Materialism").

At that still deeper level, this book proposes that we now face the intellectual breakdown of the modern atomistic-mechanical and materialist Cosmological paradigm constructed by Modern Philosophy and Modern Science. Therefore, the book argues, we need to explore not only the intellectual transition from the receding Modern Mechanical Cosmology to the emerging Postmodern Ecological Cosmology, but also the correlative transition from the receding paradigms of Modern Philosophy and Modern Science to their emerging postmodern paradigms.

As we will see later, the Modern Mechanical Cosmology of an atomistic-mechanistic and purely materialist Universe found its initially normative articulation in the sequential contributions of René Descartes (1596-1650) for Philosophy and Isaac Newton (1643-1727) for Physics, though both understood their work as "Natural Philosophy."

Descartes and Newton completed the early modern overthrow of what had been the classical Western Aristotelian-Ptolemaic Cosmology. That classical Cosmology had defined the Cosmos as geocentric, organic, hierarchical, and teleological. In addition, it had dualistically perceived the spiritual dimension as located in the higher "Celestial Spheres" of "the Heavens," with the "Terrestrial Sphere" of Earth seen as purely materialist. That classical Aristotelian-Ptolemaic Cosmology became Christianized in the late classical and medieval periods.

Yet early modern Christian "natural philosophers" (as scientists were then called) retrieved for their then "New Science" the atomistic-mechanical Materialism of the classical Greek philosopher Epicurus (341-270 BCE). The Epicurean Cosmology was not broadly accepted during the late classical or medieval Christian periods, since Epicurus had argued that the Universe was simply a collection of atoms (*atoma* in Greek and meaning "uncuttable particles" – i.e., the "atomic theory"). He had further argued that these atoms chaotically and temporarily combined in random, mechanical, and meaningless ways. He had also argued that there is no truly spiritual dimension to reality.

Today, the Modern Mechanical Cosmology is breaking down in the face of more holistic scientific data and more holistic philosophical in-sights, and a fresh Postmodern Ecological Cosmology is emerging. In contrast to the old paradigm which has been atomistic-mechanical and materialist, the emerging new paradigm is ecological-evolutionary and holistic.[26] Further, in terms of evolution, this "New Cosmology" trans-cends the modern Darwinian and Neo-Darwinian interpretation of evolution, since both have remained grounded in modern Scientific Materialism, which is now breaking down.[27]

But even this deeper cosmological level of social analysis cannot fully explain the late modern breakdown of Modern Industrial Civilization. There is a still deeper root of its erosion of life's integral ecology.

---

[26] A full articulation of the emerging postmodern "New Cosmology," as embraced in this book, may be found in Thomas Berry and Brian Swimme, THE UNIVERSE STORY: FROM THE PRIMAL FLARING FORTH TO THE ECOZOIC ERA – A CELEBRATION OF THE UNFOLDING OF THE COSMOS, Reprint Edition (HarperOne, 1994).

[27] In addition, Darwinism has had had intimate links with Eugenics. See Peter Quinn, "The Gentle Darwinians: What Darwin's Champions Won't Mention," COMMONWEAL, Volume CXXXIV, Number 05 (March 7, 2007), available at:
https://www.commonwealmagazine.org/gentle-darwinians (accessed 2017-04-12).

Level 4
Symbolic-Mythic Foundations

It is at the fourth level of symbolic-mythic foundations that Modern Industrial Civilization finds its deepest cultural grounding in spirituality, or in pathological rejections or deformations of spiritual reality. Addressing that deepest level, this book traces the correlative breakdowns of Modern Industrial Civilization and Modern Psychological Spirituality to an *oppressive deformation of sexual symbols and myths,* lodged within Modernity's cultural-spiritual foundations, and also in the earlier cultural-spiritual foundations of the Western Classical Era.

Yet this book sees that oppressive deformation as having been lodged in different ways in the cultural-spiritual foundations of the sequential Classical and Modern Eras of Western Civilization. During the Classical Era, that oppressive symbolic deformation was institutionalized in the aristocratic deformation called *"patriarchy"* (not authentically paternal). For the Modern Era, it has been institutionalized in the more expansive bourgeois deformation that may be called *"hyper-masculinism"* (not authentically masculine).

Further, while Western Modernity assigned a hyper-masculine deformation of symbolic-mythic identity to scientific-technological institutions, it also assigned a disempowering symbolic-mythic 'feminine' identity (not authentically feminine) to the societally privatized institutions of religion and family (even though deformed hyper-masculine ideologies continued to dominate both institutions).

In addition, Western Modernity undermined the entire foundational cultural-spiritual system of feminine symbols and myths from the Primal Era, which had supported the integral-ecological regeneration of Nature's webs and cycles, including the webs and cycles of our human family. Thus, we have the core example of the modern bourgeois symbolic shift from spiritual reverence for our "Mother Earth" to her materialistic redefinition as "natural resources" for industrial exploitation.

Hence, Modernity has not been only patriarchal, which means hierarchically and oppressively attempting to *demote* to a lower level women and the primal system of regenerative feminine myths and symbols. Rather, Modernity has also been hyper-masculine, which means attempting to *eliminate* the regenerative role of the ancient Primal feminine symbols and myths of regeneration (again, for example, elimination of the Primal cultural-spiritual symbol of "Mother Earth").

The modern hyper-masculine bourgeois project has been trying unsustainably to replace Nature's regenerative evolutionary-ecological *reproduction* with degenerative industrial-colonizing *production*. For the sake of maximizing wealth, power, and fame, modern bourgeois elites have been constructing over centuries a deformed scientific-technological world of exploitive industrialism that is now devastating the integral-ecological reproduction of Nature's evolving creative communion.

Within that late modern hyper-masculine framework, intellectual pressures grow to misunderstand men and women as both uprooted from the regenerative processes of natural, human, and spiritual ecology. Within that late modern misunderstanding, both women and men are then equally offered the promise of becoming 'free,' but only by accepting the late modern atomistic-mechanical, materialist – and now even nihilist – hyper-masculine drive to destroy the reproductive capacity of our loving Creator's beloved garden-planet Earth.

In ancient Asian symbolic language, Modernity's bourgeois hyper-masculinism is attempting through non-regenerative industrial production to fabricate a deformed scientific-technological world that expands *yang* by eliminating *yin*. But the imbalanced *yang* of the modern bourgeois hyper-masculine project has now become ecologically *unsustainable* across life's interwoven natural, human, and spiritual fabric.

Further, both classical aristocratic patriarchy and modern bourgeois hyper-masculinism have pathologically deformed what may be called the ancient symbol and myths of the *noble-warrior archetype*. They have deformed that ancient symbol and its myths by elevating it above, and eventually against, the primal feminine symbols and myths of communitarian cooperation. As a result, the modern hyper-masculine deformation pathologically misdirects its *industrial production* into devastating the *ecological reproduction* of life's integral ecology across its interwoven natural, human, and spiritual fabric.

Because of its hyper-masculine character, the modern Western bourgeois drive has long been conducting an *anti-ecological war against Nature*.[28] That anti-ecological war has intensified with late modern neoliberal globalization and with the growing global triumph of neoconservative industrial militarization. The current late modern global devastation of life's integral ecology thus stands as the long-term pathological outcome of the patriarchal and hyper-masculine deformations lodged within Classicism's and Modernity's symbolic-mythic foundations.

We need, however, to distinguish Modernity's philosophical-scientific appropriation of Epicurean Cosmology (again, atomistic-mechanical Materialism) from Modernity's hyper-masculine mythic-symbolic foundations. For Epicureanism is not itself hyper-masculine.[29] But

---

[28] For a recent highlighting of this "war against Nature," see the article by Agnès Sinaï, *"Guerre totale contre la nature,"* LE MONDE DIPLOMATIQUE, September 2015, *http://www.monde-diplomatique.fr/2015/09/SINAI/53706* (accessed 2015-08-15). Also, as we will see later in this book, important eco-feminine writers like eco-historian of Science Carolyn Merchant, Catholic eco-philosopher Charlene Spretnak, and eco-journalist Naomi Klein, have been intellectually uncovering the hyper-masculine, and thus anti-ecological, foundation of Modern Western Industrial-Colonial Civilization.

[29] Epicurus, who lived with intimate friends in his "garden" of Nature, would certainly disapprove of the late modern techno-scientific devastation of integral ecology that the modern Western elite project has long been inflicting on the planet. Epicurus constantly expressed a reverent attitude toward Nature. Further, he viewed Nature as symbolically feminine, and delighted in referring to "her" creativity and beauty.

Yet such a beauteous and feminine understanding of Nature cannot come from Epicurus' cosmological understanding of the Universe as only atomistic-mechanical, materialist, chaotic, random, blind, and meaningless. For how could a Universe, guided only by chaotic, random, blind, and meaningless chance, be perceived as endowed with such beauty,

where then does Modernity's hyper-masculine mythic-symbolic foundation come from?

While that is a question to be addressed more fully in the sequel book, SOCIAL ANALYSIS II, an immediate cause can be identified in Francis Bacon's (1561-1626) hyper-masculine symbolic-mythic vision that *Modern Science should conquer Nature*. In his writing about the "New Science," Bacon even called for using brutal techniques metaphorically akin to torture to "extract Nature's secrets."[30] The torture of non-human animals, and sometimes even of humans, became a key part of modern scientific research.

Bacon's hyper-masculine call for conquering Nature, and his metaphorical use of torturing techniques, thus represented a pathological deformation of the mission of the noble warrior, which is *to defend the community of life.*

A still older cause, which will be addressed later in this book, may be found in the militaristic spirit that first entered Christianity with the Constantinian turn, which took on further strength from the papal imperial alliance with Charlemagne's military power, and during the later European medieval period took on even more militarized form with

---

or be understood symbolically as so deeply feminine? To be consistent, would not the atomistic-mechanical and purely materialist Cosmology of Epicurus rather require something more like the brutal "state of nature" articulated by Thomas Hobbes (1588-1679) as the endless war of all against all? Or as the fascist philosophical style of Friedrich Nietzsche, which reduced all reality to the arrogant and conquering "will to power?"

Therefore, in order also to fully understand Epicurus, we need to distinguish his *cosmological framework* of an atomistic-mechanical and purely materialist Universe from his deeper *symbolic-mythic foundational vision* of a 'feminine' Universe filled with the constant delights and wondrous beauty of "her" boundless creativity. Further, so rich is Epicurus' feminine symbolic-mythic foundation that we might even be tempted to describe it as spiritually mystical. In such an almost spiritual mysticism, might we be hearing secularized echoes of the ancient mythic-symbolic celebration of the *Earth-Mother Goddess*, whose mystical presence so pervades ancient tribal spiritualities?

[30] On Bacon's vision of conquering, and implicitly of torturing, nature, see Carolyn Merchant, "The Scientific Revolution and *The Death of Nature*," Isis, 2006, 97:513-533.

the violently militarist and "crusading" spirit embraced by major strains of Western Christian monasticism.[31]

Tragically, it would later become an easy extension for European and European-American Christians to bring that deformed and pathological warrior-spirit to the conquering, torturing, and murdering of their human sisters and brothers within the First Nations of the Americas, as well as within the Atlantic slave system, and more widely within the Americas' lush and vibrant integral ecology of life.

POSTMODERN
ECOLOGICAL RENAISSANCE

In service of postmodern integral-ecological regeneration, this book urges Christians across the planet, and all concerned spiritual seekers, to support, and if feasible to contribute to, what the Pacem in Terris Ecological Initiative calls the "Postmodern Ecological Renaissance."[32]

Postmodern Ecological Visionaries

The Postmodern Ecological Renaissance is already being pioneered by still small networks of visionary artists, philosophers, scientists, and other intellectuals and professionals, as well as by visionary farmers, business-people, and other creative explorers. In all areas of human activity, these pioneering visionaries are advancing the emerging Postmodern Ecological Cosmology's regenerative paradigm for the evolving creative communion of life's integral ecology.

---

[31] For examples of Western monastic militarism during that period within the Iberian peninsula, see Enrique Rodriguez-Picavea, LOS MONJES GUERREROS EN LOS REINOS HISPÁNICOS: LAS ORDENES MILITA RES EN LA PENÍNSULA IBÉRICA DURANTE LA EDAD MEDIA (La Esfera de los Libros, 2008). Perhaps those militarized sectors of Iberian Christianity were copying the warrior-spirit of Islam, which earlier had conquered much of the Iberian Peninsula.

[32] See again the PACEM IN TERRIS ECOLOGICAL DECLARATION at the beginning of this book.

Visionary pioneers in this Postmodern Ecological Renaissance have been articulating a fresh postmodern cosmological paradigm for Philosophy and Science, which can provide the intellectual foundation for a regenerative Postmodern Ecological Civilization.[33] Further, at the deepest symbolic-mythic level, some of these pioneering visionaries have been exploring regenerative foundations for this Postmodern Ecological Civilization in the form of *a co-creative partnership of feminine and masculine energy*.[34] In addition, other pioneering visionaries in this Renaissance have been developing *a regenerative political economy*, which seeks to reintegrate human political-economic activity with Nature's own political economy.[35]

To further support the visionary work of such creative pioneers, this book urges Catholic-Christians and other Christians across our loving Creator's garden-planet Earth to promote in Christian circles two emerging postmodern movements, which are in fact overlapping. They are: 1) a postmodern lay-ecological and rural-centered *New Monasticism*; and 2) postmodern rural *ecovillages*. Both of these movements can humbly serve their surrounding rural communities and bioregions in regenerating the integral ecology of natural, human, and spiritual life.

Postmodern Lay-Ecological New Monasticism

To help us navigate creatively out of the breakdown of Modern Industrial Civilization toward a future Postmodern Ecological Civilization, this book calls for a postmodern lay-ecological Catholic-Christian New Monasticism, which in fact has already begun.

---

[33] On Philosophy and Science, see earlier and later references especially to the work of Thomas Berry and Brian Swimme, as well as to Fritjof Capra and Pier Luigi Liusi.

[34] On feminine-masculine partnership, see the work of Riane Eisler, as reported at: *https://en.wikipedia.org/wiki/Riane_Eisler* (accessed 2016-11-15), as well as *http://rianeeisler.com* (accessed 2016-11-15).

[35] See the later reference to the important work of organic farmer Anthony Flaccavento.

As one model for the New Monasticism, this book holds up *the rural-centered vision of Peter Maurin* – again, co-founder of the Catholic Worker movement in partnership with Dorothy Day. As both lay and implicitly ecological in its spiritual grounding, Peter's vision of this New Monasticism includes women and men, and marrieds and singles, as well as families with children.[36]

While this book proposes the lay-ecological New Monasticism as carrying Catholic-Christian eco-spiritual grounding, it also sees it as having an ecumenically Christian character. Further, it sees this New Monasticism as seeking dialogue with all human religions, and with all eco-spiritual seekers.[37] In addition, this book proposes that the Catholic-Christian form of this New Monasticism needs to seek a postmodern eco-spiritual alliance with traditional forms of Catholic-Christian "religious life" and with emerging Catholic-Christian new lay movements.

For this book's vision, the proposed *deep spiritual mission* of this New Monasticism may be described as follows.

> *The Holy Spirit is now calling us, both personally and institutionally, to embody and to preach the Good News of Jesus in and through holistic regeneration of the evolving creative communion of life's integral ecology, throughout its interwoven natural, human, and spiritual fabric, across our loving Creator's beloved garden-planet Earth.*

Again, this book sees this New Monasticism as called to ground postmodern Christian eco-spirituality in the postmodern global regeneration of life's integral ecology. It also sees this New Monasticism as called to plant regenerative seeds for a future Postmodern Ecological

---

[36] On Peter Maurin, see the moving biography by Dorothy Day & Francis J. Sicius, PETER MAURIN: APOSTLE TO THE WORLD (Orbis Books, 2004).

[37] Thomas Merton, toward the end of his life, was exploring a lay and ecological vision for monasticism, and he was linking it to the ancient Keltic monastic tradition, which we will examine in a later chapter. See the fascinating study by Monica Weiss, SSJ, THOMAS MERTON AND THE CELTS: A NEW WORLD OPENING UP (Pickwick Publications, 2016).

Civilization, and for a correlative Postmodern Ecological Evangelization. Let us now look briefly at the second overlapping movement in the Postmodern Ecological Renaissance, namely, ecovillages.

Postmodern Ecovillages & Rural Regeneration

In this book's vision, one core task for this New Monasticism, as well as for other institutions and movements, is to help to create *global networks of locally rooted regenerative ecovillages of Christian eco-spiritual inspiration,* and to do so in cooperation with ecovillages from other inspirational sources.

A spiritually diverse global network of locally based ecovillages is already emerging across planet Earth.[38] These already-existing ecovillages constitute the first glimpses of a new wave of practical micromodels for the wider macro-institutional regeneration of the creative communion of life's integral ecology.

In his helpful book on ecovillages, Jonathan Dawson – formerly Executive Secretary of Global Ecovillage Network (GEN) Europe and a sustainability educator at the Findhorn Foundation in Scotland – has quoted the following definition of ecovillages by Robert and Diane Gilman (at the time editors of IN CONTEXT magazine).

> *[Ecovillages are] human scale full-featured settlements in which human activities are harmlessly integrated into the natural world in a way that is supportive of healthy human development and can be successfully continued into the indefinite future.*[39]

---

[38] On the Global Ecovillage Network, see Hildur Jackson, ECOVILLAGE LIVING: RESTORING THE EARTH AND HER PEOPLE (UIT Cambridge Ltd, 2002); Diana Leafe Christian, CREATING A LIFE TOGETHER: PRACTICAL TOOLS TO GROW ECOVILLAGES AND INTENTIONAL COMMUNITIES (New Society Publishers, 2003); and *https://www.facebook.com/GlobalEcovillageNetwork.*

[39] Jonathan Dawson, ECOVILLAGES: NEW FRONTIERS FOR SUSTAINABILITY, Schumacher Briefings Series (UIT Cambridge Ltd, 2006), p. 13. The book provides an excellent

Jonathan Dawson has also cited the insightful words of Robert J. Rosenthal, Professor of Philosophy at Hanover College:

> *Ecovillages are the newest and most potent kind of intentional community, and in the vanguard of the environmental movement that is sweeping the world. I believe they unite two profound truths: that human life is at its best in small, supportive, healthy communities, and that the only sustainable path for humanity is in the recovery and refinement of traditional community life.*[40]

Developing a global network of ecovillages represents a return to traditional rural village life, yet one enhanced by postmodern electronic technologies like computers and solar energy. The global network of ecovillages is planting small but important seeds for reversing across planet Earth the late modern plague of slum-ridden megacities, resulting from the hyper-masculine destruction of traditional rural village life. [41]

Further, this book sees these ecovillages as called to help existing rural towns and villages, and even cities, to regenerate the evolving creative communion of integral-ecological life throughout the interwoven natural, human, and spiritual fabric of their own bioregions.

To share important examples of wider rural bioregional regeneration of life's integral ecology, Anthony Flaccavento, an organic farmer and leader in Abington, Virginia, has written a marvelous study titled BUILDING A HEALTHY ECONOMY FROM THE BOTTOM UP.[42] The book re-

---

introduction to ecovillages. Interestingly, in a manner similar to Peter Maurin, Dawson links contemporary ecovillages in part with early Medieval Keltic Christian Monasteries.

[40] Dawson, ECOVILLAGES, p. 13.

[41] On the systemic nature of late modern megacities filled with slums, see Mike Davis, PLANET OF SLUMS, Reprint Edition (Verso, 2007).

[42] Anthony Flaccavento, BUILDING A HEALTHY ECONOMY FROM THE BOTTOM UP: HARNESSING REAL-WORLD EXPERIENCE FOR TRANSFORMATIVE CHANGE (University of Kentucky Press, 2016).

ports on emerging locally-rooted networks of what elsewhere has been called "Ecological Economics."[43]

In his book, Anthony Flaccavento describes these networks as "place-based" and "living Economics." Further, he contrasts the emerging regenerative economic model with the currently dominant anti-ecological model of Neoliberal Economics. In so doing, he clarifies key practical principles that distinguish those two fundamentally different economic paradigms, and he lays out a comprehensive strategy for continuing development of the ecological paradigm for Economics.

Within this regenerative economic system, regional networks of ecovillages become connected with small-scale towns and even small cities, which then serve as hubs for regional commerce and shared cultural-spiritual development. In turn, such towns and small cities can then form part of wider global networks serving the postmodern regeneration of life's integral ecology.

OVERVIEW OF THE BOOK

In historically contextualizing the postmodern spiritual transformation, this book first traces the evolution of Catholic-Christian spiritual energy through past organizational forms traditionally called *"religious life,"* and then into the emerging *new lay forms*. The book offers its understanding of this evolution in a spirit of gratitude and hope:

- *In gratitude* for the gifts of older forms of "religious life" and of newer forms of lay movements, all of which have been wondrous gifts to the Catholic-Christian family, to the whole family of Christianity, and to the entire human family;

- *In hope* that both older Western Catholic-Christian movements of "religious life" and newer Catholic-Christian lay movements, with

---

[43] On the discipline of Ecological Economics, see Robert Costanza *et al.*, AN INTRO-DUCTION TO ECOLOGICAL ECONOMICS, Second Edition (CRC Press, 2014).

both renewed by the Holy Spirit, may help to heal both the *exterior breakdown* of Modern Industrial Civilization and the *interior breakdown* of Modern Psychological Spirituality.

In its structure, this book addresses the breakdown of Modern Psychological Spirituality by exploring first its *historical background,* then its *contemporary foreground,* and finally its *future horizon.* It offers this exploration as a humble contribution to the Catholic-Christian form of Postmodern Ecological Spirituality, as well as wider Christian and still wider human forms.

- *As historical background,* the study traces specifically Catholic-Christian spiritual energy through its evolving institutional forms from the early church to the Modern Western Era. It also critiques the oppressive deformation of sexual symbolism, as found within both late classical, medieval, and modern forms of Western Christian Civilization, and as echoed in both late classical, medieval, and modern forms of Western Catholic-Christian spirituality.

- *As contemporary foreground,* the study explores the historical-social context of the late modern Western spiritual decline of "apostolic religious life" within the 'advanced' industrial regions, and of the emerging and regenerative global postmodern Catholic-Christian spiritual energy that is lay in character.

- *As future horizon,* the study proposes an eco-spiritual alliance between traditional Catholic-Christian "religious communities" and new lay Catholic-Christian spiritual movements. It grounds that alliance in the search for holistic global regeneration of the evolving creative communion of integral-ecological life, across its interwoven natural, human, and spiritual dimensions. Finally, it points to Peter Maurin's radical-traditional vision of rural communes, urban houses of hospitality, and integrating "agronomic universities," with all seen as seeds for a regenerative Postmodern Ecological Civilization.

Let us now briefly review each of the chapters within the book's overall structure.

- *Chapter 1*, which is this Introduction, has proposed that the breakdowns of Modern Industrial Civilization and of Modern Psychological Spirituality are correlatively interwoven. It has also proposed as correlatively interwoven the emergence of Postmodern Ecological Spirituality and the already germinating seeds of Postmodern Ecological Civilization. Further, it has proposed that the postmodern mission of both spirituality and civilization is to regenerate the evolving creative communion of integral-ecological life, throughout its interwoven natural, human, and spiritual dimensions, across our loving Creator's beloved garden-planet Earth.

- *Chapter 2* analyzes *ideal types of five past long waves of Catholic-Christian mystical-prophetic communities*. Those five waves have emerged within the evolutionary journey of Catholic Christianity from the early church to the currently dominant modern model of the Western Catholic Church. They include the foundational lay movement, classical coenobitic movements, feudal monastic movements, medieval mendicant movements, and modern apostolic movements (followed today by postmodern lay movements).

- *Chapter 3* lays out *an overview of the great postmodern ecological transformation of spirituality and civilization*. It does that by exploring the postmodern cosmological transformation, the failure of modern ideologies, the modern bourgeois spiritual alienation from Nature, and the deepest roots of the late modern ecological breakdown in classical, medieval and modern deformations of sexual symbolism lodged within Modernity's mythic-symbolic foundations.

- *Chapter 4* is *the first of two chapters exploring the breakdown of Modern Psychological Spirituality*, as part of the integral-ecological breakdown of Modern Industrial Civilization. It explains how Philosophy constitutes the intellectual ground of spirituality, and it offers a reflection on the late modern spiritual "Dark Night." It also explores the roots of the late modern spiritual breakdown to the early modern Catholic and Protestant bourgeois development of urbanism, to the older aristocratic roots of classical Catholic-Platonic dualism, and to the cosmological grounding of Modern Philosophy and Modern Science in ancient Epicurean Materialism, which is atomistic and mechanical.

- *Chapter 5* continues investigating the breakdown of Modern Psychological Spirituality by *exploring the intellectual construction and subsequent deconstruction of the continental European tradition of Modern Philosophy.* On the constructive side, the chapter begins with the revised Platonic dualisms of Descartes' and Kant's philosophies. Then, on the deconstructive side, it reviews the Marxian atheistic and the Nietzschean nihilistic rejections of dualism. Finally, it reflects on the intellectual-spiritual breakdown of Modern Philosophy as the cultural triumph of Scientific Materialism and of Nietzschean voluntarist Nihilism.

- *Chapter 6, on late modern ideological degeneration and the strategic response of Catholic Social Teaching,* explores further implications of the late modern intellectual-spiritual breakdown. First, it explores the intellectual-spiritual degeneration of the late modern form of the ideology of Modern Industrial Capitalism, specifically with reference to the degenerative economic doctrine of Neoliberalism and the degenerative political doctrine of the National Security State. Second, it explores the strategic response of what I call "Postmodern Catholic Social Teaching" to that ideological degeneration, and it contextualizes that response within three historical-strategic stages of this wisdom tradition. Further, it holds up Postmodern Catholic Social Teaching as a wise societal guide for the Catholic-Christian form of Postmodern Ecological Spirituality.

- *Chapter 7* addresses *the emergence of postmodern new lay spiritual movements,* in parallel with the decline of modern "apostolic religious orders." The Chapter reflects again on institutional-spiritual evolution in the postmodern transition. It offers the proposed deep spiritual mission, centered in integral ecological regeneration, to ground and to guide the new lay movements. It also critiques the deficiencies, one-sidedness, and polarization which afflict many so called 'conservative' and so-called 'progressive' Catholic-Christian lay movements. Lastly, it calls for broad awakening to Postmodern Ecological Spirituality as foundational.

- *Chapter 8* *addresses the possibility of regeneration through "refounding" for declining, or even dying, "apostolic religious communities."* Further, it proposes an intellectual-spiritual strategic alliance, grounded in the emerging Postmodern Ecological Spirituality, between communities of the receding "religious" form and of the emerging new lay form. Such refounding could entail, according to the chapter, a postmodern ecological reinterpretation of the three "religious vows." The Chapter also outlines two counter-productive strategies that have appeared within many "apostolic religious communities, namely, continuing modernization and its opposite of pre-modern restoration. It sees both strategies as unable to provide regenerative guidance for the postmodern transition. Lastly, the Chapter proposes creating what it calls "islands of regenerative co-creativity," as core projects for refounding.

- *Chapter 9* *recommends the three-part "Green Revolution" of Peter Maurin's lay and rurally centered New Monasticism,* as a regenerative project for the proposed postmodern Catholic-Christian ecological-spiritual alliance between new lay movements and "apostolic religious communities." These three parts include: 1) "clarification of thought," to be pursued at multiple levels from "round-table discussions" to "agronomic universities;" 2) urban "houses of hospitality," to care especially for urban victims of the breakdown of Modern Industrial Civilization; and 3) "rural communes" (ecovillages), as centers of ecological, social, and spiritual regeneration. Finally, it proposes that ecovillages need to serve the wider ecological regeneration of rural life and to plant regenerative seeds for a Postmodern Ecological Civilization.

- *Chapter 10* concludes the study with a final reflection.

Readers who would not enjoy a heavy analysis of transformations in Philosophy, Science, and Cosmology, might consider skipping Chapter 3. Readers who do not enjoy heavy philosophical analyses might consider skipping Chapters 4 and 5, though Chapter 5 is very important for the argument of the book. Readers who are looking for the practical implications of the book will find those in Chapters 7, 8, and 9. Even so, I do recommend all these chapters for those who have such interests.

SOME ADDITIONAL POINTS

First, please note that this book does not consistently provide scholarly documentation throughout its text. Providing full documentation for this book's broad explorations would have made it an overwhelming project for both writer and reader. The book does, however, provide references to some books and other sources that could prove helpful for further study on its themes. These include occasional references to other writings of my own, which may further illumine what is written here.

Second, if this book is correct in stating that we are indeed facing the correlative breakdowns of Modern Industrial Civilization and Modern Psychological Spirituality, then any single analysis of such a profound historical transformation will of necessity be limited and incomplete. In addition, any such grand-scale analysis might surely contain errors.

For that reason, this book remains exploratory in nature. It explores past, present, and future developments of Western Catholic-Christian spirituality, as part of the wider development of all Christian and human spiritualities, within the correlative context of the postmodern transformation of civilization. The book thus offers a grandiose, yet still only exploratory, interpretation of the great postmodern historical transformation that our global human family and all creatures on planet Earth are now experiencing. It offers that interpretation as a modest contribution to ongoing dialogue.

Third, this book is offered with a humble and hopeful prayer that its exploration of the postmodern eco-spiritual transformation may prove of some modest service to the global Catholic-Christian family (again, including all twenty-four *sui-juris* Catholic-Christian Churches), as well as to the wider global Christian family that includes its Orthodox and Protestant branches, to the wider global family of all world religions, and to our entire global human family.

Lastly, this book is offered with a humble and hopeful prayer that it may prove of some modest service to our threatened global ecological family, including all of our loving Creator's beloved and beauteous creatures throughout the garden of life across our loving Creator's beloved and beauteous garden-planet Earth.

2

PAST LONG WAVES OF

CATHOLIC-CHRISTIAN SPIRITUAL ENERGY

T his chapter reviews the *past five historical long waves* of what I call "Catholic-Christian mystical-prophetic communities."[1] Those past long waves flow from the foundational lay roots of the early church up to the modern Western "apostolic" form of "religious life," which is now experiencing late modern decline within the 'advanced' industrialized countries. In turn, the most recent last long wave of modern "apostolic-religious" communities is now yielding to the emerging postmodern wave of new lay movements.

CO-CREATIVE ROLE OF CATHOLIC-CHRISTIAN
MYSTICAL-PROPHETIC COMMUNITIES

Catholic-Christian mystical-prophetic communities are intense centers of spiritual energy, with historically evolving institutional expressions in long waves of Catholic-Christian spirituality. Each wave arises as a strategic-spiritual response to a new wave of civilization. Again, within the present postmodern transition, the modern wave of "apostolic religious life" is in decline. At the same time, there is emerging an early

---

[1] Again, I have for the most part rounded off dating of the beginning and ending of the dominance of each post-apostolic wave to the nearest hundredth year. Of course, the emergence and decline of the past forms overlap across long historical periods. For the beginning of Christianity, I have chosen as the rounded-off date the year 30.

postmodern wave of a fresh lay form of Catholic-Christian mystical-prophetic communities. This book sees these new lay movements as called, in partnership with traditional forms of "religious life," to promote a Catholic-Christian form of Postmodern Ecological Spirituality on behalf of global regeneration of life's integral ecology.

"Religious life" is an ancient and rich tradition in Catholic Christianity, with its modern "apostolic" form being one of many forms in its evolutionary history. Further, since a new form is now emerging and its identity is lay, this new lay form requires that we examine critically the cosmologically dualist character of the concept "religious life."

Beyond "Religious" Dualism

Since the emerging postmodern form of Catholic-Christian spiritual energy is taking a distinctly lay form, and since the dualistic phrase "religious life" is not of evangelical origin, I prefer to describe all such spiritual communities in this still evolving tradition by the broader name of Catholic-Christian mystical-prophetic communities.

Although some prefer the phrase "vowed life" or "consecrated life" over "religious life," those alternatives also do not seem adequate. All Christians have a vowed and consecrated life in the sacraments of Baptism (baptismal vows) and Confirmation (consecration with oil). Further, Catholic-Christian married couples have a vowed life in the sacrament of Marriage (marriage vows). In addition, while the "religious vows" of poverty, chastity, and obedience constitute an important form of "vowed life," they do not constitute a Catholic-Christian sacrament, as do baptismal and marriage vows and the consecration of Confirmation.

Again and for those reasons, this book uses the non-dualist phrase of Catholic-Christian mystical-prophetic communities. The core institutional identity of such communities has been, throughout their evolution, *their intense personal and institutional commitment to the mystical and prophetic dimensions of Christian discipleship.*

As mentioned, however, the Western Catholic-Christian spiritual tradition is partly problematic, because its classical cosmological dualism of 'higher' ("religious") and 'lower' ("secular") "states of life" came not from Jesus' original lay movement, but from the Neo-Platonist tradition, parts of which both classical and modern forms of Western Catholic-Christian Ascetical Theology incorporated. By contrast, in Jesus' teaching, as is clear in the New Testament, spirituality is not for a "state in life" but rather it is a way of life, and there is only one foundational way of Christian discipleship, namely, *the lay baptismal "Way" of Jesus' own mystical-prophetic path.*

Special Historical Roles

Catholic Christianity is heir to a long series of distinctive and creative movements of special mystical-prophetic communities. Those movements have emerged historically in strategic spiritual response to profound historical transformations within the contextual civilization.

Those creative spiritual movements have included, for example, Desert Fathers and Desert Mothers, Irish-Keltic monasticism and Latin Benedictine Monasticism, Augustinians who began as medieval canons, medieval mendicant Franciscans and Dominicans, late medieval Beguines and Beghards, and modern apostolic communities like Jesuits, Daughters of Charity, Religious of the Sacred Heart, Sisters of Mercy, etc. Such women's and men's communities have long been the Holy Spirit's special instruments for renewing both church and society, albeit always in a limited and imperfect manner.

Catholic-Christian "religious communities" have played significant roles by providing important gifts for renewing and sustaining the vocation, communion, and mission of all Jesus' disciples throughout the wider church. In these "religious communities," some of Jesus' lay disciples have gathered together to live Jesus' call in a more intense way as a renewing service to the wider community of all Jesus' disciples, as well as to the entire human family, and even to all of creation.

Yet we need to remember that the purpose of these *special* Catholic-Christian mystical-prophetic communities is part of the wider purpose of the *general* mystical-prophetic community of all Jesus' disciples. We need also to recall that the wider and full community of Jesus' disciples, which we call "church," exists for one central purpose, namely, *to serve as the evangelical-sacramental instrument of the Holy Spirit's healing and deeper sanctification of our wounded creation and of our wounded human family within it.*

Human sin has wounded and continues to wound the Creator's beloved creation and humanity within it. The Holy Spirit's healing and deeper sanctification of all creation and of humanity within it, through the "Way" of Jesus, comes to partial fulfillment when Christians gather in love as the imperfect community of disciples that we call "church."

Further, it is the evangelical-sacramental *lay mission* of all Jesus' disciples to carry the "good news" of that healing and deeper sanctification to all peoples. Those of us who are Jesus' disciples witness to the reality of that healing and deeper sanctification by loving communion within our community of disciples, as well as with all our human sisters and brothers across planet Earth. We also witness to it by our loving communion with all our loving Creator's beloved other creatures across our garden-planet Earth and throughout the Cosmos. For Christians, this healing sanctification partly takes place now, but its full power will be revealed only in the *Eschaton.*

Six Evolving Long Waves of Spirituality

Again, within this historical framework, what may now be called *special* Catholic-Christian mystical-prophetic communities have the special historical vocation of reforming and deepening the identity and mission of the *general* mystical-prophetic community of "Church." Such special communities do that through historically distinct mystical-prophetic strategic responses to historically distinct transformations of the contextual civilization.

SIX HISTORICAL LONG WAVES

OF CATHOLIC-CHRISTIAN SPIRITUAL ENERGY

HISTORICAL CONTEXT	HISTORICAL FORM	HISTORICAL MISSION
Cities of Oppressive & Idolatrous Roman Empire	FOUNDATIONAL LAY COMMUNITIES *(30-300)*	Live as Messianic Community often under Roman Imperial Persecution
Cities of Christianized Roman Empire	CLASSICAL COENOBITICAL COMMUNITIES *(Desert Hermits)* *(300-500)*	Ascetical Flight to Rural Wilderness as Counter-point to Urban "Clergy's" Imperial Church
Rural Feudalism after Fall of Western Roman Empire	FEUDAL MONASTIC COMMUNITIES *(500-1200)*	Evangelize Migrating 'Barbarian' Tribes & with Them Rebuild Western Christian Civilization
Late Medieval Bourgeois Commercial City-States as Seeds of Modern Capitalism	MEDIEVAL MENDICANT COMMUNITIES *(1200-1500)*	Evangelize New Bourgeois Culture & Challenge its Foundational Temptations *(Defense of Poor, Ecology, & Democracy)*
Modern Western Bourgeois Industrial-Colonial Nation-States *(Initially Liberal-Capitalist & later also Scientific-Socialist)*	MODERN APOSTOLIC COMMUNITIES *(1500-2000)*	Apostolates of Health, Education, & Welfare, especially for Urban Working Class, Poor Rural Areas, & Colonized Peoples
Breakdown of Modern Western Industrial-Colonial Civilization & Emergence of Postmodern Global Electronic-Ecological Civilization	POSTMODERN LAY COMMUNITIES *(2000 ...)*	Overcome Late Modern Western Culture of Death & Seek Global Regeneration of Life's Evolving Ecology across its Interwoven Natural, Human, & Spiritual Fabric

Simplifying the complexity of this still developing tradition into what the great German sociologist Max Weber called "ideal types," we may identify within the evolving history of Catholic-Christian mystical-prophetic communities the following six successive long waves (summarized in the chart on the preceding page).[2] For the most part, the dating of these waves is rounded off here to the nearest hundredth year. These six long waves may be described as follows.

- *Foundational Lay Communities* (30-300) of the early church, including women and men, married and singles, and families with children – witnessing to Jesus' messianic vision under the oppression and persecution of the unjust and idolatrous Roman Empire;

- *Classical Coenobitical Communities* (300-500) of "Desert Mothers" and "Desert Fathers," who moved to remote rural areas beyond the urban-centered Empire and outside the ecclesial framework of the new Imperial Church with its now hierarchical urban "clergy," who

---

[2] For the history of "religious life," I am especially endebted to: Lawrence Catta, Raymond Fitz, Gertrude Foley, Thomas Giordino & Carol Lynchburg SHAPING THE COMING AGE OF RELIGIOUS LIFE (Seabury Press, 1985); Institute for Research, NEW BEGINNINGS, RELIGIOUS LIFE EVOLVES (Lumen Vitae, 1983); Gerald Arbuckle, STRATEGIES FOR GROWTH IN RELIGIOUS LIFE (ALBA HOUSE, 1987) OUT OF CHAOS: REFOUNDING RELIGIOUS CONGREGATIONS (Paulist Press, 1988); Lori Felknor CRISIS IN RELIGIOUS VOCATION (Paulist Press, 1989); Mary Jo Leddy, "Beyond the Liberal Model of Religious Life," THE WAY (Summer, 1989.

Since the time when the above-noted books were published, much more has been written about the history of "religious life," including about refounding, though the majority have been from perspectives internal to "religious life." The most recent of these books includes Diarmuid O'Murchu's magisterial text, RELIGIOUS LIFE IN THE 21ST CENTURY: THE PROSPECT OF REFOUNDING (Orbis Books, 2016). That book does a masterful job of synthesizing recent explorations on the history and present crisis of modern "religious life." It also provides a prophetic vision and process for discernment about possible "refounding" with "religious communities."

Note that this list of six leaves out some additional models – for example, medieval "canons" as well as the Beguines and Beghards, since such additional models, while important and creative, never became pervasive. Also, this listing does not agree with the distinction sometimes made between earlier modern "apostolic" communities and later modern "missionary" communities. For this listing, both fall under the "apostolic" model.

as religious legitimizers of the Empire often tended to change the Evangelical message of the Cross to an imperial military symbol;

- *Feudal Monastic Communities* (500-1200) which, after the fall of the Western Roman Empire, lived within rural Feudalism to evangelize the conquering 'barbarian' German tribes, and with them to regenerate Western Civilization by creating intellectual-spiritual centers and communitarian-agrarian foundations, many of which would later become medieval towns and modern cities (for example, the city of Vienna, founded by Irish-Keltic monks).

- *Medieval Mendicant Communities* (1200-1500), which challenged the early bourgeois temptations of the new urban culture of the high Middle Ages, and reached out especially to youth in the medieval university towns – themselves expanding from the new commercial wealth generated from the Eastern "Silk Roads" that were re-opened as trading routes by the West's violent military "Crusades;"[3]

- *Modern Apostolic Communities* (1500-2000), which ministered within the 'advanced' bourgeois civilization that was becoming Modern Western Industrial-Colonial Capitalism, and did so by providing professional "apostolates" especially to the industrial urban working class and to poor rural farming families, as well as to conquered and colonized peoples, primarily by pioneering and developing modern social-welfare institutions for education, healthcare, and other charitable services;

- *Projected Postmodern Lay Ecological New Monasticism* (2,000 ...), which is seen here as called to become grounded in the emerging Postmodern Ecological Spirituality, to promote a future Postmodern Ecological Civilization, and to plant seeds for the postmodern

---

[3] As noted earlier, in the High Middle Ages, there emerged many military forms of monasticism – a development far from Jesus' non-violent message. Again, see Rodriguez-Picavea, LOS MONJES GUERREROS.

global regeneration of life's integral ecology, especially on behalf of vulnerable humans and all other threatened living creatures across our loving Creator's beloved garden planet Earth.

Again, against the background of this historical unfolding, this book sees the new lay wave as called to celebrate the creative communion of life's integral ecology, throughout its interwoven natural, human, and spiritual fabric. But let us now review the past five long waves, including the now declining "apostolic-religious" wave.

FOUNDATIONAL LAY COMMUNITIES WITNESSING WITHIN THE ROMAN EMPIRE (30-300)

The first wave of Catholic-Christian mystical-prophetic communities is the *foundational lay period* of Christianity during its first three centuries – originally Jewish but quickly expanding into Arabian and African Christianity, as well as into Greco-Roman and Keltic Christianities, and into the Christianities of Persia, India, and perhaps even China. Within the territories of the Roman Empire, the identity and mission of the early and foundational lay communities carried a *messianic rejection of the Empire's idolatry and injustice.*

"Way" of Jesus as Lay

The brutal Roman Empire had crucified Jesus, a Jewish lay teacher ("rabbi"), as a political threat. The Empire also subsequently executed Peter and Paul, both Jewish laypersons, as well as thousands of other Christians, all of whom were lay. That foundational period has been called the "Age of Martyrs," since the Empire executed so many Christians for following the "Way" of Jesus.

In all the regions of this first wave, throughout the apostolic church and for several centuries after, Christianity was *exclusively lay*. In that first wave, there was no such thing as the "religious state in life" (with "state" meaning status or class), nor was there any such thing as the "clerical state in life." Over time, there emerged, of course, disciples who were ordained for authority-bearing offices (deacons, presbyters, and bishops), as well as disciples with special charisms for the community (including communities of virgins and widows). Yet all were lay.

Again, in the church's early centuries, these offices and charisms did not represent separate "states-in-life" (to use the language of the contemporary Canon Law of the Western or Roman Catholic Church). There was originally only the *one lay "way"* of the baptized, including ordained lay leaders and lay disciples with special charisms. There was only the New Testament's "Way" of Jesus.

The word "lay" comes from the Greek word *Laos*, which means "people." In the Greek Septuagint translation of the Hebrew Scriptures and in Greek texts of the New Testament, *Laos* means the holy, royal, priestly People of God. Further, in the New Testament the Greek work *kleros* (from which we get "clergy") means "chosen." The New Testament uses the word *kleros* to signify that everyone within the *Laos* of Jesus' disciples is "chosen."

Thus, neither the "religious state" nor the "clerical state" is a constitutive dimension of the Church, for they did not exist in the early centuries of Christianity. Further, the Catholic-Christian tradition came to understand Baptism, Confirmation, Ordination, and Marriage as "sacraments." But the canonical "clerical and religious states" are not sacraments. Even so, both often became elevated in practice above the "laity," and thus above the sacraments of Baptism, Confirmation, and Marriage. Nonetheless, the "religious and clerical states in life" represented creative legal-cultural additions to the late classical form of Catholic Christianity, and they later carried over into medieval modern forms. Yet, again, those adaptations were not part of the church's apostolic foundation.

End of Persecuted Lay Church
& Rise of Imperial Hierarchical Church

Toward the end of the foundational period, Roman imperial leaders saw the lay movement of Christianity – despite persecution, spreading rapidly and broadly throughout the Empire – as offering the possibility of holding together the externally threatened and internally disintegrating imperial society.

As external attacks by migrating 'barbarian' German tribes intensified, and as the Empire began to degenerate internally, the Christian movement appeared to imperial leaders to offer renewed and unifying organizational strength. That was because the Christian cosmopolitan vision was not limited to a specific geographic, ethnic, or class identity.

From the time of the fifty-seventh Roman Emperor Constantine the Great (272-337), ruling from Constantinople (formerly Byzantium) in what is today's Turkey, the imperial government constructed an ecclesial-political alliance with the Catholic bishops of the imperial regions (called "dioceses"). The Roman Empire, which had crucified Jesus and probably thousands of his followers, appealed to the episcopal leaders of Jesus' disciples in the desperate hope of saving itself. Most Catholic bishops accepted the opportunity, though the Coptic church of Africa resisted imperial take-over and continued to suffer persecution from the Imperial State in its new partnership with the Imperial Church.

That Catholic-Christian acceptance eventually led to Christianity becoming the official religion of the Empire, reshaped by imperial consciousness and backed by the coercive power of the Imperial State. Within that profound political shift, the first history of the Catholic Church, written by the Catholic bishop Eusebius of Caesarea (c. 263-339) who was close to the imperial household, described the Emperor Constantine ruling on his throne as reflecting an *imperial image of God*.[4]

---

[4] See EUSEBIUS: THE CHURCH HISTORY, transl. Paul L. Maier (Kraeger, 2007). Note that, contrary to GENESIS 1:27, the image does not include woman.

That imperial image, Christianized as "*Christ the King*," would dominate Catholic Christianity until recent times when Latin-American Liberation Theology recovered, for both Catholicism and Protestantism, the alternative prophetic biblical image of Jesus as proclaimed in Luke 4:18-19. That is the image of *Jesus the Liberator*, recalling not David the King but Moses the Prophet. The following lengthy quotation may be helpful for understanding how profound is that symbolic shift in Christian Soteriology.

> *In the impending collapse of Western political-economic and ecclesial-spiritual hegemony, we are now experiencing a paradigm-shift in the foundational biblical metaphor for evangelization from David to Moses, or from the Temple at Zion to the Covenant at Shechem. Since the time of Constantine, Western Catholic Christianity pursued evangelization under the symbolic image of "Yeshua Ha-Mashiach" (Jesus the Christ, or Joshua the Messiah), understood hierarchically and triumphally as Christ the King.*

> *That foundational Davidic or Zionist image understands the Word of God as coming in priestly manner to the people through the established social structures (equivalent of the king), with the established social order presumably reflecting the Divine order.*

> *Today, however, with Western de-Christianization, with the post-colonial emancipation of the formerly colonized peoples of the Global South, and with the threatened ecological destruction of at least half of the Creator's beloved species on planet Earth, the foundational biblical metaphor of evangelization is shifting.*

> *It is now swinging to the other biblical pole of the counter-cultural symbol of "Yeshua Ha-Mashiach," that is, Jesus (or Joshua) the Liberator, as proclaimed in Luke 4:18-19, which repeats Isaiah 61:11. In this foundational symbol of evangelization, the Word of God comes prophetically from the oppressed margins of society to challenge spiritually its idolatrous centers of power.*

This Western shift in the foundational biblical symbolic pole began hundreds of years ago, with the spiritual songs of the oppressed African-rooted peoples of the Atlantic slave system. More recently, it developed a newer Catholic expression with the Amerindian-rooted Theology of Liberation articulated by the Amerindian theologian Gustavo Gutiérrez (of Quechua-Inca ancestry). Now the Theology of Liberation is spreading ecumenically across the planet.[5]

Yet in the time of Constantine, while the Catholic bishops were restructuring Christianity into the new Imperial Church, persecuted Christians were still suffering in imperial prisons (again, especially Coptic Christians). The older church of the martyrs and the early Imperial Church thus co-existed for some time as alternative paths for Jesus' disciples. Eventually, however, the Imperial Church won and the Age of Martyrs ended. That also ended Christianity's foundational lay era.

At the beginning of the episcopal-imperial alliance formed in the fourth century, the Emperor Constantine gave to the Catholic-Christian bishops in many towns an imperial building for their gatherings. The Greek word for emperor is *basileus,* so those imperial buildings were called (in English translation) "basilicas," meaning buildings of the emperor. Imperial basilicas became the first large church buildings.

Prior to that gift of imperial buildings, the community of Jesus' disciples had typically gathered during three centuries for the Lord's Supper in *people's homes.* Following the donation of imperial buildings to the bishops, a tendency emerged to think of the "Church" as *holy buildings* (so today we "go to Church"), rather than as the sacred gathering of Jesus' disciples who form the holy, chosen, and priestly *Laos.*

---

[5] Adapted from Joe Holland, "See-Judge-Act: A Praxis Method for Catholic Practical Theology," keynote address to Iannone Conference II, St. Thomas University School of Theology & Ministry, Miami Gardens, Florida, 2 May 2015. Full text available via email request from *office@paceminterris.net.*

Further, with the new alliance between the Catholic bishops and the Empire, imperial leaders extended to the bishops and to their presbyters the *special class-rank of the imperial pagan priesthood*. This special imperial class rank ("state" or "status") is the legal origin of the "clerical state." That imperial "state" legally gave to Jesus' ordained disciples *certain government-granted economic and political privileges that Jesus' non-ordained disciples did not receive* – for example, exemption from imperial taxes and from military service in the imperial army, plus a legal court only for those in the "clerical state."

Again, the Greek word *kleros*, from which the word "clergy" is derived, refers in the Greek texts of the New Testament to the "chosen" character of all disciples of Jesus who form the holy *Laos* (1 Peter 2:5-10). Yet in a non-evangelical manner, the New Testament's lay term *kleros* became misidentified with a 'higher' clerical class ruling from 'above' the *Laos* of Jesus' non-clerical disciples. As a result, a non-evangelical tendency also emerged to identify clericalized bishops and presbyters as "*the Church*," rather than the full *Laos* of all Jesus' disciples.

That Constantinian episcopal-imperial alliance then expanded geographically the Catholic-Christian evangelization of Western Civilization. It often did so, however, through military force imposed on 'uncivilized' (meaning not living in cities) European tribal peoples, and later in similar manner on 'uncivilized' non-European tribal peoples.

Along with its contributions, that late classical Greco-Roman episcopal-imperial alliance created *three anti-evangelical distortions* of the original apostolic community of Jesus' disciples.

- *Loss of Lay Identity.* First, it weakened the foundational evangelical truth that Christian church was entirely a *lay community of disciples.* It did so by promoting a wrong sense that the church was a state-sponsored institution identified with set of *temple-like buildings,* and alternately with a *hierarchical clerical class* receiving state privileges that the rest of Jesus' disciples did not receive.

- *Ruling Clerical Class.* Second, it weakened the foundational evangelical command that the ordained leaders of Jesus' disciples were to function as *servant-leaders* of the wider lay community. It did that by social construction of an imperially privileged clerical class empowered by the imperial state to *rule hierarchically over the Laos.*

- *Cross as Imperial Military Conquest.* Third, as many elite clericalized leaders supported the militaristic Roman Imperial State, a hierarchical-patriarchal and military-command style of leadership was imposed on the Catholic-Christian community. That imperial style for ecclesial leadership then undermined the foundational evangelical doctrine of the *Cross* as a symbol of persecution. That undermining not only legitimated imperial, class-based, and gender-based domination. It also inverted the meaning of the Cross *from Jesus' suffering imperial execution to supporting imperial conquest.*

As a symbol of that third distortion of Christianity, we have the legend of Constantine seeing in a vision the Cross with Greek words that have been traditionally rendered in Latin as "*In hoc signo vinces*" (Under this sign you will conquer). Thus was the prophetic meaning of the Cross of Jesus inverted. Again, no longer a sign of *persecution*, the Cross became a sign of *military conquest and domination.*

That imperial identification of evangelization with imperial violence would continue for Western Catholic Christianity up to the time of the early modern European-Catholic "*Conquista*" of the First Nations of the Americas, beginning in the late fifteenth and early sixteenth centuries. It continued during the late nineteenth and early twentieth centuries into *Modern Western Industrial Colonialism.*

Catholic examples of Modern Western Industrial Colonialism included Belgian King Leopold's personally held "Congo Free State," which caused the unjust death of perhaps ten-million people, as well as the twentieth-century 'imperial' conquest of Ethiopia by the officially 'Catholic' Italian fascist state of Benito Mussolini.

Predominantly Protestant modern examples included the vast British Empire across Africa, Asia, and the Caribbean, as well as the United States' genocidal military attacks on the First Nations of the continent – most infamously in the Cherokee "Trail of Tears." It also included Modern Western Neo-Colonialism throughout Africa, the Asian/Pacific region, and the Latin American/Caribbean region.

"Cross and sword" (and later machine gun) continued in Western partnership across the twentieth century. The most famous example occurred in the late twentieth-century with the Vatican-CIA alliance, established between U.S. President Ronald Reagan and Pope John Paul II, to support the right-wing side of the "Contra Wars" in Central America. Let us hope and pray that will remain the last tragic example of the Constantinian inversion.

COENOBITICAL COMMUNITIES
AT THE MARGINS OF THE IMPERIAL CHURCH
(300-500)

Within the classical Constantinian urban-imperial setting, the Catholic-Christian episcopal shepherds of Jesus' disciples became tempted to *lose their prophetic voice*. In response, a spiritual hunger for that prophetic voice led to the next institutional wave of Catholic-Christian spiritual energy, namely, the Desert Mothers and Desert Fathers, who eventually formed what have been called coenobitical communities.

Maurice Monette, in his pioneering book titled KINDRED SPIRITS: BONDING OF LAITY AND RELIGIOUS, has provided a helpful description of that new Catholic-Christian form of spiritual energy:

Lay men and women fled to into the desert to pursue the ideal life set by holy ascetics like Anthony of the Desert (251-356 CE). The desert became for them a wondrous and life-giving milieu. Their reasons for being there were varied. For the earlier hermits, the desert was often an escape from persecution and a place to seek holiness through asceticism. For many of the fiercely independent Egyptian peasants, the desert was a route to escape from insurmountable economic burdens. For yet others, the flight from the new Christian cities was a protest against the church turned too worldly and over-institutionalized, now that it was established in the Empire and no longer persecuted.[6]

About these communities, he continues:

This movement began in the Egyptian desert and on the Eastern rim of the Mediterranean and gradually spread west to the Italian peninsula, Spain, Gaul, and the northern coast of Africa. It attracted men and women from all strata of society ... The coenobia attracted thousands of ascetics, even families. Perhaps ten thousand ascetics were networked in Egypt by Pachomius and Mary alone.[7]

Though the initial Egyptian desert movement began before the Constantinian inversion (and may even have had pre-Christian roots), and though the motives for involvement were diverse, note especially what Maurice Monette has described above as "a protest against a church turned too worldly and over-institutionalized, now that it was established in the Empire and no longer persecuted." Further, in contrast to the social construction of hierarchical "clergy" for the Imperial Church, this new form of Catholic-Christian institutional energy remained lay. Paradoxically, however, church historians and ascetical theologians would later identify it as the first stage of "religious life."

Return to the Wilderness

Thus, some disciples of Jesus, inspired by the Holy Spirit to live the "Way" of discipleship more intensely, turned to the ancient human ascetical path which rejected elite cities and the empires that grew out of

---

[6] Maurice Monette, KINDRED SPIRITS: BONDING OF LAITY AND RELIGIOUS (Sheed & Ward, 1987), p. 29.

[7] Monette, KINDRED SPIRITS, p 30.

them. Those heroic disciples first heard the call to live the Cross of Jesus in their own persons, and they abandoned life in imperial cities. Like Israel and Jesus before them, they returned to the wilderness – that is, to Nature – in order to become closer to their Creator. They also embraced spiritual martyrdom for their own bodies.

Again, like Israel and like Jesus, they sought to meet God in the harshness of Nature, but also in Nature's ecological beauty. In the natural world, they celebrated the astounding beauty of the loving Creator's beloved creation. Like Francis of Assisi many centuries later, they even befriended non-human animals. In that return to the beauty of the natural world, and within it to wider animal kingdom, they imagined themselves returning to the Garden of Eden's mystical Paradise.

Found especially in Egypt, Syria, and Palestine, this radical Christian movement also appeared far away in the Keltic church of Ireland, although in Ireland the radicals went not to the desert, but to forest and mountain, and to the rocky turbulence at the edge of the wild sea.

In their early stage, these Desert Mothers and Fathers have been called "*anchorites*," which meant that they led the stable and solitary existence of hermits. As more of these radical disciples fled to the desert, however, they established the *coenobitical* form of common life. Though they often continued to be described as "hermits," perhaps their coenobitical communities were really bioregional rural ecovillages.

Those coenobitical communities were the first form of special Catholic Christian mystical-prophetic communities, distinct from the wider institutionalized Church of the Empire. With hindsight, we can say that their mission (at least in the Imperial period) was to be a counterpoint to Constantinian imperial urbanism, with its military-imperial inversion of the meaning of the Cross. They witnessed to the Cross by living in simple poverty and in the hardships felt by their own bodies. But they also celebrated the beauty of creation and befriended its wondrous creatures. Many reportedly embraced voluntary celibacy, yet there seemed also to have been large numbers of families among them. Again, they may have been the Christian "ecovillages" of the late classical period.

Thus, on one side, many episcopal authorities of the Imperial Church lost consciousness of the lay nature of the apostolic church, of its prophetic critique of the Empire, and of the identity of the Cross with persecution. On the other side, the Desert Mothers and Fathers kept alive those themes as healing gifts to the wider church and society, and they rooted their lives in the ecological beauty of Nature.

Negative Strains of Hellenist Philosophy

While the Desert Mothers and Desert Fathers drew on the Gospel of Jesus and on the Genesis narrative of Eden's Paradise, some also drew on certain negative strains in Hellenist Philosophy. As we have seen, such negative strains wrongly expressed contempt for material creation, including for the human body, for human sexuality, and especially for the body of woman (again, whom Genesis 1:27 describes as the feminine face of the "image of God").

Negative non-evangelical teachings, including Neo-Platonist and sometimes even Gnostic teachings, had long been in circulation across the Hellenistic culture that arose in the wake of the conquests of Alexander the Great (356-323 BCE). The classical center of Christian Neo-Platonist Philosophy became the North-African city of Alexandria, to which (according to the Coptic tradition) the evangelist Mark had brought Christianity, and which became a Catholic "patriarchal" city.[8]

---

[8] Plato had viewed women's mind (*psyche* or "soul") as equal to men's mind in the spiritual pursuit of wisdom (with "Philosophy," meaning from its Greek roots the "love of wisdom"). Yet Plato had also taught that the human rational "soul" (again, mind) had no gender, and that "souls" had "fallen" into, and become trapped within, human bodies, which then constituted temporary prisons for the entrapped souls. In that corporeal entrapment, however, Plato had defined *the female body as inferior to the male body*, since he ranked it lower than the male body in the descending hierarchy of reincarnation for those

68

Contempt for material creation (again including for the human body, for human sexuality, and especially for women's bodies) had never been part of Jesus' teaching. Although most Christians believe that Jesus lived the spiritual creativity of the celibate vocation and even encouraged select individuals to follow that path, it is clear from the New Testament that Jesus did not combine his honoring of the charism of celibacy with contempt for material creation, nor for the human body, nor for human sexuality, nor for the body of woman.

In contrast to classical demeaning of women, Jesus held up women as the first hearers and proclaimers of the Gospel. We see this in his mother Mary's special role, in the refusal of key female disciples to flee from his crucifixion, and in his first appearance after the resurrection to Mary Magdalene, who was his most important female disciple.

Married Catholic Bishops & Presbyters

Similarly, regarding sexuality and marriage, Jesus' first public miracle was for a wedding feast, and he appears to have chosen mostly married individuals as his apostles. Continuing that apostolic precedent, for the first thousand years of Christian history the Catholic-Christian bishops and presbyters throughout the Catholic-Christian Churches, including within the Latin or Roman Church, were typically married. In early support for that later tradition, the New Testament presumes

---

who failed to become enlightened philosophers. Further, the misogyny of Plato's student Aristotle became notorious, for Aristotle in his POLITICS wrote that women, as well as 'uncivilized' tribal peoples, were sub-human due to an alleged lack of rationality. Aristotle's proof that 'barbarian' tribes were not fully rational was that they viewed women and men as equals. If the 'barbarian' men were equal to 'barbarian' women, he concluded, then both must be subhuman.

On the deep Western philosophical bias against women found in the writings not only of Plato and Aristotle, but also of Descartes, Rousseau, Kant, Hume, Locke, and Hegel, see the excellent book by Nancy Tuana, WOMAN AND THE HISTORY OF PHILOSOPHY (Paragon House, 1992).

that bishops or presbyters overseeing the communities of Jesus' disciples would be married. Thus, I TIMOTHY 3:2-5 states:

> *Therefore, a bishop must be irreproachable,* **married only once***, temperate, self-controlled, decent, hospitable, able to teach, not a drunkard, not aggressive, but gentle, not contentious, not a lover of money. He must manage his own household well, keeping his children under control with perfect dignity; for if a man does not know how to manage his own household, how can he take care of the church of God? (Bold font added.)*

Similarly, regarding presbyters, TITUS 1:5-7 states:

> *Appoint presbyters in every town, as I directed you, on condition that a man be blameless,* **married only once***, with believing children who are not accused of licentiousness or rebellious. For a bishop as God's steward must be blameless, not arrogant, not irritable, not a drunkard, not aggressive, not greedy for sordid gain. (Bold font added.)*[9]

Over against perhaps hundreds of later Western Catholic-Christian theological volumes defending the Western Catholic Church's second-millennium law of mandatory "clerical celibacy" for its bishops and presbyters, the clear teaching of the New Testament must certainly rank higher. In addition, of the twenty-four "*sui-juris*" Catholic-Christian churches that make up the global Catholic family in communion with the Catholic-Christian Bishop of Rome, with many having apostolic origin, practically all those churches have never required "clerical celibacy" for their presbyters.

Jesus' Cosmic Spirituality

Jesus' spirituality was not anti-worldly but rather *Earth-rooted*, celebrating the birds of the air and the lilies of the field. Further, Jesus pro-

---

[9] The above biblical quotations are from the NEW AMERICAN BIBLE. Note that, in the beginning of Christianity, bishops and presbyters were not clearly distinguished.

claimed an *eschatological renewal of all creation* that would include both the "Heavens" and the "Earth." Contrary to the Pythagorean, Platonic, and Neo-Platonist goals of only "saving souls," Jesus did not preach "saving souls." Rather, he proclaimed a "Paradise" that would include resurrected bodies and eschatological renewal of both the "Heavens and Earth," that is, of the entire Cosmos.[10]

After the foundational first centuries, however, non-evangelical and anti-material Hellenistic teachings began to infect Catholic-Christian spirituality. As a result, non-evangelical teachings – again, disparaging material creation, disparaging the human body, disparaging human sexuality, and especially disparaging the body of woman – spread across significant aspects of *classical Catholic-Christian Ascetical Theology.* That infection has continued in some sectors even up to today.

Disintegration of the Western Empire

The historical mission of the communities of Desert Mothers and Fathers made sense as a prophetic counter-point only so long as the clericalized episcopal and presbyteral authorities in the Roman imperial cities remained as religious functionaries of the Empire. Yet with the growing migrations of 'barbarian' German tribes into the Western Empire, with their military attacks on many Western imperial cities, and with the slow but relentless internal breakdown of the Western imperial organization, the Roman Empire in the West gradually fell into turmoil and decline.

Many historians have judged that, by the end of the fifth century, the Western Empire had ceased to exist, though some imperial structures continued beyond that point, and many migrating tribes integrated

---

[10] See Rebecca Ann Parker & Rita Nakashima Brock, SAVING PARADISE: HOW CHRISTIANITY TRADED LOVE OF THIS WORLD FOR EMPIRE AND CRUCIFIXION (Beacon Press, 2009).

Roman traditions into their cultures.[11] Even so, with imperial decline, coenobitical communities in the West lost a key *raison d'être*.

MONASTIC COMMUNITIES
REBUILDING CIVILIZATION WITHIN FEUDALISM
(500-1200)

As Feudalism replaced Empire in the West, a new Western wave of "religious life" called "*monasticism*" displaced the historical role of coenobitical communities as the dominant historical form of Catholic-Christian mystical-prophetic communities.

To repeat, as migrating 'barbarian' German tribes triumphed across Western Europe, they plundered imperial cities, which people then often abandoned. For survival, many people returned to rural areas and joined fortified enclaves, which became the new "feudal" form of Western European society. Decentralized and ruled over by patriarchal-aristocratic warlords, peasants in those fortified rural communities were bound in oaths of fealty to their warlords.

Within that historical context, the new strategic question for prophetic leaders within the Western Catholic-Christian community became how to evangelize the migrating 'barbarian' German tribes, and with them how to rebuild Western Christian Civilization. The strategic response of Catholic-Christian spiritual energy became the post-imperial stage of *Western monasticism*. That development represented a historically new spiritual-institutional form for Catholic Christianity, even though other forms of monasticism had existed earlier within Buddhism in the East and in Mediterranean Pythagorean communities.

---

[11] The Eastern Roman Empire, known also as the Byzantine Empire and centered in the then Greek city of Constantinople, survived until its conquest by the Ottoman Turks in 1453.

Irish-Keltic Monasticism

Following the fall of the Western Empire, the migrating German tribes settled in Western rural areas along with the existing Western tribal peoples (including Keltic tribes that had migrated earlier from Asia Minor). In response to that new social situation, the Keltic church in Ireland sent highly educated male monks (Peter Maurin's "scholars") from the Irish tribes – and often from royal or aristocratic families – as nomadic missionaries to convert, and to educate, the migrating German tribes. Those Irish-Keltic monks then worked with royal and aristocratic leaders of the German tribes to create the new medieval form of Western Christian Civilization.[12]

---

[12] Most histories of Western monasticism unfortunately give only a brief and poorly informed account of the great work of the Irish-Keltic evangelization and education of the German tribes in Western Europe. For a popular account of the intellectual-spiritual role of Irish-Keltic monasticism in evangelizing Western Europe and regenerating Western Civilization, see Thomas Cahill, HOW THE IRISH SAVED CIVILIZATION: THE STORY OF IRELAND'S HEROIC ROLE FROM THE FALL OF ROME TO THE RISE OF MEDIEVAL EUROPE (Anchor, 1996). For an older and extensively researched analysis of that achievement, see Benedict Fitzpatrick's two detailed studies, IRELAND AND THE MAKING OF BRITAIN (Funk & Wagnalls, 1922) and IRELAND AND THE FOUNDATIONS OF EUROPE (Funk & Wagnalls, 1927). Both of Fitzpatrick's books (originally planned to be one book) are based especially on Fitzpatrick's continental research of manuscripts in the Irish language. His second book was the source for Peter Maurin's three-part "Green Revolution."

Scholarly neglect of the powerful impact of Irish-Keltic monasticism in standard histories of Western monasticism may be partly due to lack of adequate research into manuscripts in the Irish language. It may also be the result of marginalization of the Irish-Keltic Church by the Imperial Roman Church (similar to what happened to the "Donatist" African Coptic Church), and of subsequent destruction of Irish manuscripts within Ireland by Viking plundering and still later by British Protestant imperialism. Saint Augustine of Hippo (354-430) contributed to the initial marginalization of the Irish-Keltic Christian tradition across continental Europe by his promotion of the Imperial Church. That happened especially through his polemic against the Irish-Keltic lay theologian Pelagius, who was his brilliant competitor for intellectual-spiritual influence in Roman aristocratic circles. (Contemporary scholars have argued that Pelagius was not a "Pelagian.") Later, the Roman-directed Synod of Whitby (664) weakened Keltic monasticism in England, in favor of the organizational model of the Latin Benedictine monasticism favored by the Imperial Church. Still later, and more ruthlessly, the

Again, the Keltic missionaries were often sons of royal or aristocratic Irish families. Further, formed in the great Irish monastic schools of higher education, they brought with them advanced training in Philosophy, Theology, and the Liberal Arts, including fluency in both Greek and Latin, and knowledge of classical works like the writings of Cicero. Other Keltic monks from across the British Isles (typically trained in the Irish monastic schools of higher education) also participated in the great Keltic mission to continental Europe.

While Latin Church intellectuals of that time were ignorant of Greek (Saint Augustine of Hippo, for example, could never learn it), the Irish-Keltic scholars carried a long tradition of fluency in Greek, and they were well schooled in the classical Greek intellectual legacy. It appears that the early Irish-Keltic Church may have been closer to the Byzantine Greek Church, and perhaps also to the African Coptic Church with its vast coenobitical movement, than to the Roman Latin Church.

That may be understandable, since the Keltic tribes had migrated out of Asia Minor, and there had been an ancient Keltic presence close to Greece. For example, in the region that is today's Turkey, the ancient province of Galatia (to whose Church Saint Paul wrote an epistle) had been Keltic. Also, a Keltic army once almost conquered Athens.

Sharing their sophisticated education with the German tribes advancing across Western Europe, the Irish-Keltic missionaries founded monasteries, promoted sedentary agriculture, built libraries and schools, and established towns. For example, the Austrian city of Vienna still honors its foundation by Irish-Keltic monks. Further, Irish-Keltic scholars became famous at the Merovingian and Carolingian courts. The Irish Kelts, of course, were great wanderers on land and sea.

---

seventeenth-century social and intellectual devastation of Ireland by the English Puritan military conqueror Oliver Cromwell included a campaign to destroy all Irish monastic libraries, and to burn all manuscripts written in the Irish language. It became a capital offense even to possess a manuscript written in Irish.

While earlier Latin missionaries had failed in their attempt to convert the German tribes, the Irish-Keltic missionaries became immediately successful – again, probably because they themselves came from tribal communities, and often carried aristocratic or even royal rank. The Irish-Keltic monks, together with leaders of the newly evangelized German tribes, then laid the intellectual and spiritual foundations for medieval Europe. As also noted earlier, the great work of those Irish-Keltic monks became in the twentieth century the regenerative model promoted by Peter Maurin in his three-part "Green Revolution."

Thus, though seldom fully explored in standard Western Christian histories, the first expanding form of Western Christian monasticism within Europe, and the early source for re-founding Western Christian Civilization after the decline of the Western Roman Empire, was the Irish-Keltic monastic evangelization and education of the German tribes. Irish-Keltic missionary foundations in Europe were not places where monks left society, but rather places where monks and local tribal leaders worked together to rebuild civilization. Their monasteries became creative centers of spiritual, social, and intellectual regeneration, and places where Western Christian Civilization began to grow anew.

Meanwhile, in Ireland from which the monks came, Keltic monasticism had long provided stable communities for women and men. In contrast to the Roman Latin model, Irish-Keltic Catholic Christians, like the original apostolic church, celebrated salvation as embracing Nature, and welcomed the leadership of strong women. Female abbesses often led closely connected male and female Keltic monasteries.

Further, in Ireland the Keltic Church had identified its monasteries not with stone buildings but rather with the beauty of Nature, as in the lush green valley of the ancient Irish-Keltic monastery of Glendalough (Valley of Two Lakes), founded within the gentle Wicklow Mountains during the sixth century by Saint Kevin. Reportedly, during the so-called European "Dark Ages," thousands of young people came every summer from the continent to study with the Irish-Keltic monks in the lush green monastic valley of Glendalough.

In addition, Thomas Cahill has claimed that the Irish-Keltic Catholic Church saw the prophetic critique of social injustice as central to the Gospel of Jesus and to authentic evangelization (in contrast to the Imperial Church, which moved away from the prophetic biblical tradition). In that regard, Cahill has stated that the Irish-Keltic church condemned slavery, while the Roman popes continued to hold slaves. Of course, Saint Patrick, active in Ireland in the fifth century (well after Christianity had been established in the South of that land) was captured as a youth by Irish pirates, and then became enslaved in Ireland. In that experience, he had learned first-hand of the terrible nature of slavery, and especially for women.

Benedictine Latin Monasticism

In a manner softer than the strongly ascetical style of Keltic monasticism, Saint Benedict of Norcia (480-543), son of a feudal lord in the Italian peninsula, developed the Latin form of monasticism that would later become the dominant Western European Catholic-Christian model. At the same time, his twin sister Saint Scholastica (480-453) founded a female branch of the order. But Benedict and Scholastica never sought to expand their foundation to other areas in missionary outreach.

Eventually, however, Benedictine monasticism displaced Irish-Keltic Monasticism in Europe and, in some cases, became complicit in the restoration of imperial consciousness within the Roman Church. From that point on, the Nature-oriented Irish-Keltic stream of Christian spirituality – continuing mainly at the Western margins of European civilization – would not broadly re-emerge with spiritual power until the late twentieth century. It was retrieved then in spiritual response to the profound global ecological crisis that grew in part out of the spiritual errors planted within the dualist-hierarchical ground of what became clericalized monastic spirituality.

In the interim, however, so powerful became the influence of more developed forms of Benedictine monasticism on the emerging European society that the great German sociologist Max Weber claimed that Modern Capitalism was an outgrowth of Benedictine monasticism's early spiritual-technological rationalization. In his classic book, THE PROTESTANT ETHIC AND THE SPIRIT OF CAPITALISM (1905), while arguing that John Calvin (1509-1564), founder of the Calvinist strain of Protestantism, was the 'father' of modern Capitalism, Weber further argued that Benedict had been the 'grandfather.'

Benedictine monasteries were originally spiritual centers of egalitarian community, presided over by loving feudal patriarchs called "abbots" (from the Hebrew word *abba*, meaning "father"). As their mission succeeded, however, some Benedictine monasteries, particularly the European monastic network of Cluny, became a powerful political-economic force of aristocratic hierarchy within Europe.

During the 'high' Middle Ages, the Benedictine community of monastic lay disciples, originally sharing together in the mutual tasks of *ora et labora* (prayer and labor), became dualistically and hierarchically divided. On one side were aristocratic "*choir monks*" of the "religious state" who were assigned to *ora*. On the other side were lower-class "*lay monks*" who were assigned to *labora*. Further, the wealthy monasteries of Cluny also hired lower-class lay workers to do the "*labora,*" while the choir monks – supposedly devoted exclusively to prayer – developed luxurious lifestyles. That more 'developed' model of Western monasticism forgot the evangelical character of the apostolic church's original Christian *Laos*.

Centuries later, in Benedictine monastic foundations within the English Midlands, lower-class lay employees also replaced lower-class lay monks as workers. Those monastic lands in the Midlands, devoted to the profitable task of raising sheep to obtain wool for textiles, later became "secularized" by King Henry VIII. Still later, that same region became the English seedbed for the modern Industrial Revolution, in which textiles played a central role.

Forgetting Sacred Immanence

Though Benedictine monasticism included separate male and female monasteries, it did not include the sacrament of Christian Marriage. Further, the dominant male side eventually centered itself in the masculine spiritual symbol of *sacred transcendence*, seeking to rise 'above' Nature – again, with lower-class lay brothers and lower-class lay employees assigned to deal with the 'lower' tasks of Nature. As a result, certain strains of Western male monasticism tended to forget the Divine revelation in Nature of the primal feminine spiritual symbol of *sacred immanence*.

Further, since Benedictine monasticism also became in the Classical Era the center of Western or Roman Catholic Theology, many teachers of the Western Roman Church theologically emphasized *sacred transcendence* as the masculine symbol of the Divine Mystery. Some later identified that male face of the Divine with men in the "clerical" and "religious" "states of life." By this time, upper-level monks were typically being ordained priests and became part of the hierarchical "clergy."

Major strains of male Benedictine monasticism, oriented to masculinized "religious" and "clerical" transcendence, gained great patriarchal political-economic power in the high Middle Ages. Again, the rich and powerful monasteries of Cluny – for a time the greatest landowner in Europe – began to reshape the papacy in the name of 'reform.'

Misogynist Contempt for Women

In their 'reforming' zeal for masculine transcendence, some Western monastic leaders from Cluny attempted to impose a Platonic antisexual model of hierarchical dualism on diocesan bishops and diocesan presbyters. In a cruel attack on the Catholic-Christian families of traditionally married Western Catholic-Christian bishops and presbyters, and on their Catholic-Christian wives and children, the popes of that time, inspired by the monasticism of Cluny, declared "clerical marriages *"heretical."* That theologically false claim also became a source of great tension with the Eastern Churches, which rejected such an anti-evangelical absurdity.

The forced imposition of the monastic celibate model on diocesan bishops and presbyters became the central task of the so-called "Gregorian Reform," identified especially by the Pope Gregory VII (Bishop of Rome from 1073 to 1085). Known earlier as Hildebrand, Gregory had been formed by the monasticism of Cluny. As pope, Gregory tried to force by coercive police-power all Western bishops and presbyters, who had continued the thousand-year old tradition of Christian marriage, *to abandon their Christian wives and their Christian children*.[13]

A central part of this brutal anti-evangelical campaign was an underlying *misogynist contempt for women*. The contemporary historian Anne Llewellyn Barstow has reported that the monastic-inspired papal campaign not only forcibly removed the wives of bishops and presbyters from their homes, but also often drove displaced wives into homelessness, prostitution, and even suicide. Barstow has described that violent papal attack on the traditional marriage and families of Catholic bishops and presbyters as the "monasticizing of the clergy."[14]

Further, Anne Llewellyn Barstow and the earlier historian Henry Lea, both distinguished scholars, stated that written records of resistance by traditionally married bishops and traditionally married presbyters

---

[13] On this period, see the classic study by Henry C. Lea, HISTORY OF SACERDOTAL CELIBACY IN THE CHRISTIAN CHURCH (Kessinger Publishing, 2003), with the original published in 1867. Lea once served as president of the American Historical Society.

[14] Anne Llewellyn Barstow, MARRIED PRIESTS AND THE REFORMING PAPACY: THE 11TH CENTURY DEBATES (Edwin Mellen, 1982). The phrase "monasticizing of the clergy" appears throughout the book.

suggested that there was a medieval homosexual clerical culture behind the 'reforming' attack on "clerical marriage."

The late and distinguished Yale historian John Boswell, in his celebrated work, CHRISTIANITY, SOCIAL TOLERANCE, AND HOMOSEXUALITY, famously pointed to a broad late classical and medieval "clerical" tolerance of homosexuality.[15] Yet it was during this same period of "tolerance" that the monastic-driven papal attack on the Christian marriages
and families of Western bishops and presbyters occurred. Why tolerance on one side, but not on the other? In response to that question,
Barstow has summarized Boswell's honest narrative:

> *The Gregorian church ... in the century 1050-1150 created no*
> *legislation against gay clergy. Indeed, it has been argued that this*
> *was a period in which homosexuality flourished among clerics,*
> *especially in monasteries, and that since monks gained the*
> *ascendency in the church at this time, the legislative centers of the*
> *church had little choice but to go light on the question of men who*
> *loved men.*

> *John Boswell claims that St. Anselm and several of his pupils, Pope*
> *Alexander II and Archbishop Lanfranc, Archbishop Ralph of Tours*
> *and his beloved "Flora," Bishop John of Orléans, Bishop William*
> *Longchamp of Ely, and most notably Ailred of Rievaulx and his*
> *Simon, all represent influential churchmen whose actions and/or*
> *writings help make this century notable for clerical homosexuality.*

> *Boswell goes so far as to claim that "there was more than a*
> *coincidental relation between gay sexuality and some of the [celibacy]*
> *reforms ... A satire against a reforming bishop specifically accuses*
> *him of hostility to clerical marriage because of his own homosexual*
> *disposition." There is some evidence of a power struggle between gay*

---

[15] John Boswell, CHRISTIANITY, SOCIAL TOLERANCE, AND HOMOSEXUALITY: GAY PEOPLE IN
WESTERN EUROPE FROM THE BEGINNING OF THE CHRISTIAN ERA TO THE FOURTEENTH
CENTURY University of Chicago Press, 2005.

and married clergy over whose predilections would be stigmatized. Indeed, we will see that several [medieval] married clerical authors will express themselves vehemently on just that point.[16]

Both Barstow and Lea's studies also reveal a hate-filled misogynist language from leaders of that 'reform.' Perhaps the worst known examples came from Pietro Damiani (c. 1007-1072), a Benedictine monk, later cardinal, still later a declared saint, and at the time lead papal agent of the Gregorian attack on the Catholic-Christian marriages and Catholic-Christian families of Western bishops and presbyters. Damiani's vicious words betray a horrendous contempt for women, and especially for the female body. As an example, Barstow has cited one of Damiani's many "fulminations" against the Catholic-Christian women who shared in the apostolic tradition of married bishops and presbyters:

I speak to you, o charmers of the clergy, appetizing flesh of the devil, that casting away from paradise, you, poison of the minds, death of souls, companions of the very stuff of sin, the cause of our ruin. You, I say, I exhort you women of the ancient enemy, you bitches, sows, screech-owls, night owls, she-wolves, blood-suckers ... Come now, hear me, harlots, prostitutes, with your lascivious kisses, you wallowing places for fat pigs, couches for unclean spirits, demigoddesses, sirens, witches.

*You vipers full of madness, parading the ardor of your ungovernable lust, through your lovers you mutilate Christ, who is the head of the clergy ... you snatch away the unhappy men from their ministry of the sacred altar ... that you may strangle them in the slimy glue of your passion ... The ancient foe pants to invade the summit of the church's chastity through you ... **They should kill you.**[17] (Bold font added.)*

---

[16] Barstow, MARRIED PRIESTS, pp. 113-114; Boswell, CHRISTIANITY, pp. 210-227.

[17] Cited by Barstow, MARRIED PRIESTS, pp. 60-61.

In other "tirades" against the wives of presbyters and bishops, Damiani repeated his hatred for women:

> *The hands that touch the body and blood of Christ must not have touched the genitals of a whore ... I have attempted to place the restraints of continence upon the genitals of the priesthood, upon those who have the high honor of touching the body and blood of Christ.*[18]

Yet Barstow also told a story about how Damiani's own mother, after his birth, had refused to nurse him, and only the intervention of a priest's wife had saved the baby.

> *As the infant Peter lay withering away, an angel of mercy came from an unexpected and ... ironic source: a neighboring priest's wife took pity on the starving infant and talked his mother into offering him her breast, thereby saving the life of the future scourge of priestly families.*[19]

In the misogynist language of that monastic-led papal 'reform,' we see clearly the infection of Western Catholic-Christian spirituality by the negative teachings still flowing from certain anti-material philosophical schools within Hellenism. Again, these negative teachings disparaged material creation, disparaged the human body, disparaged human sexuality, and especially disparaged the body of woman.

Barstow further pointed out that ecclesiastical decrees, at the papal and at regional levels, ordered that the wives and children of married clerics should be *sold into slavery.*[20] Lea also documented that Pope Leo IX (1049-1054) had ordered the enslavements of presbyters' wives when the couple refused to be separated. Leo, also a promoter of the power

---

[18] Cited by Barstow, MARRIED PRIESTS, pp. 59-60.

[19] Barstow, MARRIED PRIESTS, pp. 58-59.

[20] Barstow, MARRIED PRIESTS, p. 43.

of Cluny, brought Hildebrand with him to Rome and, according to Lea, dramatically "magnified" the distinction between "clergy and laity."[21]

Similarly, Lea noted, Pope Urban II (1088-1099) – a follower of the Gregorian 'reform,' founder of the modern papal Curia, and launcher of the first medieval military "crusade" – ordered 'recalcitrant' clerical wives into slavery. He further noted that Urban even "offered their servitude as a bribe to the nobles who should aid in thus purifying the Church."[22]

Also, the historian Earl Evelyn Sperry, dating the "beginning of a crusade against the married clergy" to 1049 (first year of Leo IX's papacy) and describing Pietro Damiani as "principal instigator," pointed out that:

> *A council at Rome decreed that the wives of the clergy should be attached as slaves to the Lateran Palace, and bishops of the church were urged to inflict the same punishments upon the wives of priests.*

In addition, Sperry reported that later the "Hungarian Council of Ofen (1279) enacted that the children of ecclesiastics should be the slaves of the church."[23]

Papal Lust for Theocratic Imperial Power

Ultimately, according to Sperry, what stood behind the cruel 'reform' was the monastic-inspired papal lust for theocratic imperial power. Thus, Sperry wrote:

> *With the election of Hildebrand to the Papal chair ... a celibate clergy was indispensable to a realization of his views concerning the position*

---

[21] Lea, HISTORY OF SACERDOTAL CELIBACY, p. 154.

[22] Lea, HISTORY OF SACERDOTAL CELIBACY, p. 198.

[23] For both preceding quotes, see Earl Evelyn Sperry, AN OUTLINE OF THE HISTORY OF CLERICAL CELIBACY IN WESTERN EUROPE TO THE COUNCIL OF TRENT (Doctoral Dissertation for Columbia University, 1905), pp. 41-43. The author had been a University Fellow at Columbia University and later became a professor of history at Syracuse University.

of the Pope in the affairs of the world. His theories are clearly set forth in the DICTATUS PAPAE *... This enunciation of Papal rights ... is tantamount to a declaration that the Pope is the autocrat of the church.*

As to the powers of the Pope in secular affairs, Gregory declared that he might depose emperors, that he might annul the decrees of all earthly authorities, but that no one could annul Papal decrees, and that he was to be judged by no one. [According to] the DICTATUS PAPAE *... all earthly rulers and powers are amenable and subordinate to the pope ...*

Sperry continued:

As spiritual chief of the world, it was necessary that the Pope should have for his agents a body of men without local attachments and without personal interests to which they might sacrifice the welfare of the church. It was necessary that their powers should be devoted exclusively to defense and aggrandizement of this great ecclesial institution.

To create a body of men with such singleness of purpose, it was also necessary, besides cutting of all personal interest, to distinguish them sharply from the people they were to rule. The indelible spiritual attributes conferred at ordination accomplished this to some degree, but celibacy was a much more obvious and striking distinction. ... [Celibacy would] deprive the clergy of the cares, ambitions, and interests which the rearing of a family involves, and it would isolate them from their fellow men.[24]

Lea concurred with this analysis:

Hildebrand ... had conceived a scheme of hierarchical autocracy ... To the realization of this ideal he devoted his life with a fiery zeal and unshaken purpose that shrank from no obstacle, and to it he was

---

[24] Sperry, OUTLINE, pp. 26-27.

ready to sacrifice not only the [people] who stood in his path, but also the immutable principles of truth and justice ... Such a man could comprehend the full importance of the rule of celibacy, not alone as essential to the ascetic purity of the Church, but as necessary to the theocratic structure which he proposed to elevate on the ruins of kingdoms and empires.[25]

Key figures related to Cluny became papal leaders in the misogynist campaign against clerical families. They did so in support of the Gregorian lust for theocratic power. Meanwhile, baptized Catholic-Christian wives of bishops and priests, their baptized and ordained Catholic-Christian husbands, and their baptized Catholic-Christian children, all became victims of misogynist lust for clerical power.

How sad the apparent medieval battle between "gay" and "straight" "clergy." In that case for the "clerical" world at least, the "gay" side won, and the non-evangelical legacy of canonically mandatory "clerical" celibacy became institutionalized in the West.[26] In the wider society over longer history, however, the "straight" prejudice against "gay" people would inflict viciousness and hatred on "gay" people. Yet all persons on both sides are our loving Creator's beloved children, and all persons on both sides bear the image of the Creator's beauty and goodness.

There were other important issues in the Gregorian reform, especially the debate over lay-investiture and the papal-imperial struggle. Nonetheless, there is no question about the misogyny. And there is no ques-

---

[25] Lea, HISTORY, pp. 181-182.

[26] The "clerical state" and mandatory celibacy on one side, and the Sacrament of Ordination on the other side, are distinct matters. The Western Catholic canonical requirement of celibacy is linked not to ordination but to the clerical state. That distinction and that linkage are clear from the fact that an ordained clerical celibate presbyter in the Roman Church may be released from celibacy by "reduction" to the "lay state" (*reducionem ad statum laicalem,* in Latin rescripts for "laicization"). Yet even after that "reduction," the individual remains a validly and permanently ordained presbyter, though he is forbidden to function as such. In addition, as noted, neither the "clerical state" nor mandatory celibacy for ordained presbyters are of apostolic origin.

tion that the papacy rejected the ancient and broad apostolic tradition of married bishops and presbyters, which is affirmed by the New Testament and which continues, at least for presbyters, in practically all of the Eastern Catholic-Christian Churches.

Postmodern Renewal of
Monasticism's Regenerative Charism

Of course, that monastic-inspired misogyny and theocratic-imperial lust for power of the 'Gregorian Reform' do not belong to the core of the ancient and still important monastic movement. The brutal Gregorian campaign against Catholic-Christian episcopal and presbyteral families stands as a pathological deformation of the monastic charism.

Fortunately, following the medieval triumph of Cluny, zeal for retrieving the true monastic charism arose especially in the medieval Cistercian and Carthusian movements. But like Cluny and in contrast to the earlier desert movement, they remained sexually segregated communities, predominately of men, and did not include families.

Jumping far ahead to today, I have already noted that the twentieth-century Catholic-Christian prophet, Peter Maurin, proposed a fresh lay and agroecological monastic movement. In Peter's vision, that lay form of the monastic movement would retrieve the civilization-building mission of the early medieval Irish-Keltic missionary scholars. It would also welcome women and men, both single and married, as well as families with children.

Later in this book, I will propose that such a postmodern lay and agroecological monasticism as envisioned by Peter needs to become a central component of the global Catholic-Christian, as well as the universally Christian, strategic response to the late modern devastation of life's integral ecology throughout its interwoven natural, human, and spiritual fabric. Again, that natural, human, and spiritual devastation is now being inflicted on the evolving creative communion of life by

86

technological projects of late modern economistic Neoliberalism and militarist Neoconservativism, both of which embody the voluntarist philosophy of Nietzschean Nihilism.

In a further development of Peter's vision, I propose that his postmodern lay and agroecological Catholic-Christian monasticism needs to recover its eco-spiritual roots in "Mother Earth." It also needs to support marginalized people by developing with them sustainable agroecological communities. In addition, it needs to create a regenerative agroecological model of education, grounded in the ecological wisdom of Nature, as well as in ancient peasant eco-spiritual traditions, and in the contemporary ecological spirituality being developed by postmodern mystics. Finally, it would hold up both the Sacrament of Marriage and the vocation of celibacy in a co-creative eco-spiritual partnership.

Again, the original form of this vision first appeared in the Catholic Worker movement's three-part "Green Revolution," as articulated by Peter Maurin in the first half of the twentieth-century. As we have seen, Peter looked back to the early medieval program of Catholic-Christian evangelization and philosophical-theological renewal developed by missionary Irish-Keltic missionary scholars, in partnership with leaders of the migrating German tribes.

Though Peter had been a member of a "religious order" (the De La Salle Christian Brothers), he preferred to describe those Irish-Keltic missionaries in lay terms as "scholars," rather than as "monks." He saw those "scholars" as integrating prayer, study, and agriculture ("*cult, culture, and cultivation*"), and not simply for monks, but more broadly for rural village communities ("communes"). Further, disillusioned by contemporary universities and even by many Catholic-university professors, Peter called for his lay monasticism of a "Green Revolution" to create "*agronomic universities*" (that is, integrated with rural agriculture).

Today, we might better describe Peter Maurin's lay ecological monasticism as grounded in rural "ecovillages" and rural "agroecological universities," even while still serving the poor and abandoned human sisters and brothers in urban centers through "houses of hospitality."

Misogynist Influence on
Modern Science & Technology

The misogynist spiritual infection of some sectors of medieval monasticism contributed indirectly yet still powerfully to the modern hyper-masculine symbolic-mythic deformation lodged within the cultural foundations of Modern Science and Modern Philosophy. For Modern Science, originally called "Natural Philosophy" and a key carrier of Modernity's hyper-masculine deformation, arose from medieval male monasteries, even though it broke out into a lay "secular" form beyond that originally narrow ecclesial framework.

In his impressive study, A WORLD WITHOUT WOMEN: THE CLERICAL ORIGIN OF WESTERN SCIENCE, the late M.I.T. historian of technology David Noble documented the intellectual roots of the West's "New Science" in medieval Latin monasticism.[27] In that book, Noble showed how important sectors of the medieval Latin monastic movement became the incubator of Modern Science's hyper-masculine culture.

Noble had been investigating the question of why there has been a hyper-masculine deformation in the foundational style of modern Western Science, which then led Western Civilization into its contemporary unsustainable ecological degeneration. Of course, Noble found earlier roots of that deformation in the classical Greco-Roman philosophical tradition. But, he argued, medieval monasticism became the immediate source for Modern Science.

Further, there also emerged an early modern Western scientific-technological vision which intensified the medieval monastic symbolic deformation with its own misogynist strains. As the distinguished his-

---

[27] David Noble, A WORLD WITHOUT WOMEN: THE CLERICAL ORIGIN OF WESTERN SCIENCE (Oxford University Press, 1993).

torian of Science Carolyn Merchant has shown, Francis Bacon adopted a misogynist metaphor, metaphorically linked to techniques of torture, to describe the modern 'masculine' scientific project of forcing 'feminine' Nature to reveal her "secrets." In addition, Descartes infamously justified the 'scientific' torture of non-human animals, on grounds that they were simply machines without feeling. Again, Carolyn Merchant has documented the intellectual construction of that disturbing misogynist mythic-symbolic strain for Modern Science in her indicting study, THE DEATH OF NATURE: WOMEN, ECOLOGY, AND THE SCIENTIFIC REVOLUTION.[28]

Thus, it should not be surprising that now, within the terminal "climax" of hyper-masculine Western Modernity, we discover that the modern Western bourgeois scientific-technological path of Scientific Materialism has become ecologically *unsustainable* throughout its natural, human, and spiritual dimensions. Again, that hyper-masculine scientific-technological drive has been achieving dramatic increases in *human technological production*, but it has been destroying *Nature's biological reproduction*.

Medieval Seeds of the Modern Bourgeois Era

Now, let us return to the medieval period. With medieval monastic celibate "clerical" power guiding the 'reforming' eleventh-century papacy, the papacy expanded its theocratic power over Western Europe and beyond. Within that development, medieval popes – again, in alliance with powerful monasteries of Cluny – supported great military

---

[28] In addition to her already noted book DEATH OF NATURE, see again her subsequent and already noted ISIS article, in which she persuasively defends against denying critics her claim that Bacon was using a metaphor linked to torture as the mythic-symbolic ground for the "New Science." By the way, the brilliant Irish scientist, theologian, and Anglican priest Alister McGrath, in his otherwise excellent book THE REENCHANTMENT OF NATURE: THE DENIAL OF RELIGION (Doubleday/Galilee, 2002), dismisses Carolyn Merchant's claim. But he does not seem to be familiar with the subsequent and persuasive defense of that claim in her ISIS article.

campaigns to invade the Middle East, and did so in the name of the Gospel. Those "Crusades" – paradoxically named after the "Cross" (*Crux* in Latin) of the non-violent Jesus – opened major commercial trading routes between West and East, which then led to the *rise of wealthy bourgeois classes* within medieval commercial cities.

Out of those medieval bourgeois classes, there later arose the modern bourgeois *"secular"* vision of society. It was earlier Neo-Platonist strains in Christian monasticism, however, that had first defined the material world as "secular." That secular vision eventually led to the bourgeois destruction of the aristocratic civilization of Christendom. In its place, elites within the rising Western lay bourgeoisie then constructed – first in liberal-capitalist form, and later in the alternative scientific-socialist form – Modern Industrial Civilization based on *Scientific Materialism,* and not reverencing matter but plundering it.

Correlatively, alongside the medieval development of bourgeois lay-secular classes, there also emerged a new post-monastic form of Catholic-Christian mystical-prophetic communities. Those communities prophetically challenged anti-evangelical and anti-human elements within the early bourgeois urban-capitalist culture of the expanding medieval mercantile city-states, and they contributed to its intellectual development through their work in emerging Western Catholic universities.

MENDICANT COMMUNITIES
CHALLENGING MEDIEVAL BOURGEOIS CULTURE
(1200-1500)

The high-medieval trading cities, grown rich from the "silk roads" re-opened by Crusades, became the *young bourgeois seeds* of the modern mercantile-capitalist form of Western Civilization. Still small and living like little islands within a sea of Feudalism, those cities became the early seedbeds of both modern bourgeois political democracy and modern bourgeois materialist culture.

Meanwhile, Benedictine monks, bound to rural monasteries by once relevant vow of stability, proved unable to provide the mobile, dynamic, and flexible forms of evangelization needed for the growing medieval bourgeois urban centers, with their prosperous bourgeois families. In particular, rural monks were unable to evangelize the many young males flocking to the new urban bourgeois educational institutions eventually known as "*universities*." (Of course, in that still patriarchal culture, women were not permitted to attend such schools.)

The Mendicant Model

In response to the new historical-societal situation, there emerged the "*mendicant*" (from the Latin *mendicare*, which means "to beg") model of Catholic-Christian mystical-prophetic communities. Rejecting the corporate wealth and magnificent buildings of the great monastic foundations, the new model initially embraced both individual and corporate poverty. The initial commitment to institutional poverty would erode, however, in the model's later development. Even so, the mendicant movement represented a new spiritual response to the new societal challenge from the seminally modern high-medieval bourgeois society.

The high-medieval development of the "mendicant" form of Catholic-Christian mystical-prophetic communities planted seeds for an evangelical challenge to foundational evils already present in that early bourgeois culture – evils later to emerge more powerfully in Modern Western Industrial Civilization. Those bourgeois evils included both psychological and technological alienation from *Nature*, exploitation and marginalization of the *poor*, and eventual erosion of the Socratic tradition of seeking *truth* beyond the empirical level.

Francis & Dominic

In response to the new bourgeois challenge, Giovanni de Pietro di Bernadone (c. 1181-1226) – son of a wealthy medieval bourgeois capitalist merchant and today known in English as Saint Francis of Assisi – became the founder of one new leading forms of Catholic-Christian mystical-prophetic communities.

That version was eventually identified in Latin as the *Ordo Fratrum Minorum*. It is now translated into English as the "Order of Friars Minor," though the social meaning of the Latin name is disputed. It is popularly known as the "Franciscans." Further, though beginning as a lay movement, Francis' initiative later developed into what are today known as the "first, second, and third orders," with the first a "clerical" order, the second an order of "religious" sisters, and the third an order of laity.

In troubadour style, Saint Francis built on the Nature-spirituality of the earlier Christian hermit-movement that grew into coenobitical life and survived into the medieval period. Like his hermit predecessors, he celebrated the beauteous creatures of Nature, befriended them, even preached to them, and continued the ancient Christian cosmic spirituality that saw all of creation as praising the Creator. In addition, Francis developed a unique *Christian mysticism of the natural world,* in which he identified all creatures as "brothers" and "sisters," and in which he lovingly embraced poor and rejected human creatures.[29]

Similarly, Domingo Félix de Guzmán Garcés (1170-1221), known today in English as Saint Dominic, became the founder of another model form, known in Latin as the *Ordo Predicatorum* (Order of Preachers) and popularly called the "Dominicans." These mendicants moved among the people, preached in vernacular languages, and soon promoted for Catholic Christianity Aristotelian scholarship, learned from African-Muslim, Jewish, and Catholic-Christian scholars in the south of Spain.[30]

---

[29] The ancient peoples of the Americas' First Nations (Native Americans) also see all of creation as family, and celebrate non-human creatures as also our "sisters and brothers."

[30] See Richard E. Rubenstein, ARISTOTLE'S CHILDREN: HOW CHRISTIANS, MUSLIMS, AND JEWS REDISCOVERED ANCIENT WISDOM AND ILLUMINATED THE MIDDLE AGES (Harvest Books, 2004).

Especially through Albertus Magnus (1306-1280) and through Saint Thomas Aquinas (1225-1274), the Dominicans shifted the philosophical foundation of the Western Catholic theologian tradition from Platonism to Aristotelianism. In addition, they introduced the modern democratic principle into their organizational life – electing a term-limited "*prior*" (first, among equals), rather than being ruled in the classical monastic and aristocratic-patriarchal manner by a life-time "abbot" (again, from the Hebrew *abba*, meaning "father").

New Mendicant Mission

Following the new mendicant model, the Franciscans and Dominicans functioned as itinerant preachers who lived partly in cloister, but also went out of the cloister to preach among the people. By so doing, they provided fresh spiritual energy for the seminally emerging modern bourgeois era of Western Civilization.

While some Dominicans and Franciscans played central roles in the repressive Inquisition, Dominicans of the Spanish School of the Catholic University of Salamanca powerfully criticized the brutal injustice of the early modern Spanish *Conquista*. They paved the way, both philosophically and theologically, for the development of a modern democratic polity based on human rights. Most famously, the Dominican Bartolomé de las Casas (1484-1566) became the pioneering prophet in the struggle against the modern slave-system of the Americas.[31] We may therefore rightfully call Las Casas the early 'father' of Modern Catholic Social Teaching.[32]

---

[31] On Las Casas, see the moving study by Gustavo Gutiérrez, LAS CASAS: IN SEARCH OF THE POOR OF JESUS CHRIST, trans. Robert R. Barr (Orbis Books, 1993). The original Spanish version is DIOS O EL ORO DE LAS INDIAS (Salamanca: Síguame, 1990). The Spanish title (God or the Gold of the Indies) is more revealing of the book's powerful message. See also Las Casas' own short but powerful work, one among many in his vast corpus of writings about the *Conquista*, THE DEVASTATION OF THE INDIES: A BRIEF ACCOUNT, trans. Herma Briffault (Johns Hopkins University Press, 1992).

[32] I am indebted to Rev. Stephen Judd MM for this insight.

The Franciscan movement in turn presented a spiritual challenge to two great evils that would become central to later modern bourgeois civilization, namely, *bourgeois greed for money* (resulting in exploitation of God's beloved humans who were *poor)* and *bourgeois loss of spiritual reverence for Nature (*leading to anti-ecological economic plundering of God's other beloved creatures within the natural world).

In solidarity with the poor, the Latin name of Francis' movement as *Fratres Menores* could be translated as the "Brothers of the Lower Class." This socio-economic interpretation resonates with Jesus' own identification with the poor and the least ones, as well as with contemporary Catholicism's evangelically rooted "preferential option for the poor." In the spirit of that translation, Francis asked his followers to wear the simple and rough clothing of the impoverished lower class.

In addition, Francis' spirituality preserved the *pre-classical ecological-feminine spirituality of divine immanence,* as sacramentally revealed in and through Nature ("Mother Earth"). Francis thus implicitly retrieved the cosmic spirituality of the Irish-Keltic missionary evangelization and of the early church, and he continued the coenobitical desire to return to the wilderness as a symbolic recovery of the biblical Garden of Eden.

Long before the Irish-Keltic missionary evangelization, Francis' native province of Umbria had been an ancient center of the Keltic tradition's Nature-oriented spirituality. Prior to the imperial Roman conquest, Keltic culture had expanded from today's Turkey across Western Europe to the British Isles, and it included a strong presence in Northern Italy. Thus, in a manner reminiscent of Keltic culture's mystical love of Nature, Francis prayed in song and dance – like Moses' sister Miriam before the Ark of the Covenant – and he embraced both human and non-human creatures as his sisters and brothers.

For these reasons, Francis symbolizes for us today a visionary Catholic-Christian spiritual leader who refused to accept the temptation from certain classical and Hellenistic strains to demean material creation. For that reason, Francis stands out still today as a special Catholic-Christian saint for the emerging Postmodern Ecological Spirituality.

Some sectors of the later Franciscan movement, however, weakened Francis' radical vision for his movement. For example, as noted, the evangelically challenging name of his movement as *Fratres Menores* has been rendered today in English as the meaningless Latinism "Friars Minor." Similarly, some have converted Francis' embrace of the clothing of the poor into a "religious habit," supposedly separating its wearers from "secular" members of society, and often costing more than the normal clothing of the "secular" middle class.

In addition, as also noted, Francis' original evangelical celebration of an egalitarian lay community became hierarchically classified into "first, second, and third orders," ranked according to the supposed "order" of superiority claimed by Latin patriarchal clericalism. Yet, on a positive note, what became the Franciscan "third order" (today also called "secular Franciscans") did welcome into its core the sacrament of Christian Marriage, albeit at a lower rung in the clerical-hierarchical ladder.

New Bourgeois Universities

Along with the dramatic growth of high-medieval bourgeois wealth, there also developed an explosion of new knowledge carried along the Eastern trading routes and from the African-Muslim kingdom in the south of Spain (*Al-Andalus* or *Andalucía*). Since the narrow limits of monastic libraries could no longer contain the medieval explosion of knowledge, there emerged the important new Western bourgeois institution known today as the *university*. Though initially often governed by cooperative communities of lay scholars, most of these new academic institutions were soon taken over by the new mendicant "religious orders."

Interestingly, there remained an historical connection between the development of those early Western universities and the surviving intellectual influence across continental Europe of the missionary scholars from the great Irish-Keltic monastic schools. For example, Benedict Fitzpatrick linked Thomas Aquinas' recovery of Aristotle to his Irish-Keltic teacher at Naples. Thus, Fitzpatrick reported:

> *Long after the period of the Irish apostolate the fame of Irish learning lingered in Italy, and in the thirteenth century when the Emperor Frederick II founded the University of Naples, he summoned from Ireland and appointed as his first rector Peter Hibernicus, among whose pupils was no less a personage than St. Thomas Aquinas.*

> *Peter was one of a group of Irish literati at the brilliant court of Frederick, where among others resided about the same period Michael the Irishman (Scotus), who learnt Arabic at Toledo and was skilled in Hebrew, and who, with Hermann the German and Andreas the Jew, was instrumental in introducing to Europe several of the philosophical works of Aristotle that before that time had remained unknown in the West.[33]*

The medieval bourgeois transformation of the knowledge system, beyond the limits of feudal monasticism, inevitably brought a powerful clash between the old monastic culture of knowledge and the mendicant-led university culture. Umberto Eco's famous novel, THE NAME OF THE ROSE, stands as a masterful journey of literary fiction into that profound epistemological and ecclesial transformation, which eventually helped to create Modern Science.[34]

APOSTOLIC COMMUNITIES MINISTERING WITHIN MODERN CAPITALISM (1500-2000)

The Modern Western Era, fully emerging in 1500 (again, a rounded-off date), gave birth to the beginnings of Modern Western Industrial-

---

[33] Fitzpatrick, IRELAND AND THE FOUNDATIONS OF EUROPE, p. 336.

[34] Umberto Eco, THE NAME OF THE ROSE (Mariner Books, Reprint Edition, 2014).

Colonial Civilization. The 'efficiently' organized modern Atlantic slave-system, with its "Triangular Trade" and its early modern stock-markets (reportedly beginning in Antwerp as speculation on profits from slave ships coming there to deposit the profits) constituted first expressions of that new era. Soon, there emerged in England the early modern Factory Revolution, which imitated the 'efficiency' of Caribbean slave plantations, but with 'free labor.' The Factory Revolution later expanded in productivity with industrial mechanization.

Such institutions established the beginnings of Modern Industrial-Colonial Capitalism. From those processes, there also developed across the colonizing countries a militarist-imperialist nationalism, along with intertwined industrial exploitation of Nature and the poor. Over the long term, that same process generated a new bourgeois individualism, centered in an anti-ecological, selfishly possessive, and destructively materialistic consumerism.[35]

In spiritual response to the historical development of this new bourgeois form of Western Civilization, there emerged yet another new form of special Catholic-Christian mystical-prophetic communities, the "apostolic" model of "religious life."[36] That new "apostolic" form eventually provided *specialized professional ministries* for the increasingly complex and uprooting bourgeois society, and especially for the millions of uprooted and migrating European peasants who were becoming the modern industrial working class, as well as for missionary evangelization across the new areas of Western imperial colonization.

---

[35] For an insightful investigation of the philosophical development of that process, see the great work of C. B. Macpherson, THE POLITICAL PROCESS OF POLITICAL INDIVIDUALISM: HOBBES TO LOCKE, (Oxford University Press Reprint Edition, 2011).

[36] Cada et al., in SHAPING THE COMING AGE OF RELIGIOUS LIFE, divide this period into two sections. They call the first the "Age of the Apostolic Orders" (1500-1800), and the second the "Age of the Teaching Congregations" (1800 ...). Others call the second the age of the missionary orders. In my analysis, however, those two periods constitute two successive phases within the one "Apostolic" model.

Professional Apostolates
for Modern Bourgeois Civilization

The naming of new modern Catholic-Christian mystical-prophetic communities as the "apostolic" form of "religious life" meant that they provided outside the cloister specialized "apostolates," eventually professional in character and designed to meet the more complex needs of Modern Western Industrial-Colonial Civilization.

The famous prototype of the modern "apostolic" form is the Society of Jesus (Jesuits), founded by the Basque military noble, Ignatius of Loyola (again, 1491-1556). Drawing on the late medieval *Devotio Moderna*, Ignatius developed his own model of psychological "Spiritual Exercises." True to the new bourgeois spirituality, these Exercises functioned as *a psychologized monastery,* cultivated within the interior psyche, yet supporting exterior "apostolates" to the 'secular' world.

In addition, the Jesuits provided Catholic-Christian shock-troops for the new battles with Protestantism and with the anti-Catholic wing of the rising bourgeoisie. They also established beachheads within Catholic bourgeois families, especially through spiritual direction of elite women and through the secondary education (and later higher education) of their elite children.

Uprooting of the Rural Peasantry

With the rise of industrial modernization in England, bourgeois capitalists began a long-term process of restructuring the countryside by uprooting rural peasants from it. Displaced peasants, desperate for work, migrated to the new industrial towns. In that migration, the uprooted peasants – initially in England and eventually across the planet – lost their communal support system from traditional rural villages. [37]

---

[37] On the uprooting of the English peasantry in the early modern English Enclosure Movement, as the first in a series of what Rubenstein calls modern (industrial-linked)

They became the "urban proletariat" or "industrial-working class," living in harsh urban-industrial slums and largely without societal care.

At least within the industrial center-countries, the mainstream of industrial-working class in the industrial-center countries would later achieve the semi-affluent status of "middle class." That would be due to their self-organization into unions, and their political support for creation of the social-welfare state. That semi-affluence would also be subsidized, however, by capital flows from the colonial periphery, and by expanding employment for increasing military production.

That semi-affluent status within the industrial center-countries peaked in the middle years of the twentieth century. With the onset of neoliberal industrial globalization (gaining strength in the 1970s), there then began a downwardly mobile process that economically and politically undermined both "blue-collar" and "white-collar" middle classes through neoliberal attacks on unions, foreign "outsourcing" of industrial jobs to regions of "cheap labor," technological "automation," and government policies of "austerity."

Further, the long-term modern bourgeois process of uprooting rural people from their traditional agrarian communities continues today across the globe.[38] For example, as a result of the Western neoliberal capitalist-financial partnership in China's industrialization, the Chinese Communist State has been undertaking what is probably the world's largest ever historical destruction of rural peasant village life.

Blossoming of Women's "Apostolic" Communities

Again, with the Western onset of modern industrialization and urbanization, the new urban industrial working class lost many of the social functions that *women* had provided within the traditional rural village

---

"genocides" that included the nineteenth-century Irish Famine (actually an empire-forced starvation), see Richard Rubenstein, THE AGE OF TRIAGE (Beacon Press, 1984).

[38] See Mike Davis, PLANET OF SLUMS, Reprint Edition (Verso, 2007).

community: care for the sick, education of the young, sustenance for the poor, provision for the elderly, and charity for the poor. These functions were no longer immediately available within the anonymous, fragmented, and impoverished context of early urban working-class life constructed by hyper-masculine Modern Western Industrial-Colonial Capitalism.

In strategic spiritual response to hyper-masculine industrialization exploding across the late eighteenth, nineteenth, and early twentieth centuries, there emerged countless new Catholic-Christian mystical-prophetic communities founded by women. These new feminine "apostolic" congregations launched heroic social-service ministries of health, education, and welfare – again, especially for the exploited and impoverished working class of the industrializing countries, as well as for migrating farm families.

In addition, "apostolic" communities of women, as well as of men, provided missionary services within the regions violently conquered by Western Industrial Colonialism, though frequently without critiquing their supportive role for the colonizing powers, and sometimes even participating in the cruelty of that colonization.

In summary, those "apostolic" communities created what I humorously, but with great admiration, have called the "Catholic Department of Health, Education and Welfare." Their "apostolates" have included schools, hospitals, orphanages, and charitable enterprises. Such "apostolic works" were forerunners of the secular social-welfare state.

Sacrament of Marriage Still Excluded

Yet, as with the earlier forms of "religious life," the core of those "apostolic" communities" did not include the Sacrament of Marriage. Indeed, for a long time in some apostolic orders, those who entered were typically not allowed during their novitiates, and sometimes later as well, to share a meal with their Catholic-Christian parents who raised them, or to sleep in their own parents' home. How profound the loss of the original evangelical *Laos*.

The Irish historian John Bossy has claimed that the "clerical" architects of the Catholic Counter-Reformation (out of which the "apostolic" model of "religious life" arose) *deliberately tried to break the organic link between evangelization and the familial kinship system*, even though the kinship system had been the primary and fundamental vehicle of evangelization since the time of Jesus' original apostles.

According to John Bossy, the reason for that attempted break between the modern Western Catholic evangelization and the ancient kinship system was that *the family relatives became a powerful network for Protestant penetration into the Catholic lands*. Within that context, uprooting "apostolic religious" from their biological families of origin, and then training them as uprooted professional evangelizers, served the anti-Protestant goals of the Catholic Counter-Reformation.[39]

Something similar happened with the Catholic Counter-Reformation's creation of the modern seminary system for training candidates to the the Catholic-Christian presbyterate. It uprooted "seminarians" from the locally rooted kinship system.

By contrast, the Reformation's promise of legalizing the common-law marriages of Catholic-Christian presbyters, and of legalizing their (so-called) canonically 'illegitimate' children, presumably became for many Catholic presbyters and their families an attractive feature of the new Protestant movement. At the time, large numbers of European diocesan presbyters maintained common-law marriages and fathered children for whom they provided and whom they loved.

---

[39] See John Bossy, "The Counter Reformation and the People of Catholic Europe," THE PAST AND PRESENT SOCIETY, Number 47 (Oxford University Press, 1970), pages 51-70. I am indebted to Cardinal Francis Stafford for this information, which he shared when, as a young priest, he served as Director of the Family Life Office of the Catholic bishops' conference of the United States.

The Protestant Reformation's return to the ancient apostolic tradition of married bishops and presbyters, forcibly suppressed within the Roman Church since the eleventh-century 'Gregorian Reform,' may in part explain the Reformation's success in Northern Europe. At the time of the Reformation, police-power was no longer available in the northern European regions for the papacy to suppress that apostolic tradition.

Late Modern Corporatization

As we have seen, "apostolic religious communities" provided evangelical prototypes for how social-welfare institutions could creatively function in the industrialized center-countries, and in the invaded countries of the colonial or neo-colonial periphery. In recent times, however, at least within the United States, many of these "apostolates" have become *corporatized by lay trustees*, who by and large are capitalist business owners and executives following the neoliberal ideology.

As a result, many Catholic hospitals and universities in the United States now follow the neoliberal corporate-business model. The most obvious example occurs when managers of Catholic hospitals, schools, and charitable enterprises – in violation of Catholic Social Teaching – try to prevent their employees from organizing into a labor union.

During the first half of the twentieth century, Catholic-Christian leaders in the United States created close to *two hundred labor schools or union training programs* to educate leaders for the labor movement at every level.[40] Yet today, to my knowledge, the only such schools still existing in the United States are the Labor Guild and Institute of Industrial Relations of the Archdiocese of Boston and the Labor Studies Program at

---

[40] See Rev. Patrick Sullivan, CSC, FIVE GIANTS IN THE BISHOP'S SOCIAL ACTION DEPARTMENT AMONG MORE THAN FOUR HUNDRED U.S. CATHOLIC LABOR PRIESTS (Pacem in Terris Press, 2014), Volume One in a forthcoming series titled CATHOLIC LABOR PRIESTS IN THE UNITED STATES: A 20TH CENTURY STORY OF SOLIDARITY.

New York City's Manhattan College (a program created by Dr. Joseph Fahey, founding chairperson of Catholic Scholars for Worker Justice).[41]

In place of those two-hundred labor schools, Catholic educational leaders in the United States have now created at Catholic colleges and universities close to *two hundred business schools or business training programs*. We might describe this strategic class-shift from approximately two-hundred labor schools to approximately two hundred business schools as the "bourgeois captivity" of so many leaders of American-Catholic higher education.[42]

Again, even though many "apostolic religious communities" once sought to serve the *industrial working class*, some current leaders of "religious apostolates" now follow the *anti-worker prejudice* of the neoliberal corporate business class that fills the boards of trustees of their hospitals and universities. That reality reveals a sad institutional loss of prophetic spirituality.

Historical Decline of
Modern Apostolic Religious Communities

The modern period of dominance for the "apostolic" model of "religious life" lasted approximately from 1500 to 2000 (again, rounded-off to centuries). At least for the 'advanced' industrial countries, we now see the sunset of the "apostolic" model of Catholic-Christian mystical-prophetic communities, which the Holy Spirit had prophetically inspired to address the societal challenges emerging from the rise of Modern Western Industrial-Colonial Civilization.

In a similar manner across earlier forms of Western Civilization, earlier periods of Western church history saw the sunset of their dominant spiritual model – of the mendicant model for medieval bourgeois socie-

---

[41] For information on the Labor Guild, see *http://laborguild.com*, and for information on Catholic Scholars for Worker Justice, see *http:cswj.us* (both accessed 2017-04-30).

[42] See Chapters 1 and 7 of Joe Holland, 100 YEARS OF CATHOLIC SOCIAL TEACHING DEFENDING WORKERS AND THEIR UNIONS (Pacem in Terris Press, 2012).

ty, of the monastic model for feudal-aristocratic society, of the coeno-bitical model for late classical imperial society, and even of the foundational lay model with its messianic spiritual challenge to the idolatrous and oppressive Roman Empire. All these models long ago entered their historical decline.

In ending this chapter, let us recall that we have seen how the late modern form of Modern Industrial Civilization is precipitating a breakdown of integral ecology throughout its interwoven natural, human, and spiritual fabric, across our loving Creator's beloved garden-planet Earth. That is happening even as the late modern neoliberal global expression of Liberal Capitalism appears to triumph technologically and ideologically. Yet visionary pioneers are already planting creative seeds for an alternative Postmodern Ecological Civilization.

Understanding the emerging Postmodern Ecological Era with its new historical challenge for human spirituality, and within it for Catholic-Christian spirituality, becomes essential for discerning the vocation, identity, and mission of the emerging postmodern *lay form* of Catholic-Christian mystical-prophetic communities. It also becomes essential for discerning what *revised role* modern Catholic-Christian "apostolic religious communities" seeking "refounding" might play in the emerging Postmodern Era, as well as for discerning how to develop a postmodern "New Evangelization" that will draw on the emerging Postmodern Ecological Spirituality.

This chapter has reviewed the first five stages of what this book calls Catholic mystical-prophetic communities. The next two chapters will explore the late modern breakdown of Modern Psychological Spirituality, which arose in correlation with the rise of Modern Industrial Civilization. It was that receding spirituality, in Catholic-Christian form, that provided the spiritual grounding for the modern, and yet now receding, "apostolic" form of "religious life."

☙ ❧

3

GREAT POSTMODERN

ECOLOGICAL TRANSFORMATION

H Aving reviewed past long waves of Catholic Christian spiritual energy, we will now examine some of the core themes of what I call in the title of this chapter "The Great Postmodern Transformation." Many of these core themes are woven throughout the book, while some are more fully addressed in separate chapters.

CORE THEMES IN THE TRANSFORMATION

To some degree, this outline of core themes is a repetition. Yet, since the interpretation of this book is broad and for some readers new, repetition may help to implant the interpretation in readers' consciousness. Core themes identified in this chapter include the following.

- *Correlative Transformation of Civilization & Spirituality.* Again, this is the passage from Modern Industrial Civilization to Postmodern Ecological Civilization and, correlatively, from Modern Psychological Spirituality to Postmodern Ecological Spirituality. As we have seen, the late modern global industrial devastation of life's integral ecology, across its interwoven natural, human, and spiritual fabric, constitutes the historical breakdown of Modern Industrial Civilization and it precipitates those transformations.

- *Transformation of Philosophical-Scientific Cosmology.* On one side there is the intellectual breakdown of the Modern Mechanical Cosmology. That "Old Cosmology" was based on a retrieval of the ancient Philosophy of Epicurean Materialism and it initially emerged as the materialist side of the matter-spirit dualism of Descartes' revised Platonic paradigm. Later, that Cartesian dualism was reduced to the monism of Scientific Materialism, and now it is disintegrating into Nietzschean Nihilism. On the other side, there is the emerging "New Cosmology," or the Postmodern Ecological Cosmology. It holistically views the Cosmos as an evolving creative communion, which may be described analogously as alive, and which this book sees as also mystical.

- *Breakdown of Modern Ideologies of Scientific Materialism.* Accompanying the intellectual breakdown of the Modern Mechanical Cosmology has been the derivative intellectual breakdown of Modern Industrial Civilization's two competing ideologies of Materialism – again, Liberal Capitalism (Liberalism), and Scientific Socialism (Marxism), and across their various forms. The Epicurean philosophical errors shared by those two ideologies of Materialism have been misguiding society into the late modern global devastation of life's integral ecology.

- *Modern Bourgeois Spiritual Alienation from Nature.* At its deep sociological level, Modern Industrial Civilization has been grounded in a fundamentally *bourgeois* (urban) consciousness. The relentless bourgeois drive for urbanization has been uprooting humans across the planet from their ancient symbiotic relationship in rural life with the natural world. That drive is now producing a global plague of anti-ecological megacities, which typically warehouse

106

vast masses of uprooted rural migrants, often unemployed or underemployed.

- *Deep Roots in Oppressive Deformation of Sexual Symbols & Myths.* Undergirding the entire modern bourgeois project of urbanization stands a profound spiritual alienation from the immanent revelation of the Divine Mystery in and through the natural world. In the Primal Era, this revelation was known through the powerful spiritual image of "Mother Earth." Beginning in the Classical Era and becoming more intensive in the Modern Era, the bourgeois project of urbanization has been the anti-ecological outcome of a long spiritual flight from the feminine image of the Divine Mystery, and from its revelation in and through the natural world. During the Classical Era, that deep cultural-spiritual alienation from the feminine face of the Divine Mystery took the aristocratic form of patriarchy. During the subsequent Modern Era, it has taken the more intensive bourgeois form of hyper-masculinism.[1]

- *Spiritual Healing by Retrieving Ancient Christian Teachings.* Late modern Christians can begin postmodern spiritual healing by retrieving three ancient Christian teachings: 1) the sacred or *sacramental* understanding of the natural world; 2) the Holy Spirit, and in a related way woman, as the *feminine* face of the "image of God," and 3) the "Way" of Jesus as the sacred *lay path* of Christianity.

In addition, there are two more core themes not outlined in this chapter. To be addressed in later chapters, they are the following:

- *Planting Seeds of Regeneration* - the Holy Spirit's call for Christian communities across planet Earth to plant integral-ecological seeds for a regenerative Postmodern Ecological Civilization, and the need

---

[1] The forthcoming book titled SOCIAL ANALYSIS II will propose that the Classical Era and the Modern Era constituted two sequential developmental phases of what it calls the "Masculine Revolution." That book will also propose that the Primal Era constituted what it calls the "Feminine Revolution – all within the long historical evolution of the human journey.

for an eco-spiritual alliance between traditional "religious orders" and new lay movements to promote that task;

- *Peter Maurin's "New Monasticism"* - his lay and agroecological three-part "Green Revolution" as a visionary project for the above eco-spiritual alliance that urges us (in contemporary language) to create rural ecovillages (helping to regenerate the integral ecology of rural life in general), urban eco-houses of hospitality, and eco-universities linking work and study as well as urban and rural life.

CORRELATIVE TRANSFORMATION OF CIVILIZATION & SPIRITUALITY

In its foreground, this book explores the postmodern ecological transformation of Catholic-Christian spirituality, as part of the wider Christian and wider human postmodern spiritual transformation. It does so against the correlative background of the postmodern transformation of civilization. As we have seen, the book describes the foreground transformation as the historical passage from *Modern Psychological Spirituality* to *Postmodern Ecological Spirituality*. And, as we have also seen, it describes the background transformation as the historical passage from *Modern Industrial Civilization* to *Postmodern Ecological Civilization*.

Again, from its spiritual perspective, this book also describes the emerging postmodern cosmological ground -- underlying the transformation of both civilization and spirituality – as the *evolving creative communion of integral-ecological life,* throughout its interwoven natural, human, and spiritual fabric, across our loving Creator's beloved planet Earth. Again, this book sees this "creative communion" as *integrally (that is, holistically) ecological,* Thus, the adjective "ecological" provides here a comprehensive metaphor, in the human realm, for the creative communion of all life on planet Earth across its interwoven natural, human, and spiritual fabric.

Further, like a tree trunk growing new rings, the emerging postmodern spiritual transformation is not a replacement, but rather an expansion. Not eliminating prior forms of spirituality but moving them to a recessive place, the transformation is adding a partly new and partly old dimension to Christian and wider human spiritual consciousness. What is new is not the ecological dimension itself. For that dimension has ancient human and biblical roots that are still strong in indigenous spiritual traditions and in Eastern Christian spiritual traditions.[2] What is new is rather our recent discovery of ecology's *evolutionary* character.

SUMMARY OF POSTMODERN
SOCIETAL-SPIRITUAL TRANSFORMATION

HISTORICAL PERIOD	GEOGRAPHIC BASE	SPIRITUAL ENERGY	SOCIETAL FORM
RECEDING MODERN ERA: *(1500-2000)*	WESTERN *(Globalized as Neoliberal Capitalism)*	BREAKDOWN OF MODERN DUALISTIC PSYCHOLOGICAL SPIRITUALITY *(Subjective Consciousness)*	BREAKDOWN OF MODERN INDUSTRIAL-COLONIAL CIVILIZATION *(Objective Materialism)*
EMERGING POSTMODERN ERA: *(2000 ...)*	GLOBAL *(Networking Diversity of Regional Civilizations)*	EMERGENCE OF POSTMODERN HOLISTIC-ECOLOGICAL SPIRITUALITY *(Holistic Co-Creativity)*	SEEDS OF POSTMODERN ELECTRONIC-ECOLOGICAL CIVILIZATION *(Holistic Regeneration)*

The chart on the next page gives a preview of the contextual historical transformation of civilization described in this and following chapters.

---

[2] On the ancient Christian roots for ecological spirituality, see Jame Schaefer, THEO-LOGICAL FOUNDATIONS FOR ENVIRONMENTAL ETHICS: RECONSTRUCTING PATRISTIC & MEDIEVAL CONCEPTS (Georgetown University Press, 2009). See also Roger D. Sorrell, ST. FRANCIS OF ASSISI AND NATURE: TRADITION AND INNOVATION IN WESTERN CHRISTIAN ATTITUDES TOWARD THE ENVIRONMENT (Oxford University Press, 1988).

INTELLECTUAL-SPIRITUAL RISE & FALL OF
MODERN INDUSTRIAL CIVILIZATION

**HYPER-MASCULINE
SYMBOLIC-MYTHIC FOUNDATION**
(Misogynist Spiritual Deformation of Noble Warrior Symbol)

↓

MODERN MECHANICAL COSMOLOGY
*(Cartesian Revision of Epicurean Philosophy as Atomistic-Mechanical-Materialist "New Science"
Schizophrenically Combined with Cartesian Revision of Platonic Mind/Soul
as Philosophical Foundation for Modern Psychological Spirituality)*

↓

MODERN EUROPEAN ENLIGHTENMENT
*(Application of Atomistic-Mechanical-Materialist
"New Science" to Society as Social Sciences & Ideologies)*

↙ ↘

LIBERAL-CAPITALIST IDEOLOGY   **SCIENTIFIC-SOCIALIST IDEOLOGY**
(Liberal Privatization of Spirituality)   *(Marxian Rejection of Spirituality)*

↘ ↙

**PROGRESSIVE EROSION
OF LIFE'S INTEGRAL ECOLOGY**
(Natural, Human, Spiritual)

↓

**PHILOSOPHICAL COLLAPSE INTO
SCIENTIFIC MATERIALISM
& NIETZSCHEAN VOLUNTARIST NIHILISM**
(Intellectual-Spiritual Breakdown)

↓

**INTEGRAL-ECOLOGICAL BREAKDOWN OF
MODERN INDUSTRIAL CIVILIZATION**

↓

**EMERGENCE OF
POSTMODERN ECOLOGICAL SPIRITUALITY**
*Grounded In Emerging Postmodern Ecological Cosmology
& Called to Plant Regenerative Seeds for Postmodern Ecological Civilization)*

PARADIGM SHIFT IN
PHILOSOPHICAL-SCIENTIFIC COSMOLOGY

Let us now explore further the *cosmological grounding* of Modern Psychological Spirituality, and how this cosmological ground is shifting at the foundational level. As we have seen, since Cosmology is philosophical-scientific in character, the Modern Mechanical Cosmology has been jointly constructed by Modern Philosophy and Modern Science.

The Modern Mechanical Cosmology has sometimes been called the "Cartesian-Newtonian Paradigm." In that name, "Cartesian" refers to René Descartes (1596-1650), often called the 'father' of Modern Philosophy, and "Newtonian" refers to Isaac Newton (1643-1727), often called the 'father' of Modern Physics, which for Modernity has functioned as the foundational Science.

Modifying the classical Neo-Platonist dualism of Augustine of Hippo, Descartes constructed the most widely accepted initial philosophical articulation of the modern cosmological paradigm. He did so by replacing *classical Platonic temporal-spatial dualism* with a *modern Cartesian objective-subjective dualism.* Descartes split reality between what he defined as atomistic-mechanical "matter" (in Latin *Res Extensa,* or Extended Reality) and spiritual-cognitive "thinking" (in Latin *Res Cogitans,* or Thinking Reality).

- *Extended Reality* (*Res Extensa*) *as Objective.* On one side of his modern objective-subjective split, Descartes defined the material Universe as *objective* reality, which he understood as composed of blindly voluntarist aggregates of material particles (atoms), functioning mechanically and known only through quantitative mathematical measurements of their extension (including motion).

- *Thinking Reality* (*Res Cogitans*) *as Subjective.* On the other side of his modern objective-subjective split, Descartes defined cognitive thinking as *subjective* reality, understood as separate from the material world and including both the mind of God and the human mind. (Since thinking is an active process, Descartes' *Res Cogitans* became identified with *consciousness*.). Further, in Platonic fashion, he proposed that the Divine Mind infused substantive knowledge into the human mind, from which the human mind could deduce additional substantive knowledge. Meanwhile, he saw quantitative knowledge as coming from empirical observation.

Subsequently, Newton – building on the earlier astronomical work of Copernicus, Brahe, Galileo, and Kepler – articulated definitive mathematical formulas for cosmologically unifying the formerly differentiated "terrestrial mechanics" and "celestial mechanics" into a single reality, with the same mechanical laws applying to both regions. Yet Newton was not a pure cosmic materialist, nor a complete mechanist, since he understood gravity to be the "hand of God" active within the Universe. Further, the corpus of his religious writings is reportedly larger than the corpus of his scientific writings.

The early modern Cartesian-Newtonian Cosmology contrasted with the classical Western Aristotelian-Ptolemaic Cosmology, which had reflected Platonic spatial-temporal dualism by hierarchically distinguishing "terrestrial mechanics" (again, the lower material-temporal order of Earth) from "celestial mechanics" (again, the higher spiritual-eternal order of the Heavens).

In the classical Cosmology, those two "orders, one 'lower' and terrestrial and the other 'higher' and celestial, were seen as guided by entirely different laws. The lower terrestrial "temporal order," understood as purely material, was seen as subject to temporal decay and death. The higher celestial "eternal order," understood as ascending in grades to ever higher spiritual spheres, was seen as eternally beyond decay and death. In a late classical, medieval, and modern Christian parallel, lay members of the Church were linked to the terrestrial "material-temporal order," while "religious" and "clergy" were linked to the celestial "spiritual-eternal order."

Over time, proponents of the Cartesian-Newtonian Cosmology, after dropping Newton's spiritual interpretation of gravity, came to understand the Universe in reductionist fashion as purely materialist, without any Divine presence or spiritual meaning within it. For that reason, the maturely modern philosophical-scientific paradigm may be named (again, in perhaps too complex language) as the Modern Western Atomistic-Mechanical-Materialist Cosmology. As noted, this book refers to it in simpler terms as the *Modern Mechanical Cosmology.*

In the early twentieth century, as also noted, the great English mathematician and philosopher, Alfred North Whitehead, who taught at both Cambridge and Harvard Universities, boldly pointed out – in his pioneering 1926 book SCIENCE AND THE MODERN WORLD – that the modern Western Cosmology saw matter as "senseless, valueless, purposeless." In that book, Whitehead called the modern cosmological paradigm "*Scientific Materialism.*"[3]

Descartes' modern revision of Platonic dualism was fundamentally different in two ways from classical Platonic dualism. First, the modern Cartesian division was between matter as objective and mind as subjective, while Platonic dualism had seen matter as lower and temporal (terrestrial) and mind as higher and eternal (celestial). Thus, Descartes dualism was objective-subjective, while Platonic dualism was temporal-spatial.

Second, for Platonic dualism, although matter and mind were hierarchically ordered into a lower-temporal realm of matter and a higher-eternal realm of spirit, matter was understood to be a reflection of spirit. Thus, the two were unified into *a single ontology* of the "great chain of being," as described by Arthur O. Lovejoy's book of that title.[4]

---

[3] Alfred North Whitehead, SCIENCE AND THE MODERN WORLD (Cambridge University Press, 1926). The content was originally presented in his 1925 Lowell Lectures.

[4] See Arthur O. Lovejoy, THE GREAT CHAIN OF BEING: A STUDY OF THE HISTORY OF AN IDEA (Harvard University Press, 1936).

Descartes' modernized objective-subjective philosophical dualism of *Res Extensa* and *Res Cogitans* thus represented a fundamental rupture of the original ontological unity of classical Platonic Philosophy. In Descartes' modernized revision, matter was no longer a reflection or image of spirit (mind or consciousness). Rather, the two became ontologically unrelated – split into entirely different objective and subjective realities. Thus, while for Plato matter and spirit had been linked in a single ontological whole, for Descartes the relationship became purely extrinsic in what might be called *an ontologically schizophrenic dualism.*

Because of that schizophrenically dualist character, Descartes' system of matter and spirit eventually became philosophically unsustainable. Again, that unsustainability revealed itself in subsequent modern philosophical-scientific reformulations that collapsed the 'subjective' mind of Cartesian dualism into the 'objective' reductionism of Scientific Materialism. In that process, the spiritual dimension vanished.[5]

In addition to late modern philosophical interpretations of mind as collapsed into Scientific Materialism, others have recently proposed a rejection of the very idea of an objective human nature, in favor of plastically flexible and technologically manipulable "posthumanist" or "transhumanist" scenarios. In such proposals, not only is spirituality collapsed into "naturalistic" accounts, but human nature, and indeed all of Nature, is dissolved into a plasticity shaped only by arbitrary will.[6]

---

[5] For a charmingly written narrative account of the evolutionary emergence of consciousness, as understood from within the framework of Scientific Materialism, see the distinguished Cambridge-based psychologist Nicholas Humphrey's A HISTORY OF THE MIND (Simon & Schuster, 1992). For a widely-noted critique of such reductionist accounts by the distinguished philosopher Thomas Nagel, see his MIND & COSMOS: WHY THE MATERIALIST NEO-DARWINIAN CONCEPTION OF NATURE IS ALMOST CERTAINLY FALSE (Oxford University Press, 2012).

[6] For a sympathetic account of posthuman projections, and one arguing for a "neo-human cosmopolitanism" freed from "Natural Law," see Rosi Braidotti, THE POSTHUMAN (Polity, 2013). For a critical analysis of such developments, see Francis Fukuyama, OUR POST-HUMAN FUTURE (Farrar, Straus, & Giroux, 2002).

The extreme "transhuman" version has been powerfully laid out by Ray Kurzweil in his earlier book, THE AGE OF SPIRITUAL MACHINES, and in his later book, THE SINGULARITY IS NEAR.[7] (In 2012, Kurzweil became director of engineering at Google.) His techno-futurist projections represent a totalizing, and even totalitarian, culmination of the Modern Mechanical Cosmology. Laying out the ultimate hyper-masculine fantasy, such projections threaten increasing devastation of integral ecology across loving Creator's beloved garden-planet Earth.

Critically examining the still expanding modern hyper-masculine Modern Mechanical Cosmology, we discover that it has long been misguiding the human journey onto an ecologically unsustainable technological path. Now, to a catastrophic degree, it threatens life's integral ecology with both the rapid devastation of nuclear war and the slow but relentless devastation of ecological erosion.[8]

On the hopeful side, however, contemporary visionary philosophers and scientists, working at the frontiers of intellectual exploration, have been reaching beyond the modern reductionist paradigm of Scientific Materialism. Their emerging postmodern "New Cosmology" (again, the Postmodern Ecological Cosmology) is arising from fresh holistic data provided by early postmodern Science and from fresh holistic interpretations provided by early Postmodern Philosophy.

---

[7] Ray Kurtzweil, THE AGE OF SPIRITUAL MACHINES: WHEN COMPUTERS EXCEED HUMAN INTELLIGENCE (Penguin Books, 2000) and THE SINGULARITY IS NEAR: WHEN HUMANS TRANSCEND BIOLOGY (Penguin Books, 2006).

[8] For a critical scientific analysis of the late modern global ecological breakdown of Scientific Materialism, with a profound theological reflection on it, see the powerful book by the scientist and theologian Joshtrom Kureethadam, CREATION IN CRISIS: SCIENCE, THEOLOGY, AND ETHICS (Orbis Books, 2014). For a rich summary of societal and ecological breakdowns from the perspective of a radical Mennonite Spanish theologian, see "Chapter One – The Globalized Empire" in Antonio González Fernández, GOD'S REIGN AND THE END OF EMPIRES (Convivium Press,2012), pp. 17-55. For a fictional but scientifically ecological account of the "End of the Modern World," see Naomi Orestes and Erik M. Conway, THE COLLAPSE OF WESTERN CIVILIZATION (Columbia University Press, 2014).

This emerging postmodern cosmological paradigm has become technologically feasible because of the Electronic Revolution, which in turn has made feasible the postmodern of electronic information system, including advanced electronic telescopes, advanced electronic microscopes, and advanced electronic computers.[9]

The now "Old Cosmology" (again, the Modern Mechanical Cosmology) had arisen from fragmented data provided by early modern Science and from fragmented interpretations provided by early modern Philosophy. That cosmological paradigm had become technologically feasible because of the then new modern information system based on the mechanical printing press, in combination with simple optics of mechanical telescopes and mechanical microscopes.

Now, however, the receding Modern Mechanical Cosmology, as the materialist cosmological ground of Modern Science and Modern Philosophy, is yielding to the emerging Postmodern Ecological Cosmology. In turn, the emerging postmodern forms of Postmodern Science and Postmodern Philosophy are creating this fresh and holistic cosmological ground.

In this transforming philosophical-scientific context – again, made feasible by the Electronic Revolution – visionary scientists and philosophers (sometimes joined by visionary scholars of various spiritual traditions) have been proposing that the Cosmos does not any longer appear to be simply atomistic and mechanical or blindly materialist.

Rather, in a richer comprehension, these visionaries are proposing that the Cosmos appears to be *holistically relational and cognitively creative.*[10]

---

[9] For early insightful studies of the Electronic Revolution, see the late Daniel Bell's academic analysis, THE COMING OF POST-INDUSTRIAL SOCIETY: A VENTURE IN SOCIAL FORECASTING (Basic Books, 1976) and Alvin Toffler's popular analysis, THE THIRD WAVE (Bantam, 1984). See also the late Zbigniew K. Brezinski's, BETWEEN TWO AGES: AMERICA'S ROLE IN THE TECHNOTRONIC ERA, Revised Edition (Praeger, 1982).

[10] For a ground-breaking intellectual analysis of the historical unfolding of Science through development of modern atomistic-mechanistic and materialist paradigm, which

Further, Catholic-Christian scholars like Thomas Berry, as well as scholars from other spiritual traditions, find the Cosmos as understood in the "New Cosmology" to be *mysteriously mystical*.

Thus, in contrast to the increasingly dysfunctional Modern Mechanical Cosmology of Scientific Materialism,[11] we see emerging for the Post-modern Era the philosophical-scientific development of the *Postmodern Ecological Cosmology*.

BREAKDOWN OF MODERN
IDEOLOGIES OF SCIENTIFIC MATERIALISM

Let us now look briefly at the *ideological dimensions* of the late modern cosmological breakdown of Scientific Materialism. As we have seen, the dominant modern ideologies of Scientific Materialism are Liberal Capitalism (Liberalism) and Scientific Socialism (Marxism). Within the late modern collapse of life's integral ecology across Modern Industrial Civilization (again, now globalized), these two modern ideologies are now breaking down globally.

---

defined Physics as the foundational scientific discipline, into the emerging postmodern relational-cognitive and holistic paradigm, which (according to the authors) needs to have Biology as the foundational scientific discipline, see the magisterial book by Fritjof Capra and Pier Luisi, THE SYSTEMS VIEW OF LIFE: A UNIFYING VISION (Cambridge University Press, 2014).

[11] On the dysfunctionally destructive *psychological effects* of the modern Materialism, see the disturbing global empirical data reported by Knox University's Psychology Professor Tim Kaser in his insightful book, THE HIGH PRICE OF MATERIALISM (MIT Press, 2002). On the dysfunctionally destructive *sociological effects* of modern Materialism on youth within the United States, see the also disturbing empirical data reported by the University of Notre Dame's Sociology Professor Christian Smith, with Kari Christoffersen, Hilary Davidson, & Patricia Snell Herzog, in their insightful book LOST IN TRANSITION: THE DARK SIDE OF EMERGING ADULTHOOD (Oxford University Press, 2011). On the also disturbing impact of contemporary Materialism on the *sexual mores* of many college youths in the United States, see Donna Freitas, THE END OF SEX: HOW HOOKUP CULTURE IS LEAVING A GENERATION UNHAPPY, SEXUALLY UNFULFILLED, AND CONFUSED ABOUT INTIMACY (Basic Books, 2013).

TWO DOMINANT IDEOLOGIES
OF MODERN SCIENTIFIC MATERIALISM [12]

MODERN IDEOLOGY:	LIBERAL CAPITALISM *(Liberalism)*	SCIENTIFIC SOCIALISM *(Marxism)*
PHILOSOPHY OF PERSON IN SOCIETY:	AUTONOMOUS INDIVIDUALISM *(Fragmented Atoms)*	IMPERSONAL COLLECTIVISM *(Massified Atoms)*
FOUNDATIONAL INSTITUTION:	BLINDLY VOLUNTARIST MARKET	INSTRUMENTALLY RATIONALIST STATE
CENTER OF POWER:	CORPORATE POWER	STATE POWER
ANTI-DEMOCRATIC TEMPTATION:	ECONOMIC DICTATORSHIP	POLITICAL DICTATORSHIP
TOTALITARIAN VERSION:	DICTATORIAL FASCISM	DICTATORIAL COMMUNISM

Again, both modern Western ideologies contain *similar philosophical-scientific errors,* derived from their common cosmological ground of Scientific Materialism. Because of those errors, the negative side of both dominant modern ideologies has been misguiding much of the global human family deeper and deeper into the late modern devastation of life's integral ecology, throughout its interwoven natural, human, and spiritual fabric, across our loving Creator's beloved garden-planet Earth. Thus, the immediate underlying source of the late modern ideo-

---

[12] As noted earlier, there is a wide range of diverse forms for both ideological sides of Scientific Materialism. What are presented here are only Weberian "ideal-types" of the two dominant modern ideologies.

logical breakdown is the erroneous philosophical-scientific assumptions misguiding the late modern form of these materialist ideologies.

Capitalist-Communist Convergence

Further, some Western financial-capitalist elites are now paradoxically integrating contemporary industrial-capitalist globalism with the industrial-communist nationalism of contemporary China, as well as of Vietnam and Cuba. In that alliance, both materialist ideologies of Modern Industrial Civilization are entering *a bizarre historical convergence.*

Again, we see this capitalist-communist convergence in the cross-ideological global centralization of wealth and power revealed by massive capitalist investment in communist China, and beginning also in communist Vietnam and communist Cuba, and simultaneously in massive Chinese communist investment across industrial-capitalist countries. This convergence constitutes threatens a late-modern "merger" of contemporary Capitalism's *non-democratic economic power* with contemporary Communism's *non-democratic political power.*

For some time now, global elites of both modern ideologies of Scientific Materialism appear to have been integrating what Pope Pius XI (1922-1939) once described as Capitalism's "economic dictatorship," with what we know as Communism's political dictatorship.[13] The former carries the dictatorial temptation to deny to humans as workers their economically democratic human right to form free labor unions or to develop workers' self-management or cooperative enterprises. The latter carries the dictatorial temptation to deny to humans as citizens their politically democratic human right to elect governmental leaders.[14]

---

[13] In his 1931 social encyclical QUADRAGESIMO ANNO, Pius XI used the phrase "economic dictatorship" or "this dictatorship" six times to describe Capitalism's concentration of economic wealth. See pars. 188, 105, 106, 109, and 110.

[14] In contemporary US Capitalism, since 1970 the corporate economic linkages with the political state have become dramatically intensified. For example, Metro-Washington DC

Because of this global ideological convergence, many political-economic elites across the ideologies of Scientific Materialism are now working jointly – no doubt unintentionally but nonetheless relentlessly – to devastate the creative communion of integral ecological life, throughout its interwoven natural, human, and spiritual fabric across our loving Creator's beloved garden-planet Earth.

Uprooted Fantasy of a "Free Market"

It is important to point out, however, that Modern Industrial Capitalism and "business" are not identical. Modern Industrial Capitalism became the modern way of organizing business, but it has carried only a few hundred years of now failing experimentation. By contrast, business, with thousands of years of history, is far older than Modern Industrial Capitalism. Business will presumably continue, in postmodern electronic-ecological form, long after the breakdown of Modern Industrial Civilization.[15]

In a famous 1944 book, the Austro-Hungarian thinker Karl Polanyi argued that the fantasy of a 'Free-Market' for Modern Capitalism was a new and disruptive invention different from earlier markets that carried thousands of years of history. He saw the new capitalist 'Free-Market' fantasy as destructively uprooted from its traditional embeddedness in human and natural community.[16]

---

has become one of the highest per-capita incomes of such regions across the world – not because of the salaries of government employees, whose salaries remain modest and whose numbers have been declining for some time, but rather because of the dramatic in-migration of extremely high-paid personnel across the metro-region who are directly or indirectly linked to for-profit corporations. See Mike Lofgren, THE DEEP STATE: THE FALL OF THE CONSTITUTION AND THE RISE OF A SHADOW GOVERNMENT (Penguin Books, 1916), especially pp. 21-47.

[15] On a post-capitalist business future, see the late Peter F. Drucker's (known as the 'father' of modern management theory) POST-CAPITALIST SOCIETY (HarperBusiness, 1994).

[16] Karl Polanyi (1886-1964), THE GREAT TRANSFORMATION (Farrer & Rinehart, 1944).

As anyone who has spent time among indigenous peoples of the planet knows, *women* have traditionally controlled local economic markets.[17] Confirming that ancient control, Aristotle in his famous book POLITICS described men as being in charge of Politics (*Politiká*) and women as being in charge of Economics (*Oíkonomía*).

Modern Industrial Civilization thus not only has uprooted the fantasized 'Free-Market' from the traditional natural embeddedness of markets in local bioregional community (both human and natural). It has also transferred control of traditionally rooted local markets from rural peasant women to urban bourgeois male elites. Over past centuries, urban elites have been uprooting Economics from its ancient bioregional roots, and expanding that uprootedness up to the global level.

Defending Democracy
in a Local-Global Framework

But let us return to the growing late modern "merger" of the dictatorial temptations of both modern materialist ideologies, in which an authoritarian (and perhaps even dictatorial) form of capitalist governments could become the pervasive late modern model.

Faced with that challenge, Western Civilization, along with other ancient human civilizations, now needs to move beyond the philosophical errors of Modernity's reductionist Cosmology of Scientific Materialism. It needs to prove resilient beyond its late modern bourgeois form.

---

[17] For many years, during summer recesses from my home university in Florida, I had the honor of teaching in the *Altiplano* (High Plains of the Andes Mountains) region of Bolivia and Peru, and predominantly with students from the Aymara tradition which has its roots in the ancient Tiahuanaco civilization surrounding the great Lake Titicaca. Still today, across the Aymara culture, traditional local markets are still dominated by women – reflecting Aristotle's ancient claim that *Oikonomiá* (Economics) belonged to women, while *Politiká* (Politics) belonged to men. The fusion of Economics and Politics into the single modern system of "Political Economy," with both under hyper-masculine control, certainly did not begin with Modern Industrial Civilization. But, in the modern bourgeois system, it has reached its fullest form and now its final "climax."

In symbiotic partnership with other ancient civilizations, Western Civilization needs to help birth the seminally emerging and regenerative Postmodern Ecological Civilization, which then needs to develop locally rooted yet globally networked electronic-ecological markets.

In addition, and despite the late modern breakdown, we need to remember that Modern Western Industrial Civilization has produced important gifts that we need to preserve, particularly *democracy*. Once more, as with spirituality, it is not a matter of replacement but rather of expansion. We now need to defend democracy against acute threats from expanding centralized economic power and expanding centralized political power. Further, we need to integrate all of Modernity's positive gifts, as well as the positive gifts of the Primal and Classical Eras, within the emerging Postmodern Ecological Civilization, even while overcoming the dysfunctional philosophical errors of the modern Cosmology of Scientific Materialism.

Above all, we need a *local-global perspective*. That is because postmodern electronic technologies of communications and transportation have been midwifing a local-global human community, which is an important achievement in the human journey. For the first time in human history, following the great human diaspora that developed from the early human migrations out of Africa, the dispersed branches of our human family are now being reconnected by global electronic networks of communications and transportation. We are having our first global family reunion.[18]

Yet, while technological globalization has become possible and even essential because of the Electronic Revolution, that revolution and its consequent globalization should not be guided by the reductionist imagination of Scientific Materialism. Our global human family needs to reach beyond the materialistic imagination of modern ideologies, by

---

[18] On the human migrant out of Africa and across the planet, see my earlier book, HUMANITY'S AFRICAN ROOTS: REMEMBERING THE ANCESTORS' WISDOM, Volume I of AFROCENTRISM AND THE EMERGING GLOBAL CIVILIZATION (Pacem in Terris Press, 2012).

consciously pursuing an integral-ecological vision that seeks the holistic regeneration of natural, human, and spiritual ecology.

MODERN BOURGEOIS
SPIRITUAL ALIENATION FROM NATURE

To understand the breakdown of modern materialist ideologies, we need to remember that Modern Industrial Civilization and Modern Western Psychological Spirituality have both been *bourgeois in character.*

Uprooting & Fragmenting Urbanism

In contrast to its later and narrower identification in Marxism of the word "bourgeois" with owners of capital, its original meaning referred to people who live in towns or cities. In that older and broader sense, bourgeois means "*urban.*" Today, the word should also include what we call "suburban," since suburbs now form an integral part of urban metropolitan systems. Thus, we may also speak of Modern Industrial Civilization as *Modern Bourgeois Civilization.* In addition, we may speak of Modern Psychological Spirituality as *Modern Bourgeois Spirituality.*

Since "bourgeois" means "urban," we should not be surprised that one of the implicit but fundamental goals of bourgeois modernization has been to uproot our human family from its ancient roots in pre-modern rural ecovillages, and to migrate our human family into uprooting and fragmenting cities. Within the breakdown of Modern Industrial Civilization, however, such cities across the planet – often megacities filled with slums[19] – already face the proximate threat of becoming anti-ecological death-traps.

We find an early intellectual critique of that anti-ecological urban uprooting and fragmenting – still pursued by both Liberal Capitalism and Scientific Socialism – in the prophetic book by Simone Weil (1909-

---

[19] See again Davis, PLANET OF SLUMS.

1943), THE NEED FOR ROOTS. Weil, a French Jew raised as an agnostic, was an eccentric but deep intellectual, an activist "fellow-traveler" with the communist and anarchist Left, a close friend of Leon Trotsky, a combatant in the Spanish Civil War on the Republican side, a covert agent for the French resistance during World War II, and a spiritual mystic ultimately drawn to Catholicism.[20]

Weil wrote THE NEED FOR ROOTS to argue her challenging critique of the uprooting bourgeois character of both the liberal and Marxian ideologies. Her critique is summarized in following quote from her book.

> *Under the same name of revolution, and often using identical slogans and subjects for propaganda, lie concealed two conceptions entirely opposed to one another. One consists in transforming society in such a way that the working-class may be given roots in it; while the other consists in spreading to the whole of society the disease of uprootedness which has been inflicted on the working-class. It must not be said or supposed that the second operation can ever form a prelude to the first; that is false. They are two opposite roads which do not meet.*[21]

Ecological Alienation

The first deep problem with modern bourgeois consciousness remains that it has *philosophically misunderstood humanity as not organically part of Nature's ecology.* The other deep problem with modern bourgeois consciousness is that it has *philosophically misunderstood Nature as itself not organically ecological.* Instead, following the modern philosophical-scientific Cosmology, it has misdefined Nature as only atomistic, mechanical, and materialist.

---

[20] See Simone Weil, THE NEED FOR ROOTS: PRELUDE TO A DECLARATION OF DUTIES TOWARD MANKIND, trans. Arthur Wills, Preface by T. S. Eliot (Routledge Kegan, 1952). For reflections on the political significance of Simone Weil's insight for the start of the late modern period, see my monograph, FLAG, FAMILY, FAITH: ROOTING THE LEFT IN EVERYDAY EXPERIENCE (New Patriot Alliance, 1979).

[21] Weil, NEED FOR ROOTS, P. 45.

Modern bourgeois consciousness further distorted the meaning of Nature by abandoning the primal and mythic-symbolic feminine vision of "Mother Nature." In her place, it has mythically-symbolically constructed its *modern hyper-masculine deformation of the noble warrior archetype*. For that deformation, "Mother Nature" constitutes only inert "natural resources" to be conquered, even tortured, and ultimately exploited for human utility, without regard to the devastating consequences for integral ecology.

For that reason, within the modern bourgeois (urban) paradigm of Economics, our human economy is not understood as embedded within, or as an organic part of, Nature's foundational ecological economy. Also for that reason, in modern atomistic-mechanical and materialist paradigm of Economics, industrial pollution and the wider ecological devastation of life's integral ecology are considered "externalities" that need not be included in "cost-accounting."[22]

Further, and as noted, both modern bourgeois philosophical misunderstandings became canonized in the foundations of modern bourgeois consciousness – first *cosmologically* in Modern Philosophy and Modern Science, and second *ideologically* in Liberal Capitalism and Scientific Socialism.

Cosmological Errors
& Mythic-Symbolic Deformation

Also, as has been noted already and as we will explore further in a later chapter, we find the ancient philosophical roots for those modern misunderstandings in the atomistic-mechanical and materialist Cosmology of the Greek philosopher Epicurus (again, 341-270 BCE), who drew on the earlier Greek philosopher Democritus.

---

[22] For another now classic philosophical critique of the bourgeois worldview, albeit from a partly Platonic philosophical perspective, see Nicolas Berdyaev, BOURGEOIS MIND AND OTHER ESSAYS, Facsimile Edition (Ayer, 1934). Berdyaev's especially spiritual critique had a strong spiritual influence on Dorothy Day, co-founder of the Catholic Worker Movement.

Yet, at the deepest mythic-symbolic level, as we have also seen, Epicurus' gentle and poetic feminine interpretation of the atomistic-mechanical and materialist Cosmology was discarded by modern bourgeois Economics. Modern Science, and within it modern Economic Science, pursued the metaphorical torture and plunder of Nature – something that would have horrified Epicurus.[23]

Again, "Mother Nature" was officially de-spiritualized and her poetic beauty commodified into objective "natural resources" that were to be conquered, tortured, and exploited for human "utility." There is no poetry or beauty in modern bourgeois Economics.

Again, that violent modern economic process has been legitimated by the modern bourgeois and hyper-masculine deformation of the noble warrior archetype. Originally honoring defenders of the community of life, that archetype was distorted to legitimate the conquering, torturing, and killing of Nature, and sometimes also of exploited and colonized human beings.

Of course, that deformed hyper-masculine archetype had antecedents in classical patriarchal civilizations. But it did not achieve hegemonic

---

[23] On Epicurean Materialism as the philosophical foundation of Modern Philosophy and Modern Science, see the Canadian philosopher Catherine Wilson's brilliantly and lyrically written text, EPICUREANISM AT THE ORIGINS OF MODERNITY (Reprint Edition, Oxford University Press, 2010). See also the fascinating (albeit anti-Catholic) book by Harvard's famous Shakespeare scholar Stephen Goldblatt, THE SWERVE: HOW THE WORLD BECAME MODERN (W.W. Norton, 2012). Goldblatt so titles his book because Epicurus, to explain human freedom, arbitrarily introduced the "swerve" concept into Democritus' atomistic Materialism.

On Postmodern Catholic Social Teaching's critique of Modernity's roots in the ancient materialist Philosophy of Epicurus, see my essay, "Pacem in Terris & Philosophy: The Encyclical's Stoic Vision of Global Order versus Modern Ideologies Rooted in Epicurean Chaos," in Francis Dubois & Josef Klee, Editors, PACEM IN TERRIS: ITS CONTINUING RELEVANCE FOR THE TWENTY-FIRST CENTURY (Pacem in Terris Press, 2013). That book gathered papers presented at a Symposium at the United Nations in New York City, in preparation for the 50th Anniversary of Pacem IN TERRIS, Saint John XXIII's most famous papal encyclical.

power over civilization until the advent of Modernity, which is now globalized. That entire process of de-spiritualizing Nature has led to the modern industrial-colonial goal of technologically replacing Nature's *organic reproduction* with hyper-masculine *mechanical production.*

Such philosophical-scientific errors and mythic-symbolic deformations constitute the deep roots of Modernity's devastation of integral-ecological life, throughout its interwoven natural, human, and spiritual fabric, and across our loving Creator's beloved garden-planet Earth.

Healing & Regenerative Truths

The healing and regenerative philosophical-scientific and mythic-symbolic truth is that our human family and our human development exist organically within Nature's ecology, and that Nature is not simply atomistic, mechanical, and purely materialist. Rather, as we are now discovering from postmodern scientific and philosophical advances (again, thanks in part to electronic instruments), "Mother Nature" is showing "herself" as *holistically relational and cognitively co-creative.* Further, across our entire planet Earth, and across our entire Cosmos, "she" appears to be analogously alive.

Along with discovering this regenerative postmodern cosmological framework, Christians in the West are also re-discovering ancient Eastern Christian traditions that liturgically celebrate Nature as spiritually mystical. For that reason, the Christian expression of Postmodern Ecological Spirituality celebrates our human family, and its ongoing evolution, as an integral part of the holistically relational, cognitively creative, analogously living, and mysteriously mystical process of cosmic evolution.

Because of still emerging discoveries of Quantum Physics, Chaos Theory, Systems Theory, and the Santiago School of Cognitive Science, and thanks to the development of electronic instruments, visionary scientists and visionary philosophers are declaring that the reductionist cosmological paradigm of Scientific Materialism cannot adequately explain the wonder of the Cosmos.

Yet, many late modern bourgeois philosophers and bourgeois scientists, still bound to the Modern Mechanical Cosmology, have been trying to perpetuate beyond its time the paradigm of Scientific Materialism. They have been attempting to force fresh insights from Quantum Physics, Complexity Theory, and Systems Theory into the narrow and collapsing modern bourgeois "Old Cosmology" of atomistic-mechanical Materialism.

By contrast, scientific visionaries like physicist Fritjof Capra and biologist Pier Luigi Liusi have been developing a truly postmodern form of Systems Theory that reaches beyond the reductionist framework of Scientific Materialism. As noted already, Capra and Luisi have proposed that, in this transformed cosmological understanding of Science, Biology (rather than Physics) needs to become the foundational Science for the emerging global ecological future.[24]

Late Modern Temptations
of Eugenics & Authoritarianism

Yet, the emerging global human community faces *powerful temptations* from still surviving modern bourgeois philosophical errors and mythic-symbolic deformations. One strong temptation is to revive the discredited abomination of 'scientific' Eugenics, allegedly in the name of "ecology," and falsely to blame the global poor, rather than the global rich, for the late modern global ecological crisis.

That temptation should not be surprising, since Charles Darwin (1809-1882), principal founder of the modern reductionist form of the scientific theory of evolution, was himself a eugenicist. The original 1859 subtitle for Darwin's most famous book, ORIGIN OF THE SPECIES BY NAT-

---

[24] See again Capra & Luisi, SYSTEMS VIEW OF LIFE.

URAL SELECTION, was THE PRESERVATION OF THE FAVORED RACES IN THE STRUGGLE FOR LIFE. Also, it was Darwin's cousin, statistician Francis J. Galton (1822-1911), who coined the term "Eugenics." In addition, Darwin's son, Major Leonard Darwin, became President of the First International Congress on Eugenics, held in London in 1912. Thus, the claim that "Social Darwinism" had nothing to do with Darwin's scientific understanding of evolution is untrue.

The investigative journalist Edwin Black has documented this disturbing Darwinian family history in his extensively researched book, WAR ON THE WEAK.[25] Further, at the end of that book, Black has warned that what he calls "Newgenics" is already underway, and is camouflaged within the legitimate science of Genetics.

A second temptation, already noted, is for elites to try *to eliminate Modernity's great contribution of democracy*, and to replace it with authoritarianism or even dictatorship, perhaps as a "merger" of communist political dictatorship with capitalist economic dictatorship. Again, the powerful global partnership between Western capitalist investors and the communist government of China, as well as with other dictatorial governments, suggests that some global capitalist elites do not carry a sustained commitment to political democracy.

Postmodern Ecological Spirituality needs to struggle prophetically against these temptations. Here, Catholic Social Teaching, in both its social-ethical side and its bio-ethical side, could prove an important resource.

On a more hopeful note, let us again recall that there are already emerging small but promising seeds of regeneration, also made feasible in part by the Electronic Revolution. These seeds can eventually bear fruit in an emerging Postmodern Ecological Civilization. This Civilization needs to link in creative communion all human cultures and all

---

[25] Edwin Black, WAR ON THE WEAK: EUGENICS AND AMERICA'S CAMPAIGN TO CREATE A MASTER RACE Expanded Edition (Dialog Press, 2012).

human spiritual traditions, to seek grounding in the Postmodern Ecological Cosmology," and to drink from the living waters of ecological wisdom traditionally preserved by indigenous cultures and by many women.

Let us now look further at the deep cultural-spiritual roots of the breakdown of Modern Industrial Civilization, as found in the deformed and oppressive interpretation of sexual symbols and myths lodged at the cultural-spiritual foundations of both classical and modern forms of the Western tradition.

OPPRESSIVE DEFORMATION
OF SEXUAL SYMBOLS & MYTHS

As noted, at the deep cultural-spiritual level, this book proposes that the historical breakdown of Modern Industrial Civilization is due to an oppressive and deformed system of sexual symbols and myths. Again, that deformation has been lodged at the cultural-spiritual foundations of both classical-aristocratic and modern-bourgeois forms of Western Civilization.

Patriarchy & Hyper-Masculinism

Again, while we know well the classical-aristocratic form of that deformation as *patriarchal*, this book has proposed that we need to understand its more expansive modern bourgeois form as *hyper-masculine*. Again, central to both forms of that deformation have been ancient and persisting Western spiritual alienations from Nature.

- *Patriarchy.* The Classical Era's cultural construct of patriarchy represented the aristocratic spiritual alienation from Nature. It attempted hierarchically to *subordinate* human sexuality, the human body and especially the body of woman, and ultimately Nature itself. Yet again, in the vision of GENESIS 1:27, woman represents the feminine "image of God."

- *Hyper-Masculinism.* The deep cultural construct of hyper-masculinism undergirds the modern bourgeois spiritual alienation from Nature. Again, it attempts technologically to *replace* Nature's organic biological reproduction with bourgeois mechanical production, and sociologically to convert women to the male pattern.

As a result, in the late modern period, the bourgeois spiritual alienation from Nature has led to an undermining of human biological reproduction among the dominant social classes of Modern Industrial Civilization. For example, among the middle and upper classes of Europe and across the European Diaspora, biological reproduction has for some time fallen below replenishment levels. There has also been the notorious example of the Communist government of China brutally attempting to limit couples to one child, including by coerced abortions.

Extractive Industrial Production
Devastating Natural Reproduction

The insightful Canadian journalist Naomi Klein, in her widely-read book THIS CHANGES EVERYTHING, has implicitly identified the modern fossil-fuel industry as hyper-masculine.[26] More broadly, she has implicitly pointed out that Modern Industrial Civilization's extractive industries have long carried a hyper-masculine character. She has clearly demonstrated that modern extractive industries have plundered Nature for the sake of industrialism's *productive* capacity, but in so doing they have devastated Nature's *reproductive* capacity.

That Naomi Klein was herself pregnant while working on her book brought that insight home to her in a profoundly personal manner. She realized that a truly feminine Economics would never forget, and would always remember, the reproductive function of Nature. Yet the late modern hyper-masculine "penetration" of "Mother Nature" by

---

[26] Naomi Klein, THIS CHANGES EVERYTHING: CAPITALISM VS. THE CLIMATE (Simon & Schuster, 2014).

Modern Industrial Civilization – guided by modern hyper-masculine bourgeois Economics and grounded in the anti-ecological bourgeois absurdity of industrial production that destroys ecological reproduction – is now devastating the integral ecology of life across our loving Creator's beloved garden-planet Earth.

In addition to Naomi Klein's eco-feminine critiques of Modern Industrial Civilization, it may be helpful to recall an earlier eco-feminine critique of the classical and the modern deformations of sexual symbols and myths. In her now classic 1980 book, THE DEATH OF NATURE, University of California Berkeley historian Carolyn Merchant told the terrible tale of how Western elite male prejudices against woman became projected onto Nature.[27] She narrated how that happened first with the Classical Era's theories of hierarchal patriarchy, and later in more destructive form with the construction of Modern Science and its technological exploitation of Nature. She provided scholarly documentation to demonstrate that the early modern Baconian scientific-technological goal became to force "Mother Nature – *by violent technological means akin to torture* – to produce for human "utility," without caring for "Mother Nature" or her myriad creatures.[28]

In relation to such eco-feminine critiques, we might also describe the late modern *absentee-owner system of electronic stock-markets* as central to the hyper-masculine devastation of life's integral ecology. Long ago, as part of his cult of elevating intellectual abstraction above the concrete world, Plato (following Pythagoras) claimed that Mathematics is the highest language of reason. Today, in a modernized but degraded Platonic cult of reason as mathematical, financial investors across the globe remotely buy and sell on electronic stock-markets. Yet they typi-

---

[27] Carolyn Merchant, THE DEATH OF NATURE: WOMEN, ECOLOGY, AND THE SCIENTIFIC REVOLUTION (HarperOne, Reprint Edition, 1990).

[28] See again Carolyn Merchant, "The Scientific Revolution and *The Death of Nature*," ISIS, 2006, 97:513-533.

cally abstract their financial decisions from the bioregional impact of their financial investments on life's integral ecology.

Most current investors in electronic stock-markets have only one criterion: the mathematically monetarized maximization of return on investment. That criterion typically does not include concern for, or even awareness of, any natural, human, or spiritual devastation inflicted on concrete local bioregions inhabited by our loving Creator's beloved and beauteous creatures, including human creatures.

In that hyper-masculine process imposed by Modern Industrial Civilization, "Mother Nature" has not simply been *demoted* philosophically to the lower hierarchical level of the material world below aristocratic male transcendence, as happened with patriarchy in the Classical Era. Nor has "Mother Nature" been simply *stripped* philosophically of all spiritual meaning by the bourgeois secularization of the material world, as happened with the "New Science" in the early phase of the Modern Era. Now, in the late phase of the Modern Era, "Mother Nature" completely *disappears* from the abstracted mathematical symbols and algorithmic conclusions appearing on absentee-investors' electronic computer screens.

Ecological Devastation
Endemic to Modern Bourgeois Economics

Again, the principal yet erroneous bourgeois intellectual guide for this devastating process has been modern 'scientific' Economics, which first took on strength in Western Europe during the late eighteenth century, and now has become globalized in both liberal-capitalist and scientific-socialist forms. Further, the wider late modern bourgeois forms of Science and Engineering (despite exceptions) still generally accept the erroneous guidance of modern 'scientific' Economics.

Through hyper-masculine "hard" Science and "hard" technologies, modern Economics still seeks to exploit – exclusively for human "utility" – the "natural resources" of "Mother Nature," whom modern bourgeois business elites imagine to be only a meaningless and materialistic collection of commodified objects. In that process, modern business elites are simply following the misguidance of modern bourgeois 'scientific' Economics, which misdirects modern scientific-technological *production* into devastating "Mother Nature's *reproduction* of life's integral ecology.

Modern bourgeois consciousness misunderstands the very meaning of "Economics, which from its Greek roots means the "ordering of the home/Earth." That misunderstanding flows from the ancient and deep Western elite male biases against human embodiment, and through that embodiment against woman, and through woman against Nature. With those ancient and modern biases canonized in modern bourgeois Economics. its erroneous dogmas have been misguiding our human family into the late modern scientific-technological devastation of the creative communion of life's integral ecology, throughout its interwoven natural, human, and spiritual dimensions, across our loving Creator's beloved garden-planet Earth.

Further, that bourgeois misunderstanding is not simply ignorance, for it also produces *massive ecological sin.* Such sin is the direct result of classical-aristocratic and modern-bourgeois blocking of the primal revelation for the feminine face of the Divine Mystery. But that hyper-masculine and sinful misunderstanding is now achieving its anti-reproductive and thus unsustainable "climax."

Relational Consciousness & Ecological Economics

We find cultural-spiritual insight for a healing alternative to the contemporary hyper-masculine ecological devastation in a powerful book, THE RESURGENCE OF THE REAL, written by the brilliant Catholic-Christian eco-feminist philosopher Charlene Spretnak. In that book, Charlene Spretnak has at the deepest level critiqued the late modern

hyper-masculine devastation.[29] Further, in her subsequent book RELA-
TIONAL REALITY, she has held up innovating and successful examples of
healing experiments that already embody *feminine relational consciousness.*[30]

Consistent with Charlene Spretnak's rich insights on relationality is
what may be called the emerging postmodern ecological reform of scientific Economics. It is the pioneering work of the *International Society
for Ecological Economics.*[31] In this regenerative school of thought, the
human economy is understood as holistically embedded within, and as
called to live in symbiotic relation with, Nature's foundational and sustaining economy, which is the sustainable ordering of our common
global home of planet Earth.

Paradoxically, the much-needed phrase "Ecological Economics" is etymologically redundant. For "Economics" – from its Greek roots of
"*oíkos*" (meaning Earth/home) and "*nomos*" (meaning custom/law) –
signifies the custom/law of Earth/home. Meanwhile, "Ecological," again
from its Greek root of "*oíkos*" and "*logos*" (meaning logic/reason), signifies the logic/reason of Earth/home. Thus, the phrase "Ecological Eco-

---

[29] Charlene Spretnak, RESURGENCE OF THE REAL: BODY, NATURE, AND PLACE IN A HYPER-
MODERN WORLD (Routledge, 1999).

[30] Charlene Spretnak, RELATIONAL REALITY: NEW DISCOVERIES OF RELATEDNESS THAT ARE
TRANSFORMING THE MODERN WORLD (Green Horizon Books, 2011). See also her earlier
books, STATES OF GRACE: THE RECOVERY OF MEANING IN A POSTMODERN AGE (Harper San
Francisco, 1983), and THE SPIRITUAL DIMENSION OF GREEN POLITICS (Bear & Company,
1986).

[31] See the Society's website at *www.isecoeco.org*, as well as Robert Costanza et al., AN
INTRODUCTION TO ECOLOGICAL ECONOMICS, Second Edition (CRC Press, 2014).
"Ecological Economics" is distinguished from "Environmental Economics." The latter
does utilitarian cost-benefit analyses of economic actions in relation to the environment,
but it does not understand that the human economy is nested and enmeshed within
Nature's foundational economy. The former considers the human economy part of
Nature's foundational economy, and requires understanding Ecological Science as the
context and foundation for human Economics. The two contrasting paradigms of
Economics are thus based on entirely different cosmologies, as well as entirely different
anthropologies.

nomics," according to its Greek roots, means "the logic/reason of Earth/home for the custom/law of Earth/home."

SPIRITUAL HEALING BY
RETRIEVING ANCIENT CHRISTIAN TEACHINGS

According to the vision of this book, all Catholic Christians, all other Christians, and all humans are now being called by the Holy Spirit to help in *healing the bourgeois hyper-masculine attack on "Mother Nature's" reproductive sustainability*. This means awakening to the emerging postmodern spiritual thirst for holistic regeneration of the evolving creative communion of life's integral ecology.

For that reason, according to this book's vision, all Catholic Christians, all other Christians, and all humans are also being called by the Holy Spirit to drink from the life-giving waters of the emerging Postmodern Ecological Spirituality, which is already being stirred up among us and within us. In those calls, I believe that the Holy Spirit is now urging all Christians – Catholic, Protestant, and Orthodox, and across our Creator's beloved garden-planet Earth – to retrieve three ancient Christian teachings to ground the Christian form of Postmodern Ecological Spirituality.[32]

- *First, the mystical-sacramental character of Nature,* which Saint Augustine, among others, described as the "Book of Nature," meaning the first sacred book of revelation (followed by the Bible as the second sacred book of revelation), which sacramentally reveals the Divine Mystery in and through Nature;

---

[32] On the ancient Eastern-Christian roots of this ecologically centered Christian spirituality, on the classical Western Christian antagonism toward material creation, and on the modern Western Christian forgetfulness of the ancient Christian belief that the material world is mystical-sacramental, see John Chryssavgis, COSMIC GRACE + HUMBLE PRAYER: THE ECOLOGICAL VISION OF THE GREEN PATRIARCH BARTHOLOMEW I, second edition (W. B. Eerdmans, 2009).

- *Second, woman as the sacred feminine "Image of God,"* as proclaimed by GENESIS 1:27 in partnership with the masculine "Image of God," as the two equal images of the Divine Mystery;"[33]

- *Third, the "Way" of Jesus as the holy lay Christian path,* which all of Jesus' disciples are called to follow – be they ordained or not, and be they members of "religious communities" or not. Again, and of course, the New Testament's use of the Greek term "*Laos*" refers to all disciples of Jesus

---

[33] On the biblically grounded feminine Divine image, see again Burgess, THE HOLY SPIRIT: EASTERN CHRISTIAN TRADITIONS. See also Donald Gelpi SJ, THE DIVINE MOTHER (University of America Press, 1984); Virginia Ramey Mollenkott, THE DIVINE FEMININE: THE BIBLICAL IMAGERY OF GOD AS FEMALE (Crossroad, 1987) and April D. DeConick, HOLY MISOGYNY: WHY SEX AND GENDER CONFLICTS IN THE EARLY CHURCH STILL MATTER (Continuum, 2011).

4

PHILOSOPHICAL ROOTS OF
LATE MODERN SPIRITUAL "DARK NIGHT"

T his and the remaining chapters first explore the late modern journey of Modern Psychological Spirituality from its early modern
emergence through to its current breakdown in the late modern spiritual "Dark Night" of Modern Industrial Civilization. They then explore
the regenerative emergence of Postmodern Ecological Spirituality in
Catholic-Christian form, with its spiritual hope and searching for the
global "Dawn" of a Postmodern Ecological Civilization.

This chapter and the next sketch the development, erosion, and collapse of Modern Psychological Spirituality," by providing background
analyses of *the construction and deconstruction of the continental European
side of Modern Philosophy.* That philosophical stream has undergirded
the early modern emergence and late modern breakdown of Modern
Psychological Spirituality.

After these two philosophically oriented chapters, the following chapter explores the late modern anti-ecological ideological degeneration of
Liberal Capitalism and the postmodern pro-ecological strategic response by Catholic Social Teaching. After that background chapter, the
book's last three chapters (prior to a final reflection) explore the emergence of Postmodern Ecological Spirituality in relation to:

- The proposed regenerative ecological mission of Catholic-Christian *new lay movements;*

- The centrality of the emerging Postmodern Ecological Spirituality for Catholic *"religious communities"* seeking refounding by allying with the emerging lay energy;

- Peter Maurin's prophetic vision of a lay and integral-ecological *"New Monasticism,"* which is seen here as calling its participants to plant regenerative seeds for a Postmodern Ecological Civilization.

PHILOSOPHICAL GROUND
OF SPIRITUALITY

To understand the breakdown of Modern Psychological Spirituality in correlation with the breakdown of Modern Industrial Civilization, it is essential to understand the intellectual breakdown of the underlying Modern Mechanical Cosmology. Then, since Cosmology represents a synthesis of scientific data and philosophical interpretation, it is also essential to understand the breakdown of the correlative the paradigms of Modern Philosophy and of Modern Science.

Traditional Linking
of Philosophy & Spirituality

Until the rise of Modernity, Western Philosophy was generally considered *a spiritually therapeutic exercise.* For example, classical schools of Western Philosophy, especially Stoicism and Neo-Platonism, were understood as spiritual paths for their followers. Even the materialist Epicurus understood his anti-religious school as a psychological therapy that would enable the "soul" (*psyche*) – which he considered purely material but made of "lighter atoms" -- to achieve tranquility (*ataraxia*). Further, the Eastern philosophies of Buddhism and Daoism are still schools of spiritual practice.

It was this soul-based therapeutic character of premodern Philosophy that explains why early Christianity so easily embraced important Stoic and Neo-Platonist ideas and practices. Indeed, still to this day, Western Catholic-Christian Ascetical Theology continues to teach the three spiritual stages of Neo-Platonist spiritual purification, known as the purgative, illuminative, and unitive ways.

Early Modern Philosophy's Schizophrenic Dualism of Science & Spirituality

As the initially correlative spiritual form for Modern Industrial Civilization, Modern Psychological Spirituality limited spiritual energy to the self's psychological interiority. Thus, it philosophically defined spiritual energy as having *no relationship with the material Universe*, which was to be studied by Modern Science. As a result, Modern Western Spirituality and Modern Western Science from the beginning pursued schizophrenically divergent paths, and later often mutually antagonistic ones.

The late modern tendency for Modern Science to abandon any relationship with spirituality made the later development of 'scientific' attacks on Religion inevitable. The reason for the inevitability is that Modern Western Science had adopted as its philosophical ground the ancient atomistic-mechanical Cosmology of Epicurean Materialism, which itself had been anti-religious.

At the same time, Modern Western Psychological Spirituality, reflecting the early modern revision of Platonic dualism, had continued the subjective side of its ancient Neo-Platonist roots. But it did so in a way that abandoned the Platonic ontological unity of matter and spirit.

That modern schizophrenic form of dualism, with matter and spirit no longer seen as having any ontological relationship, could not be sustained over the long run. Inevitably, Modern Science's reductionist paradigm of the Modern Mechanical Cosmology would pull the rug out from under the schizophrenically dualist paradigm of Modern Psychological Spirituality. The result across modern culture, which we now see, has been the secularizing triumph of Scientific Materialism.

Holistic Postmodern
Philosophical & Scientific Insights

Beginning with Quantum Physics and continuing into more recent times with Systems Theory, Chaos Theory, and the Santiago School of Cognitive Science, scientists have been discovering data that goes beyond the imagination of the Modern Mechanical Cosmology and beyond its paradigm of atomistic-mechanical Scientific Materialism.[1]

Again, these more recent advances in Science have been made feasible by the Electronic Revolution. That Revolution has led to the development of new and more powerful electronic instruments for observation, data-collection, and data-analysis (electronic microscopes, electronic telescopes, electronic computers, etc.).

On the other side of the postmodern cosmological transformation, the new scientific data is being interpreted by new philosophical insights that are both holistic and evolutionary in character. Both of these developments (again, new scientific data and new philosophical interpretations) are converging in what this book calls the emerging Postmodern Ecological Cosmology.

The focus of this chapter and the next, however, is not on the scientific side, but rather on the philosophical side. Further, this and the next chapter explore that philosophical side's early modern past through to the late modern present. But, before beginning that exploration, let us

---

[1] On recent transformation of the modern paradigm of Science, see again the magisterial work by Capra & Luisi, SYSTEMS VIEW OF LIFE. On the nature of "scientific revolutions," which are typically cosmological revolutions, see the now classic work of Thomas Kuhn, THE STRUCTURE OF SCIENTIFIC REVOLUTIONS: FIFTIETH ANNIVERSARY EDITION, Fourth Edition (University of Chicago Press, 2012).

briefly look at the contemporary impact of the triumph of Scientific Materialism and the spiritual "Dark Night" that it is generating.

GROWING ATTACKS ON
INTEGRAL ECOLOGY OF LIFE

This study of the late modern spiritual breakdown does not elaborate on biological, sociological, and psychological details of the breakdown of integral ecology underlying the late modern spiritual "Dark Night." Such a detailed analysis would be both an enormous and a depressing task. Yet it would be a superficial exploration that did not point out how enormous and depressing is the "Dark Night" of the now globalized stage of Modern Industrial Civilization, and especially for many young people.

Such a superficial exploration would ignore the deep historical pain that so many young people, through no fault of their own, have inherited from prior generations. Again, fully exploring that "Dark Night" would especially require studying the *great spiritual depression,* from which so many young people in 'advanced' industrial societies today secretly suffer. So, let us note here at least some of the growing attacks on the integral ecology of natural, social, and spiritual life that young people face today, and will face even more in the future:

- *Growing global ecological devastation of Nature,* which in its myriad forms would take pages to inventory, but whose death-dealing impact is already beginning what has been called "the sixth great extinction of life of planet Earth;"[2]

- *Growing global economic destruction of rural life,* including the destruction of small family farms and local farming communities, by giant global corporations pursuing fossil-fuel extraction and mineral mining, and by giant global corporations pursing industrialized agriculture through anti-ecological "mass production" of

---

[2] See again Kolbert, THE SIXTH EXTINCTION.

food by means of toxic petrochemical fertilizers and pesticides, and by means of genetically modified organisms designed for profitable mono-cropping – all for the sole instrumental purpose of maximizing monetarized return on investment;

- *Growing global political attacks on workers*, by denying workers' human right to organize free labor unions, as well as by attempting to weaken or to destroy existing workers' unions, and by eliminating increasing numbers of workers by technologies of automation, robotics, and Artificial Intelligence (AI);

- *Growing global undermining of extended and nuclear families*, including attacks on human life in the form of state-promoted abortion, euthanasia, and perhaps "posthuman" and "transhuman" bioengineering, probably to be combined with a new future wave of Eugenics that could attempt to eliminate across the planet vast numbers of 'non-useful' poor, elderly, and handicapped persons;

- *Growing global plagues of advanced technological warfare*, devastating human life and the life of the rest of Nature, and even religiously supported torture and mass technological murder of noncombatant civilians, including so many children, all of which Pope Francis has described as a covert "third world war;"

- *Growing global industries of personal devastation,* including arms-sales, addictive drugs, pornography, and human trafficking, all of which are immensely profitable;

- *Growing global spiritual emptiness* within the 'advanced' industrialized regions, generated by the globalized consumer-culture of possessive Materialism, with which giant global culture industries "brainwash" the minds of youth, including small children; [3]

---

[3] On such cultural threats to young people, see again Tim Kaser, THE HIGH PRICE OF MATERIALISM and Christian Smith et al., LOST IN TRANSITION: THE DARK SIDE OF EMERGING ADULTHOOD. For a critical Christian perspective on the global culture

- *Growing global failure by so many cultural, educational, and religious institutions* to provide a regenerative spiritual vision of ecological hope, with so many such institutions explicitly or implicitly holding up only the materialist idol of "success," which few young people will ever achieve and whose name Luke 16:13 tells us is "Mammon."

In the face of the above attacks, and especially the *increasing spiritual emptiness of materialist secularization*, let us recall the prophetic words of Pope Emeritus Benedict XVI:

> *The external deserts in the world are growing,*
> *because the internal deserts have become so vast.*[4]

Again, all of this contributes to the breakdown of Modern Psychological Spirituality within the 'advanced" industrialized regions, as part of the globalized integral-ecological breakdown of Modern Industrial Civilization.

Yet even amidst the spiritual emptiness of this late modern "Dark Night" in the 'advanced' industrial regions, our spiritual "Sister Moon" is beginning to appear, and she reveals to us that her name is *Holy Spirit*. From within the regenerative shadows of womb-like darkness, she is beginning to console us, to sustain us, and to guide us, so that we may humbly help to birth regenerative life-giving spiritual paths of ecological hope.

More broadly across the planet, she is inspiring our global human family, and within it our global Christian family, with a *mystical-prophetic spiritual awakening* that beacons us to journey beyond the integral-ecological breakdown of Modern Industrial Civilization. That also means journeying beyond the collapse of Modern Psychological Spirituality.

---

industries, see Michael L. Budde, THE (MAGIC) KINGDOM OF GOD: CHRISTIANITY AND GLOBAL CULTURE INDUSTRIES (Westview Press, 1998).

[4] Cited by Francis in LAUDATO SI', Par. 217.

Late Modern Western Collapse
of Modern Psychological Spirituality

During the second half of the twentieth century, Modern Industrial Civilization entered the fully globalized scale of its ecologically degenerative course. At the same time, the Western form of Modern Psychological Spirituality in the 'advanced' industrialized regions began for many to retreat narcissistically into a *privatized self.*

Further, that spiritually narcissistic retreat also began to collapse into the subjective side of schizophrenic dualism that Robert Bellah and colleagues insightfully described as the inner-directed *"therapeutic ethos"* and the objective or outer-directed *"managerial ethos."*[5] In that late modern degenerative phase, the initial privatization and later secularization of Modern Psychological Spirituality has functioned as a co-dependent inner-directed *psychological enabler,* covertly legitimating the destructive addiction of late Modernity's outer-directed anti-ecological ravaging.

In that covert addictive-codependent dualism, both pathologies amplified Modernity's atomistic individualism, undermined organic human community, and blocked out Christian consciousness of Nature's sacramental character. Now, that pathological dualism threatens the biological viability of vast numbers of species among our loving Creator's beloved creatures across planet Earth, including countless numbers of poor, handicapped, elderly, and unborn human creatures.

Within that late modern degenerative process, the privatization and secularization of bourgeois individualism have also jointly undermined consciousness of communitarian justice, as we see in the pathological spread of *economic, political, and cultural libertarianism.* As a result, within the 'advanced' industrialized regions, many late modern bourgeois

---

[5] See Robert Bellah et al., HABITS OF THE HEART: INDIVIDUALISM AND COMMITMENT IN AMERICAN LIFE, New Preface Edition (University of California Press, 2007).

individuals are abandoning compassionate ethical responsibility for the objective reality of our global ecosystem, for the myriad and beauteous creatures within it, and even for our own human family (again, an organic part of our wider ecological family of creatures).

In that late modern degenerative process, the secularized bourgeois psyche finally loses consciousness of the spiritual dimension of its own inner self. It thus abandons the last vestige of bourgeois spiritual meaning. With that secularizing conquest of the inner psyche, the degenerative triumph of modern bourgeois Scientific Materialism becomes complete.

In that late modern negative triumph, not only has Scientific Materialism secularized the objective technological dimension. It has now also reached into the inner sanctum of the subjective psychological dimension. With that pathological secularization of both *techne* and *psyche*, any healthy public cultural foundation for the modern bourgeois psychological spirituality of interiority comes to its historical end.

Supporting the late modern materialist conquest of the inner self stands the overwhelming global corporate control of electronic communications media over our human family's cultural symbols and myths. Those media now successfully propagandize, by their global electronic and mythic-symbolic power, the unsustainable hyper-masculine symbols and myths underlying at the deepest level the modern philosophical-scientific Cosmology of Scientific Materialism. In so doing, they legitimate the globalized consumer society, and direct the human family ever deeper into global devastation of life's integral ecology.

The corporate global culture industries now use electronic media to maximize profit for their investors by "brainwashing" the human family on behalf of materialist consumerism. That "brainwashing" is directed even at little children – indoctrinating them to distrust their parents, and *to trust the giant global corporations in place of their parents.*

Those giant global corporations promise little children that they will provide them with the abundant and exciting commodities of capitalist mass consumerism. Yet they do not tell little children that the late modern corporate-consumerist path is destroying their very ecological future, and the ecological future of so many of our other wondrous sister and brother creatures across our loving Creator's beauteous and beloved garden-planet Earth.[6]

Again, for Catholic Christianity in the 'advanced' industrialized regions, the late modern breakdown of Modern Psychological Spirituality is revealed in the decline of the modern Catholic "apostolic" form of "religious life" and in the wider breakdown of the modern Western Catholic-Christian industrial-colonial model of evangelization. Yet another dimension of that breakdown, as we have seen, is the institutional crisis of the modern Catholic-Christian clerical-celibate-seminary model of the presbyterate and episcopate. But let us limit here our focus on the breakdown to the "apostolic" form of "religious life."

Late Modern Western Decline of
Apostolic Religious Life

As we have seen, it is within this historical and geographic context (the late modern phase of the 'advanced' industrialized regions) that we need to understand the current decline of the modern "apostolic" form of Catholic "religious life." Again, this book proposes that the deep reason for the decline is that their contextual grounding in Modern Psychological Spirituality is also collapsing. That spiritual collapse constitutes the subjective side of the objective integral-ecological breakdown of Modern Industrial Civilization.

---

[6] On the corporate "brainwashing" of little children against their parents, see Ralph Nader, THE SEVENTEEN SOLUTIONS: BOLD IDEAS FOR OUR AMERICAN FUTURE (Harper, 2012), Chapter 4 titled "Protect the Family Unit", pp. 68-98. Nader calls the executives of such corporate "brainwashing of little children "child-abusers."

"Apostolic religious communities" had traditionally avoided individualism, privatization, and secularization by their inner-directed communal life of prayer, and by their outer-directed communal "apostolates" to "secular" society. Now, however, with the late modern bourgeois secularization of both *techne* and *psyche*, secularization undermines many religious institutions. With declining recruitment, it becomes difficult for their mystical-spiritual energies and their prophetic-ethical works to survive in institutional form.

Even so, let us not forget that the ancient spirituality of interiority remains important and essential. But its modern Western bourgeois form can no longer serve as the leading spirituality for the emerging Postmodern Ecological Era. We now need to re-synthesize its ancient gifts within the emerging framework of Postmodern Ecological Spirituality.

LATE CLASSICAL ARISTOCRATIC ROOTS IN CATHOLIC-PLATONIC DUALISM

Both the eventual privatization of Modern Psychological Spirituality and more radical secularization of *psyche* have old and problematic roots in the hierarchical matter-spirit dualism adopted by the aristocratic elites of classical Western Christian Civilization from the ancient and aristocratic Platonic tradition.

As we have seen, during the late classical and medieval periods, Western Catholic-Christian monasticism canonized Neo-Platonist hierarchical dualism as the cosmological paradigm for Catholic-Christian Ascetical Theology, and for aristocratic legitimization of European Christian Civilization. Further, during the medieval period, that hierarchically dualist self-understanding defined monasticism as an allegedly *'higher'* "religious" state in life. At the same time, it correlatively reduced the non-monastic life of the laity to its allegedly *'lower'* definition as "secular."

Still later, the Modern Era – through its outer-directed scientific secu-larization of the *Cosmos* and its inner-directed spiritual privatization of the *psyche* – revised those late classical Neo-Platonist foundations into what we will explore more fully in the next chapter as the Cartesian bourgeois schizophrenia.[7] But, because the modern Cartesian form of the psychological spirituality of interiority lacked ontological unity with Modernity's materialist understanding of the exterior world, it was only a matter of time before Modern Science secularized the *psyche*. That development then undermined Modern Psychological Spirituali-ty, and it also heralded the intellectual triumph across both *techne* and *psyche* of what Whitehead called Scientific Materialism.

Because Catholic-Christian Theology could not accept the Modern Me-chanical Cosmology of Scientific Materialism, official Vatican docu-ments continued – in a pre-Copernican style – to describe the laity as responsible for the "temporal order" of planet Earth. At the same time, it continued to describe "clergy" and "religious" as linked to the "eternal order" of the "Heavens."

In addition, official Vatican Catholic-Christian terminology (codified in its Canon Law) also continued to perpetuate the pre-Copernican Cos-mology by hierarchically distinguishing between "religious priests" (belonging to "religious orders") and "secular priests" (belonging to a diocese). That hierarchical ordering implied that "religious" priests supposedly functioned at a 'higher' spiritual level. For example, "reli-gious priests" traditionally gave spiritual "retreats" to "secular priests." Hardly ever did the opposite occur.

Again, the classical Platonic hierarchical dualism of matter and spirit had grounded the scientific paradigm of the pre-Copernican geocentric Cosmology. As we have seen, that classical pre-Copernican paradigm had viewed the "sub-lunar region" as a 'lower' corrupt material sphere of temporal change, subject to cycles of death and decay. And it had

---

[7] Again, the term "Cartesian" refers to René Descartes.

defined the "Heavens" as a 'higher' realm of spiritual spheres, with the cycles of heavenly bodies supposedly moving in unchanging eternal circles, and with the heavenly bodies themselves being supposedly perfect and unblemished spheres.

Further, since that classical Western cosmological paradigm understood the supposedly eternal and perfect "heavenly spheres" as not subject to decay and death, it logically defined them as not needing sexual reproduction. Symbolically then, the monastic and later more broadly "religious" vow of chastity (or Western "clerical" celibacy) came to be understood as linking its adherents, in an anticipatory manner, with the "eternal order of the Heavens."

In addition, as we have also seen, during the eleventh century the papacy violently and unjustly – and through coercive police-power – imposed monastic celibacy on diocesan bishops and presbyters, and on their Catholic-Christian families, even condemning bishops' and presbyters' Christian wives and children into slavery.

EARLY MODERN ROOTS IN
BOURGEOIS CATHOLIC & PROTESTANT URBANISM

We also need also to understand the early modern roots of Modern Psychological Spirituality in the bourgeois (urban) form of early modern Catholic and Protestant spirituality, as well as in the bourgeois Protestant Reformation's doctrine of "total depravity."

The bourgeois anti-rural bias that emerged during the early modern period, and the modern Protestant doctrine of "total depravity" that also emerged during that period, both constitute important roots of the late modern intellectual-spiritual breakdown and of the attack by Modern Industrial Civilization on the integral ecology of life.

Bourgeois Character
of Modern Psychological Spirituality

The late medieval and early modern urban Catholic-Christian form of the psychological spirituality of interiority (again, known in Latin as the *Devotio Moderna*), as well as the late medieval and early modern philosophical innovation of empirically oriented Nominalism (known in Latin as the *Via Moderna*) took on fully modern strength in both Catholic-Christian and Protestant-Christian forms with the modern Print Revolution. Rooted in urban university towns and cities and promoted by the printers' guild, mechanical printing became the dominant new medium of communication for the emerging modern bourgeois civilization.

It has not been coincidental to Modern Psychological Spirituality that one reads a printed book *alone*, and reflects on it within one's psychological interior. That means apart from communion with other humans and apart from communion with Nature. Thus, mechanically printed literature provided the technological communications platform for the modern individualistic and ecologically uprooted bourgeois form of the spirituality of interiority.

The mechanically printed book most widely read in the early and middle phases of the West's Modern Era was of course the Christian Bible, promoted in vernacular languages first by Protestant-Christian leadership, and centuries later by Catholic-Christian leadership. In turn, abundant mechanically printed Christian devotional literature supplemented the mechanically printed Bible.

But in its turn to the Bible and to other print literature, Modern Psychological Spirituality began to lose touch with the ecologically grounded 'Book of Nature." Further, with the increasing scientific-technological uprooting of modern bourgeois life from the world of Nature, urban bourgeois consciousness began to lose awareness of the very ecosystem in which it remained embedded and on which it depended.

Modern Psychological Spirituality found a bourgeois inner-oriented literary parallel in the modern genre known as the novel, as well as an outer-oriented scientific parallel in Psychology and professional counseling. The literary novel, scientific Psychology, and professional counseling all remain important, yet in their modern bourgeois forms they became uprooted from the ecosystem, and thus do not serve as creative resources for helping us to navigate toward a regenerative Postmodern Ecological Civilization. Nonetheless, postmodern ecologically grounded explorations in literature, Psychology, and counseling do prove resourceful for guiding us through the turbulent and even dangerous postmodern passage.[8]

The Reformation's Anti-Ecological Doctrine of "Total Depravity

In early Modernity, the bourgeois form of the spirituality of psychological interiority (*Devotio Moderna*) gained further strength with the Protestant Reformation, which was also promoted by the printers' guild and spread in Northern Europe primarily in urban (bourgeois) towns and cities.[9] Within the Protestant Reformation, Martin Luther's *sola Scriptura* (Bible alone) and his neo-Augustinian emphasis on *interior conversion*, as well as his training in the Philosophy of Nominalism (*Via Moderna*), all provided uprooted and individualistic bourgeois foundation stones for constructing the Protestant-Christian form of the West's Modern Psychological Spirituality.

---

[8] An example of postmodern ecological breakthrough in clinical-pastoral Counseling is the late Howard Clinebell's book, ECOTHERAPY: HEALING OURSELVES, HEALING THE EARTH (Routledge, 1996). Clinebell was a founding member of the American Association of Pastoral Counselors, and is considered one of the 'fathers' of the clinical-pastoral counseling movement.

[9] See Steven E. Ozment, THE REFORMATION IN THE CITIES: THE APPEAL OF PROTESTANTISM TO SIXTEENTH-CENTURY GERMANY AND SWITZERLAND (Yale University Press, 1975).

Further strengthening the turn to bourgeois interiority, Martin Luther (1483-1546) and John Calvin (1509-1564) *denied the possibility of Natural Theology*. That meant they denied what the classical Christian tradition had seen as the Divine Mystery immanently revealed in and through the sacramental "Book of Nature."[10] Further, Luther's and Calvin's rejection of Natural Theology, based on the Reformation's doctrine of "total depravity" for all things natural, may have encouraged early modern Christian "natural philosophers" to welcome the de-spiritualized Materialism of Epicurus.

Luther's and Calvin's denial of Natural Theology intensified the uprooting of bourgeois Christian spirituality from its essential nourishment by spiritual revelation in and through the beauty of Nature. Again, that nourishment comes to us in and through our loving Creator's garden-planet Earth, with her myriad and beauteous creatures, and in and through our loving Creator's vast and beauteous Cosmos.

Luther and Calvin's cosmological secularization also gave implicit theological permission for Modernity's later scientific-technological devastation of "Mother Nature." Certain early modern millenarian English Calvinists even called for scientific-technological violation of 'feminine' Nature to force "Mother Nature," through techniques metaphorically linked to torture, to reveal her "Divine secrets."[11]

Yet the problem was not only on the Protestant side, but also on the Catholic side, at least in part. Though not supported by Catholic Theology, the problem was nonetheless compounded by the Catholic-Christian René Descartes' scientific Cosmology. Resonating with the

---

[10] See in John C. Rao, Editor, LUTHER AND HIS PROGENY: 500 YEARS OF PROTESTANTISM & ITS CONSEQUENCES FOR CHURCH, STATE, AND SOCIETY (Angelico Press, 2017), the Introduction by John C. Rao, pp. 1-23, and Rev. Richard A. Munkelt's essay, "Religious Evolution and Revolution in the Triumph of *Homo Economicus*" (Chapter 7), pp. 143-174. See also T. Richard Snyder, THE PROTESTANT ETHIC AND THE SPIRIT OF PUNISHMENT (W. B. Erdmanns, 2001), especially pp.11-12, 35-37, 41-43.

[11] See again Carolyn Merchant's indicting book, DEATH OF NATURE, and her ISIS article.

Protestant rejection of Natural Theology by Luther and Calvin, he philosophically defined Nature as devoid of spiritual meaning.

As we have seen, Descartes even infamously justified vivisection, which is torture of non-human animals for 'scientific' purposes. Consistent with the Modern Mechanical Cosmology, Descartes claimed (as noted) that the tortured animals were machines without feeling, and that their screams, while being tortured, were the mechanical result of squeaky machine parts.

It should be no surprise, then, that half a millennium after the dawn of bourgeois Modernity, we now find gargantuan capitalist and communist business and government enterprises globally plundering "Mother Nature" by corporate and military scientific-technological paths that threaten vast communities of life, including human life, across our loving Creator's beloved garden-planet Earth.[12]

In response to such global ecological plundering, the "green" Greek Orthodox Patriarch, Bartholomew I, has called contemporary ecocide not only a sin against stewardship, but more fundamentally a *sin of blasphemy*.[13] Contemporary ecocide is indeed blasphemous, because it fundamentally attacks the Divine Mystery immanently revealed in and through "Mother Nature's" sacramental and integral ecology of natural, human, and spiritual life.

MODERN PHILOSOPHICAL-SCIENTIFIC
GROUNDING IN EPICUREAN MATERIALISM

At the birth of the Modern World, the mathematical and observational work of Copernicus, Kepler, Galileo, and Newton disproved the pre-Copernican hierarchical Cosmology of 'higher' spiritual and 'lower'

---

[12] See, for example, Edward O. Wilson, THE CREATION: AN APPEAL TO SAVE LIFE ON EARTH (W.W. Norton, 2007). Wilson, a retired Harvard professor, is one of the world's most distinguished biologists.

[13] See again Chryssavgis, COSMIC GRACE + HUMBLE PRAYER.

155

material spheres. In its place, their mathematical and observational work produced the modern heliocentric Cosmology. To ground that Cosmology, "natural philosophers" embraced the Renaissance's retrieval of Epicurean Philosophy and interpreted the Universe as purely materialist.

Yet Epicurus' Cosmology of a purely materialist Universe presented profound intellectual-spiritual problems. Where was the spiritual dimension? And how did a spiritual "soul" relate to a material body? And what was the role of God as pure spirit within a purely material Universe? It was those questions which Descartes set out to answer.

However, before examining further Descartes' proposed philosophical-scientific solution for those haunting spiritual questions, let us first revisit how Modern Philosophy and Modern Science displaced the pre-Copernican Aristotelian-Ptolemaic Cosmology.

Again, they did so by retrieving for the intellectual construction of Modernity's cosmological foundation the ancient atomistic-mechanical Materialism of the ancient and anti-religious Greek philosopher Epicurus. Prior to the birth of Modernity, Epicurus' materialist Cosmology had never achieved Western intellectual dominance, though it had been an important philosophical school in the classical period. Further, during the late classical and medieval Catholic-Christian periods, Epicurean Materialism as an anti-religious philosophy was repressed.

Lucretius' De Rerum Natura

Then, in 1417, just before the dawn of the Modern World, the papal book-hunter Poggio Bracciolini discovered in an old German monastery a rare copy of the book-length poem DE RERUM NATURA (On the Nature of Things), written by the classical Roman Epicurean philosopher Lucretius (Titus Lucretius Carus, c. 99-55 BCE). With that extended work, late medieval European scholars recovered Lucretius' lyrical explanation of Epicurus' atomistic-mechanical, purely materialist, and anti-religious understanding of the Universe.[14]

Eventually, vernacular translations of Lucretius' DE RERUM NATURA became an intellectual sensation across Europe, with the Italian version playing a major role in the Florentine Renaissance. From there, Epicurean Materialism, along with the simultaneous Florentine revival of Neo-Platonist Philosophy, became foundational for the emerging modern Western bourgeois cosmological paradigm of Philosophy and Science. It also became foundational, as Catherine Wilson and Steven Goldblatt have shown, for all modern scientific disciplines and for the entire Modern World.[15]

From Classical Spiritual Cosmos to
Modern Mechanical Universe

With the philosophical-scientific birth of Modern Era, the word "Cosmos" began to fall out of favor. In its place, the word "Universe" began to move to center stage. The Greek word *Cosmos* means "order" and contrasts with the Greek word *Chaos,* which indicates disorder and constituted Epicurus' chosen understanding of reality.

The classical philosophical idea of creation as *Cosmos* had been linked to the ancient Greek vision of *Logos* (reason). It had seen all created re-

---

[14] For a helpful summary of Epicurus' Materialism, see Catherine Wilson, EPICUREANISM: A VERY BRIEF INTRODUCTION (Oxford University Press, 2016), as well as her already cited brilliant and lyrical study, EPICUREANISM AT THE ORIGIN OF MODERNITY. See also the comprehensive article in Stanford University's INTERNET ENCYCLOPEDIA OF PHILOSOPHY at: *http://www.iep.utm.edu/epicur* (accessed 2015-07-01).

[15] See the earlier reference to Goldblatt's THE SWERVE – HOW THE WORLD BECAME MODERN. Both Wilson and Goldblatt tell the fascinating story of the discovery of Lucretius' book, the sensation it later caused among "natural philosophers," and its foundational impact on the "Modern World." As mentioned, however, Goldblatt's book carries a strong bias against the Catholic intellectual tradition, and polemically supports modern Western Scientific Materialism as a comprehensive explanation for all reality. Wilson is also a supporter of Epicurus, though more gracefully so in terms of Epicurus' appreciation for the beauty of Nature and of "her" endless creativity.

ality as carrying within its nature an internal rational order of *Logos,* flowing from the rational order of *Logos* within the Divine Mind. In turn, it had seen that Divine rational order of *Logos* as reflected within the human mind.[16]

Thus, when classical thinkers used the word *Cosmos* to describe the Universe, they meant that the structure and process of the Universe revealed an "order" (*Cosmos*) embodying "reason" (*Logos*). In addition, they saw the created *Cosmos* and *Logos* as permeating both the macro-cosmic level and the micro-psychic level, again with both revealing the order and reason of the Divine Mind.

By contrast, Modern Philosophy and Modern Science have preferred the word "Universe" rather than Cosmos. It reportedly was Lucretius who had coined the term "Universe," and it would have been from Lucretius that the term arose within the Renaissance. From its Latin roots, the word means "turning as one." It presumably refers to the Epicurus' claim, repeated by Lucretius, that the Universe was a "vortex" which turned as a whole within a "void."[17]

Epicurus' Cosmology of
Atomistic-Mechanical Materialism

In his lengthy and lyrical DE RERUM NATURA, Lucretius poetically narrated Epicurus' atomistic-mechanical, materialist, and anti-religious teachings. Again, Lucretius' teachings had been a Latin poetic sharing of the earlier materialist teachings of the ancient Greek philosopher Epicurus and his predecessor Democritus.

---

[16] The earliest known use of the term *Logos* in relation to *Cosmos* is found with the ancient Greek philosopher Heraclitus of Ephesus (c. 535 - c. 475 BCE). His *Cosmos-Logos* tradition flows through the Greek Socratics and into the Roman Stoics, and from there into early Christianity, including New Testament.

[17] Modern Western Philosophy and Modern Western Science have sometimes continued to use the word "Cosmology," but not in the original meaning of *Cosmos* as "order." Also, contrary to its etymological root, the term is sometimes still used to embrace Epicurean *chaos* – as in the late Carl Sagan's once famous TV show "Cosmos."

Epicurus, like Democritus, had claimed that the entire Universe was not an ordered and rational structure and process of *Cosmos* revealing *Logos*, but only the irrational and meaningless *Chaos"* of *"atoma,"* which in Greek means "uncuttable particles" and is translated today as "atoms." Thus, the classical Democritean and Epicurean atomistic-mechanical and materialist Philosophy is the intellectual source for the modern scientific phrases of "Atomic Theory" and "Particle Physics."

While Democritus had proposed that the *Chaos* of atoms moved in a "vortex" within a "void," Epicurus added the claim that each atom within the vortex followed a spontaneous and random "swerve" (*clinamen*), which made its motion unpredictable. He then used his concept of the random "swerve" to explain "freedom." Yet, in his paradigm, freedom was nothing more than arbitrary and unimpeded movement or, in human terms, arbitrary and unimpeded "free choice" without substantive meaning.

In the seventeenth-century European philosophical-scientific formation of the modern Western Cosmology, European "natural philosophers" enthusiastically embraced Epicurus' atomistic-mechanical and materialist vision, with its substantively empty understanding of "freedom."[18] Epicureanism's substantively empty concept of freedom then became central to modern Scientific Materialism's rationally empty psychosocial concept of "freedom" as voluntarist choice, including economic, political, and cultural "freedom" (or alternately "liberty").

According to Epicurus, the only role for "reason" in "free choice" is instrumental and quantitative. Its function, he argued, is limited to calculating the quantity of pleasure or pain entailed by a particular "free choice." That Epicurean voluntarist doctrine of "freedom" is the deep root of modern Utilitarian Ethics, though the Utilitarians altruistically expanded the calculation to recommend the greatest amount of pleasure and the least amount of pain for the largest number.

---

[18] See again Wilson's, EPICUREANISM AT THE ORIGINS OF MODERNITY.

Apart from its altruistic expansion, Utilitarianism still flows directly from the early modern appropriation of Epicurus' atomistic-mechanical and materialist Cosmology as the intellectual foundation for Modern Western Philosophy and Modern Western Science. Thus, the bourgeois Modern World, at least in part, may be seen as a vast Epicurean historical project.

MODERN POLITICAL-ECONOMIC IDEOLOGIES OF SCIENTIFIC MATERIALISM

Epicurean Materialism, with its voluntarist and thus philosophically empty concept of "freedom," soon and inevitably became foundational for Modernity's two dominant ideologies of Scientific Materialism. Again, these are *Liberal Capitalism and Scientific Socialism*, both of which, via Newtonian Mechanics, found their philosophical-scientific ground in Epicurean Cosmology.

Liberal-Capitalist Ideology

As we have seen, during the eighteenth century, Adam Smith, a Scottish professor of Moral Philosophy, became the founding philosopher for the modern bourgeois voluntarist *market-centered* political-economic ideology of Liberal Capitalism. Applying Epicurean atomism (again, via Newtonian Mechanics) to the modern bourgeois political economy, Smith philosophically and scientifically constructed his atomistic-mechanical and materialist fantasy of the "Free-Market." Smith's individualist and competitive doctrines of "self-interest" and "economic freedom" may thus be traced immediately to Newtonian Mechanics, and ultimately to Epicurean Materialism.

Yet, just as Newton was not a pure mechanist since he saw gravity as the hand of God active within the Universe, Smith was not a pure free-marketer. He saw a significant role for state regulation and taxation in matters beyond internal justice, defense of private property, and external defense. For Smith, such matters requiring state intervention included protection of workers and the poor.

In addition, Smith was influenced, like his close friend David Hume, by the Stoic tradition of virtues, although both saw the virtues as grounded not in reason (*logos*), but rather in emotions – as addressed in Smith's other book, THE THEORY OF MORAL SENTIMENTS. But for Smith and Hume, Stoicism's reason-based virtues were reduced to non-rational *feelings,* which were easily accommodated by his grounding in non-rational Epicurean Cosmology.

Scientific-Socialist Ideology

As we have also seen, during Modernity's following nineteenth century Karl Marx became the founding philosopher of the modern bourgeois and instrumentally rationalist *state-centered* political-economic ideology of Scientific Socialism. Marx challenged Smith's and other early political-economists' liberal dogma of autonomous (atomistic) individualism, but he still embraced Newtonian Mechanics and its underlying Epicurean mechanical atomism.[19]

Marx developed his embrace of Epicurean atomism into the alternative modern bourgeois ideology that Friedrich Engels called "Scientific Socialism."[20] Engels praised Marx's modern "scientific" version of Socialism, and he contemptuously contrasted it with the quite different and earlier competitor known as "Christian Socialism," as well as with other also supposedly "utopian" forms of Socialism.[21]

---

[19] In his doctoral dissertation at the University of Berlin, Marx had compared the philosophical atomism of Democritus with that of Epicurus, and he had praised Epicurus' addition of the "swerve" as supporting human freedom.

[20] See Friedrich Engels, SOCIALISM SCIENTIFIC AND UTOPIAN (International Publishers, 1972), with the original published in 1883. In this text, Engels made destruction of the Catholic Church a *sine qua no* for the advance of Scientific Socialism

[21] On the history of Christian Socialism, which as noted is older than and different from Marxism, see the late John Cort's CHRISTIAN SOCIALISM: AN INFORMAL HISTORY (Orbis

In his embrace of Epicurus, Marx rejected Liberal Capitalism's individualistic dogma of *Homo Economicus* ("Economic Man," supposedly functioning as an autonomous "atom" guided only by "self-interest"). He saw that concept as a laissez-faire liberal dogma favoring the power of owners of capital. Holding up instead a revolutionary vision of *workers' solidarity*, Marx called upon industrial workers (seen as socially uprooted and atomized by Liberal Capitalism) to aggregate into a "mass" movement of working-class revolutionary "force" against capitalist owners. The terms "mass" and "force" reveal the ideology's 'scientific' roots in Newtonian Mechanics.

Thus, the modern bourgeois ideology of Marxism, still drawing on Epicurean atomism, also sought empty Epicurean "freedom," albeit on a different path from Liberal Capitalism. Marx sought that "freedom" by aggregating the atomized industrial working class into a Newtonian "mass force," framed by the application of Newtonian Mechanics to class-conflict. Marx also combined his concept of workers' revolutionary "mass force" with the materialist inversion of the idealist Hegelian dialectic, developed by his fellow "left-Hegelian" Ludwig Andreas von Feuerbach (1804-1872).

Using Feuerbach's materialist dialectic, Marx sought to guide the "mass" workers' revolution through the transformative "force" of class-conflict toward what he claimed would eventually become a communist utopia. Yet, paradoxically for a "socialist," Marx viewed his communist utopia as individualistically *libertarian*. He claimed that, after rationally directed industrial power overcame economic scarcity, the instrumentally 'Rationalist State' would "wither away," and "mass" revolutionary movements would no longer be necessary. Humans could then, he claimed, pursue their unbridled desires in libertarian

---

Books, 1998). Also, Pope John XXIII, as a young priest, had described himself as a "Christian socialist." Interestingly, Francis Bellamy, author of the United States "Pledge of Allegiance" and a Baptist minister, also had considered himself a "Christian Socialist."

fashion as *autonomous individuals* – again, with no need for "mass" solidarity. To repeat, Marx was ultimately and paradoxically a libertarian.

Two Paths Predicting a Libertarian Utopia

Again, the two competing modern ideologies of Liberalism and Marxism have both been seeking *a utopian future of atomistic-mechanistic libertarianism* grounded in Epicurean Materialism, though by different and competing strategic paths:

- *Liberal Capitalism* has sought its libertarian future by trying to organize society around its blindly *voluntarist fantasy* of the 'Free Market;'

- *Scientific Socialism* has sought its libertarian future by trying to organize society around its instrumentally *rationalist fantasy* of the 'Rationalist State' (which ultimately was to disappear).

Yet both share the common ultimate goal of libertarian "freedom" as grounded in the substantively empty doctrine from Epicurean Materialism of atoms "swerving" in arbitrary and unimpeded motion.

Both Modern Ideologies as Bourgeois

True to their bourgeois (again, urban) prejudices, both modern philosophical ideologies of Epicurean Materialism have sought their philosophically empty "freedom" by "emancipating" human individuals from their natural-ecological roots in organic bioregions, and from their social-ecological roots in organic rural human communities. Further, both have sought their empty "freedom" by emancipation from religion. (Again, Epicurus was militantly anti-religious, though his understanding of religion was limited to religious consciousness based on fear of punishment by the "gods.")

Both modern ideologies of Materialism have thus sought their philosophically empty "freedom" through the uprooting and fragmenting

163

means of industrializing and secularizing urbanization. Both have been *modern bourgeois (urban) ideologies.* Again, both have pursued modernization by means of uprooting and fragmenting urbanization, industrialization, and secularization. Thus, both materialist ideologies have ultimately been seeking human 'emancipation' from the evolving creative communion of life's integral ecology, across its interwoven natural, human, and spiritual fabric.

Shared Philosophical Dysfunctions

In summary, we have now seen that, because Liberal Capitalism and Scientific Socialism have both been grounded in the atomistic-mechanical and secularizing reductionism of Epicurean Materialism, both have carried *the same philosophical dysfunctions.* Further, as we have also seen, those dysfunctions are the direct outcome of the philosophical errors of their underlying Modern Mechanical Cosmology.

- *Humanity.* First, the Modern Mechanical Cosmology has not understood *humanity's integral-ecological rootedness in Nature.*

- *Nature.* Second, the Modern Mechanical Cosmology has not understood the *integral-ecological character of Nature itself.*

- *Spirituality.* Third, the Modern Mechanical Cosmology has not understood the *spiritual dimension of the integral ecology of all Creation*, including the heightened spiritual dimension of human creatures gifted with reflective consciousness.

Further, the shared ideological failure to understand "spiritual ecology" continued the anti-religious program of Epicurean Materialism into Modernity's Scientific Materialism. Boldly rejecting religion, Epicurus had taught that the "soul" was only a purely materialist part of a purely materialist body, albeit made of subtler or lighter material atoms.

Similarly, many late modern bourgeois intellectuals now seek to reduce the *psyche* to what they see as the mechanical *techne* of the brain. They also seek to reduce the entire human body to a mechanical *techne* within the wider mechanical *techne* of the Epicurean "Universe." Within that Universe of randomly "swerving" atoms, according to this late modern vision, everything, including the human mind and the human body, can be deconstructed and reconstructed according to arbitrary desires of empty voluntarist "freedom."

Three haunting spiritual questions are left to us by the breakdown of Modern Psychological Spirituality before the triumph of the modern ideologies of Scientific Materialism, and especially of its liberal-capitalist version. It is that Modern Western philosophical devolution that has generated major philosophical questions that we will address in the next chapter.

- **Individualistic Subjectivity.** First, how are we to respond to the challenge of an *unsustainable individualistic and subjectivist spirituality*, flowing from the schizophrenic philosophical dualism first constructed by René Descartes and later revised by Immanuel Kant?

- **Atheistic Materialism.** Second, how are we to respond to the left-wing rationalist challenge from Karl Marx, the revolutionary pro-worker German philosopher who claimed that the rationalist Materialism of Modern Science requires humans to *abandon the very idea of God*?

- **Voluntarist Nihilism.** Third, how are we to respond to the right-wing voluntarist challenge from Friedrich Nietzsche, the counter-revolutionary anti-worker German philologist who claimed that the entire Western tradition of rationalism (initially in the Socratic tradition, later in Christianity, and finally in Modern Science), must yield to the *voluntarist Nihilism of the "Will to Power"*?

Within the global integral-ecological breakdown of Modern Industrial Civilization, the intellectual-spiritual challenge of those haunting questions becomes urgent. But to respond, we need first to understand the construction and deconstruction of Modern Philosophy as central to the late modern collapse into spiritual emptiness, and to the wider late modern devastation of life's integral ecology.

5

PHILOSOPHICAL UNFOLDING

OF MODERN SPIRITUAL EMPTINESS

A gain, since Philosophy provides the underlying intellectual ground for human spirituality, this chapter seeks to understand the emergence and breakdown of the continental European tradition within Modern Philosophy, as they underlie the emergence and breakdown of Modern Psychological Spirituality.

To do that, the chapter examines four central and sequential figures in the continental European tradition of Modern Philosophy: Descartes, Kant, Marx, and Nietzsche. While many other philosophical figures could be added, these four have been chosen because of their strongly positive or negative relationship to the modern form of the Catholic-Christian intellectual-spiritual tradition.

A full review of Modern Western Philosophy would require also examining major figures in the modern Anglo-American philosophical tradition, which has carried a more empirical-pragmatic heritage. But, until recently, the main positive or negative philosophical dialogue partners for the Catholic intellectual-spiritual tradition have been primarily continental European.

FOUR KEY FIGURES IN
MODERN CONTINENTAL EUROPEAN PHILOSOPHY

Let us begin with a brief overview of the selected four major figures. After this overview, we will examine each figure in greater detail.

Rene Descartes, 1596-1650

First, this chapter will explore more deeply how the seventeenth-century French philosopher René Descartes, a Catholic-Christian trained by the Jesuits and often considered the 'father' of the Modern Philosophy, developed a modern schizophrenic revision of Platonic dualism as objective-subjective, in place of its original form as temporal-spatial.

As we have seen, Descartes' revision divided reality into objective *Res Extensa* (Extended Reality), which he saw as including the Universe and everything in it, and subjective *Res Cogitans* (Thinking Reality), which he saw as including the human mind and the Divine Mind. For objective *Res Extensa,* which was to be studied empirically by Science, Descartes accepted the early modern Epicurean materialist and thus secularized interpretation of *Cosmos* (again, now called "Universe").[1] For subjective *Res Cogitans,* he defined *psyche* (soul) as mental, with its "thinking" (*cogitans*) derived not from empirical knowledge of the Universe, but rather from transcendent infusion by the Divine Mind, or from "clear and distinct" logical deductions from that infusion.

Thus, for Descartes, empirical knowledge as quantitative measurement belonged to objective Science, while substantive truth belonged independently to Divine or human ideas within the subjective human mind (again, infused by God or correctly deduced from that infusion). As a distinguished mathematician reflecting Plato's ancient claim that Math-

---

[1] Yet Descartes was not a pure Epicurean, for he rejected Epicurus' concept of the "void."

ematics is the highest form of knowledge, Descartes identified substantive truth in human thought with "clear and distinct ideas."

Descartes' framework continued to provide a place for human spirituality, but only subjectively through *psyche* in the form of disembodied thought. His Philosophy thus supported Modern Psychological Spirituality's bourgeois limitation of spirituality to its psychological dimension. His spiritual *psyche* was no longer linked to pre-Copernican spiritual "Heavens" of the *Cosmos*, since the latter had now become the secularized "Universe" of Epicurean Materialism, and he saw the entire material Universe as devoid of spiritual energy. Thus, for Descartes, only *psyche* remained transcendently spiritual, and it did so by sharing in the Divine Mind.

Immanuel Kant, 1724-1804

Second, we will explore how the eighteenth-century German philosopher Immanuel Kant, formed as a child in Lutheran-Christian pietism, completed the philosophical secularization of Descartes' objective-subjective dualism. Accepting Descartes' secularized *Cosmos* as the "Universe" to be studied by what had now become Newtonian Science, Kant extended modern philosophical secularization to include also the human *psyche* (no longer called "soul," but now only "mind"). He did so by disconnecting "transcendence" from the Divine Mind, and by embedding it within a now "autonomous" human mind.

Kant secularized *psyche* by claiming that it had its own internal and only humanly transcendent "categories," through which it constructed a purely mental order out of unordered empirical "phenomena" appearing within the internal mind. He claimed that humans possess through mind an *internal and autonomous transcendence* that constitutes a secular reason (*logos*) autonomous from any Divine reason (*Logos*).

Yet Kant allowed his internally secularized human reason no substantive knowledge of the assumed Epicurean *chaos* of the external world. Again, that presumed external world was to be studied "objectively" by

Newtonian Science, but only through empirical measurement of humanly experienced "phenomena," with no cognitive access to unknowable external "noumena."

For Kantian Philosophy, the Divine *Logos* disappeared not only from the Cartesian secularized "Universe," but also from the now secularized human *psyche* as only "mind" and no longer "soul." Again, the transcendence of reason (*logos*) was no longer fundamentally the transcendence of the Divine reason (*Logos*) beyond creation, but only the autonomously human mental transcendence of a substantively unknowable exterior physical world.

Within the Kantian framework, even the Cartesian reduction of human spirituality to *psyche* disappeared. In place of spirituality, followers of Kant turned either to modern Secular Humanism, which was no longer linked to religion, or to Liberal Protestantism, which eliminated spirituality and (like Secular Humanism) reduced religion to Ethics as deontological reason (Kant's "Categorical Imperative").

Karl Marx, 1818-1883

Third, we will explore how the nineteenth-century German philosopher, Karl Marx, a secularized Jew descended from two long lines of distinguished Polish rabbis but raised in a nominally Lutheran-Christian household, rejected the entire Western dualist tradition. As an alternative to Descartes' dualism of matter and spirit and to Kant's dualism of matter and mind, Marx developed an historically dialectical and atheistic Materialism, based on a radical model of instrumental reason that sought social justice for the exploited industrial proletariat through a left-wing, pro-worker, revolutionary movement.

Within Marx's framework, there was of course no place for spirituality or even for religion, and Christianity became the enemy. A rational Ethics remained for Marx, however, but it was reduced to the utilitarian project of dialectical class conflict. Further, echoing Epicurus' instrumentally rational calculation of pleasure and pain, reason for Marx's philosophical vision also remained only instrumental. For Marx, its ultimate purpose was "scientifically" to guide human action through "Scientific Socialism" toward the final voluntarist libertarianism that he called "Pure Communism."[2]

Friedrich Nietzsche, 1844-1900

Fourth, we will explore how the later nineteenth-century German philologist Friedrich Nietzsche, raised in a strongly Lutheran-Christian household, unleased a voluntarist assault on reason itself. He did that through his construction of an anti-rationalist and will-based Nihilism that was right-wing, anti-worker, and counter-revolutionary. Within Nietzsche's framework, there was no place for Cartesian spirituality, or for Kantian "transcendental" ethics, or for Marxian solidarity.

Instead, Nietzsche's framework promoted in voluntarist form a nihilistic domination of the majority "herd" by a selfish and arrogant elite minority. Nietzsche's elite minority, contemptuous of the majority, constituted for him a post-bourgeois "new aristocracy," but one without classical communitarian responsibilities of *noblesse oblige*. The highest symbol for Nietzsche's neo-aristocratic elite was his anti-democratic superman *(Übermensch)*.

---

[2] In many ways, though this is not the place to explore it, Marx's emancipatory vision represented a secularized version of Jewish messianism. It also resonated, albeit in secularized form, with the liberationist side of the New Testament, found especially in the Gospel of Mark, where Jesus initially presented himself as a new spiritual Moses leading a new spiritual Exodus for oppressed Galilean peasants suffering under Roman imperial exploitation. Thus, contemporary Liberation Theology, still growing across the global Christian family, represents not a collapse into secular Marxism, but rather a biblical retrieval of the Book of Exodus and of the liberating dimensions of Jesus' own teachings. Those teachings were forgotten or even repressed in the classical Western Imperial Church, but they were retrieved in secularized and atheistic form by Marx (again, the secularized and atheist descendant of two long lines of distinguished Jewish rabbis).

Nietzsche rejected the entire Western humanistic reason-based ethical tradition from Socrates forward, defined Judaism and Christianity as "slave morality," and called for societal domination by a ruthless elite. Again, Nietzsche's neo-aristocratic elite was to be guided neither by Jewish or Christian ethical traditions, nor by secularized humanist or rationalist ethics, but only by his elitist, individualist, voluntarist, and anti-democratic "will to power."

PHILOSOPHICAL UNDERMINING OF SPIRITUALITY

REALITY	DESCARTES (17TH Century)	KANT (18th Century)	MARX (Mid 19th Century)	NIETZSCHE (Late 19th Century)
PSYCHE: *(Internal Subjective Reality)*	**SPIRITUAL** *(Res Cogitans as Soul or Mind Linked to the Divine Mind)*	**SECULAR** *(Categories of Natural Transcendental Mind)*	**ATHEIST** *(Mind as only Materialist and Instrumentally Rational)*	**NIHILIST** *(Mind as only Voluntarist Will to Power – Not Rationalist)*
COSMOS: *(External Objective Reality)*	**SECULAR** *(Res Extensa as Universe of Mechanical Materialism)*	**SECULAR** *(Unknowable External Noumena Studied only through Mental Phenomena)*	**ATHEIST** *(Physical World as only Materialism of Newtonian Physics)*	**NIHILIST** *(Physical World as only Blind Will or Blind Instincts)*

Summary & Implications

In summary, we see the following pattern for the intellectual emergence and breakdown of Modern continental European Philosophy, as it underlies the emergence and breakdown of Modern Psychological Spirituality:

- *Descartes.* First, in the seventeenth century, the Catholic-Christian Descartes modernized Platonic dualism in bourgeois form by disconnecting spirituality from *Cosmos* (defined scientifically as the

172

secularized "Universe") and by limiting spirituality to *psyche* as soul/mind/consciousness.

- **Kant.** Second, in the eighteenth century, Kant, carrying a Lutheran-Christian background, completed the modern philosophical secularization by removing spirituality from *psyche*, by redefining *psyche* only as "mind" (no longer "soul"), and by replacing spirituality with an autonomous ethics of deontological reason that found a home in either Secular Humanism or Liberal Protestantism.

- **Marx.** Third, in the nineteenth century, Marx, a secularized Jew with a distinguished rabbinical ancestry yet raised in a nominally Lutheran household, rejected the entire Western dualistic heritage, and with it all religion. In its place, he promoted what his close collaborator Friedrich Engels described as "Historical Materialism," which was atheistic but still 'scientifically' rationalist.

- **Nietzsche.** Fourth, later in the nineteenth century, Nietzsche, raised in a Lutheran-Christian household, rejected reason entirely. In its place, he called for a voluntarist Nihilism to be realized by a neo-aristocratic elite, whose "will to power" would be unrestrained by any spiritual, humanist, or rationalist ethics of altruism. For Nietzschean Nihilism, there is no longer any *Logos* or *Sophia*.

Nietzschean voluntarist Nihilism, triumphing in much of Western Philosophy only during the end of the twentieth century, marked the final philosophical breakdown of the modern Western rational tradition. Nietzschean Nihilism rejected the deep rational meaning of Philosophy as "love of wisdom" (*philia-sophia*). It represented the antithesis not only of spirituality, but even of reason itself. Nietzschean Nihilism also implicitly stood as the antithesis of the creative communion of life's integral ecology.

Let us now undertake a more detailed examination of these four major figures in the modern continental European tradition of Western Philosophy. We begin with Descartes.

DESCARTES' MODERN OBJECTIVE-SUBJECTIVE
REVISION OF PLATONIC DUALISM

Again, René Descartes, the Catholic-Christian 'father' of modern Western Philosophy, established the early form of the modern Western bourgeois Cosmology. Cartesian dualism remained normative for some time, as the philosophical-scientific foundation for the early modern understanding of matter on one side and of mind (as soul) on the other.

Ghost in the Machine

In his 1949 book THE CONCEPT OF MIND, the distinguished Oxford philosopher Gilbert Ryle famously ridiculed Descartes' concept of "soul" for his modernized mind-body dualism by naming it "the dogma of the Ghost in the Machine."[3] As we have seen, Descartes' "ghost in the machine" combined the subjective spiritual soul of Platonic dualism with the objective Universe of Epicurean atomistic-mechanistic Materialism.[4] Again, that modernized objective-subjective revision of classical Platonic spatial-temporal dualism included:

- **Res Extensa** (Extended Reality), constituting *objective material reality*, referred to the entire Universe (including the physical bodies of humans and of other living entities), which Descartes saw as mechanical, and as lacking any spiritual dimension or meaning;

- **Res Cogitans** (Thinking Reality), constituting *subjective spiritual reality*, which Descartes identified as "thought," again including both the human "soul" (originally conceived by Descartes as extrinsically connected to the human body only through the pineal gland), and God, whom (in a repeat of Augustine's Platonic Epis-

---

[3] Gilbert Ryle, THE CONCEPT OF MIND, Sixtieth Anniversary Edition (Routledge, 2009).

[4] Again, Descartes' mechanistic Materialism was not completely Epicurean, since he rejected Epicurus' concept of the "void." For Descartes, there were no empty spaces in the Universe.

temology) he saw as infusing truth into the human mind without mediation of the senses.[5]

Further, in terms of knowledge, Descartes understood the "Extended Reality" of matter (*Res Extensa*) as known only quantitatively by 'objective' empirical measurement. Correlatively, he understood "Thinking Reality" (*Res Cogitans*) as known only by 'subjective' spiritual thought, with that knowledge infused by God or deduced from that infusion.

The early modern Copernican revolution had scientifically discredited the *classical aristocratic spatial-temporal dualism* of a single Cosmos, constituted by a hierarchical division between the lower material-temporal order and the higher spiritual-eternal order. In its place, Descartes developed his *modern bourgeois objective-subjective dualism,* constituted by the schizophrenic division between external "Extended Reality" (matter) and internal "Thinking Reality" (spirit as thought).

In so doing, Descartes accepted the reduction of the Cosmos, and everything within it, to the "Universe" of Epicurean Materialism. Again, that required stripping spirituality of any embodied cosmological dimension, and then collapsing spirituality into the disembodied subjective *psyche* of human thought, understood as ontologically disconnected from the material world.

Modern Cartesian dualism thus abandoned classical Western spirituality's once powerful cosmological dimension of spirituality, while retaining its powerful psychological dimension. Yet, during later centuries, as indicated by Ryle's ridicule, Descartes' spiritual understanding of *psyche* would not hold. As we have seen, it became first secularized by Kant, next atheized by Marx, and finally nihilized by Nietzsche.

---

[5] Later in his life, perhaps because of his reportedly passionate love for Princess Elisabeth of Bohemia, Descartes expanded his notion of the "soul" to connect it with the human passions, and even with the entire human body.

Descartes' Debts to Augustine of Hippo
& Ignatius of Loyola

Descartes had studied at the Jesuits' Collège Henri-IV de La Flèche in France, where he had learned about the Neo-Platonist tradition via the writings of Saint Augustine of Hippo (354-430), the great late classical Western Christian theologian, as well as about the psychologically oriented SPIRITUAL EXERCISES of Saint Ignatius Loyola (1491-1556), the great early modern Basque founder of the Jesuits.[6]

Augustine had been a Neo-Platonist (albeit under the shadow of Manichaeism), and Ignatius' SPIRITUAL EXERCISES continued the classical Christian tradition of the Neo-Platonist three stages of the spiritual life (again, the purgative, illuminative, and unitive ways). Further, although Ignatius had favored the Aristotelian-Thomist tradition for Philosophy and Theology, his SPIRITUAL EXERCISES still referred in the dualist Platonic fashion of Western Christianity to the "salvation of souls."

In 1641, Descartes published his most famous philosophical work, MEDITATIONS ON FIRST PHILOSOPHY. In that work, he laid out his modernized bourgeois objective-subjective revision of the ancient Platonic temporal-spatial dualism of matter and spirit. In so doing, he modeled his MEDITATIONS on Ignatius' SPIRITUAL EXERCISES' continuation of the Neo-Platonist three stages of the spiritual life. But Descartes' MEDITATIONS, followed those three stages in epistemological rather than spiritual terms.[7]

---

[6] For the influence of Augustine's spiritual legacy on Descartes' paradigm, see Stephen Menn, DESCARTES AND AUGUSTINE (Cambridge University Press, 2002). For the influence of Ignatius, see Zeno Vendler, "Descartes' Exercises," CANADIAN JOURNAL OF PHILOSOPHY, Volume 9, Number 2, 1989, pp. 193-224. For a 1909 English translation of the original 1548 text, see Ignatius of Loyola, THE SPIRITUAL EXERCISES, trans. Elder Mullan (CreateSpace, 2016).

[7] A student once showed me his SparkNotes study-guide for Descartes' MEDITATIONS. It explained Descartes' debt to Ignatius as follows: "

Descartes' bourgeois revision of Platonic dualism, despite its objective-subjective modernization, continued the classical Platonic detachment of a spiritual "soul" from a material body. What was different, however, was his acceptance of Epicurean Materialism for Science. That shattered the ontological unity of classical Platonic dualism. Of course, neither Augustine nor Ignatius had ever accepted Epicurean Materialism within their Catholic-Christian adaptations of the Platonic Ontology.

With classical Christian spiritual writers like Origin, Augustine, and Pseudo-Dionysius, a Catholic-Christian school of Ascetical Theology had reformulated Neo-Platonist hierarchically dualist spirituality into a Catholic-Christian hierarchically dualist spirituality. Those Neo-Platonist roots (again carried into Christian Spirituality as the purgative, illuminative, and unitive ways) were most famously stated in in Pseudo-Dionysius' ECCLESIASTICAL HIERARCHY (c. 500).

Such hierarchically dualist interpretations of spirituality reflected Plato's claim, and Pythagoras' earlier claim, that the "soul" did not really belong to the material body, but rather had been imprisoned within the body. To be "saved," the "soul" needed philosophically (for Plato) or mystically (for the Neo-Platonist tradition) to escape in death from the material body, and more widely from the material world. That philosophical-spiritual escape, to be anticipated symbolically in this life by those committed to the 'higher' intellectual-spiritual way, became known in Western Christian asceticism by the Latin phrase "*fuga mundi*" (flight from the world). At the same time, Western Christian dualist interpretations of evangelization continued that ancient Pythagorean-Platonic dualist teaching of "saving souls."

[Descartes'] MEDITATIONS in many ways resemble St. Ignatius of Loyola's Spiritual Exercises. Both are framed in a meditational form meant to span six days' meditation. Descartes also imitates Loyola's three stages of purgation (skeptical doubt), illumination (proof of the existence of God), and union (linking this knowledge to the material world).

See: *https://nook.barnesandnoble.com/products/9781411473355/sample?sourceEan= 9781411473355* (accessed 2015-07-13).

Yet such dualist spiritual teachings stood as fundamentally opposed to Jesus' holistic teaching about the integral ecology of life. For Jesus taught that *salvation includes the resurrection of the body and the eschatological renewal of both "the Heavens and the Earth."* Salvation for Jesus' holistic teaching thus embraces the entire human person (in Platonic terms "body and soul") and the entire *Cosmos*.

A contemporary spiritual recovery of Jesus' authentic teaching would constitute a move away from Platonic dualism toward a holism that celebrates the integral ecology of life. It would celebrate the integral ecology of life throughout its interwoven natural, human, and spiritual fabric, across our loving Creator's beloved garden-planet Earth, and throughout our loving Creator's beloved and majestic *Cosmos*.

Before such a recovery could happen, however, modern bourgeois Cartesian dualism would need to collapse philosophically on both of its sides. As noted, that process would take centuries. Its breakdown would finally be revealed in the late modern global devastation of integral ecology, underlying the correlative global breakdown of Modern Industrial Civilization and Modern Psychological Spirituality.

Again, in its early development of the philosophical foundations for Modern Industrial Civilization, Cartesian dualism had laid the intellectual foundation for the revised modern bourgeois version of the ancient spirituality of interiority, which has been called here Modern Psychological Spirituality. That bourgeois spirituality lost consciousness of the sacred and ecological nature of the outer world, that is, of our loving Creator's beauteous and beloved garden-planet Earth and our loving Creator's vast and majestic Cosmos.

Yet Descartes' objective-subjective dualism for Modern Science and Modern Philosophy, though comprehensive and stunning for its time, would not hold for long within Modernity's bourgeois philosophical-scientific evolution. A series of philosophical-scientific challenges to its spiritual-psychological side, stretching across centuries, would culminate in the later modern collapse of spiritual consciousness first into the Kantian liberal secularization of *psyche*, then into Marxian historical-materialist Atheism, and finally into Nietzschean voluntarist Nihilism. The first philosophical challenge came from Kant.

KANT'S DUALIST TRANSCENDENTAL SECULARIZATION OF DESCARTES' RES COGITANS

As noted earlier, the first step in that long process of the breakdown of modern Cartesian paradigm for Philosophy came from Immanuel Kant, the great eighteenth-century German rationalist-humanist philosopher of the modern European Enlightenment. In the century after Descartes' death, and in response to David Hume's (1711-1776) more consistently Epicurean rejection of Metaphysics and promotion of empiricist Skepticism, Kant developed the first philosophical step in undermining Descartes' spiritual understanding of *psyche*.

While continuing to accept the embrace by early modern "natural philosophers" of the Epicurean atomistic, mechanical, and materialist understanding of the Universe, Kant framed his philosophical transformation with yet another revision of Platonic dualism, which he described as "transcendental." Yet Kant's transcendence was a secularized one, for he abandoned Descartes' Platonic claim of the Divine infusion of rational truth into the human mind.

Responding to Hume's "naturalistic" challenge, Kant proposed his own "naturalistic" claim that human knowledge was subjectively constructed through an internal autonomous ordering by innate "transcendental" categories. Those categories, he argued, subjectively organized into rational forms the non-rational "*phenomena*" of bodily sense perceptions, which he saw as triggered by the external yet unknowable objective "*noumena*" ("things in themselves") of the materialist Universe

In his fully secularized dualist proposal, Kant implicitly continued the early modern scientific acceptance of the Epicurean Cosmology that interpreted external objective reality as atomistic, mechanical, and materialist chaos. But he deviated epistemologically from Epicureanism by defining that external reality of "noumena" as cognitively unknowable to the human mind. Kant thus both disconnected Descartes' *Res Cogitans* from the Divine Mind, and reduced human knowledge of rational truth to the mental experience of *pure subjectivity*, with no true cognitive knowledge of objective reality.[8]

By declaring that ideas of logical order came only from the subjective human mind, and that objective "noumena" were unknowable in themselves, Kant undercut the Platonic, and more broadly Socratic, concept of objective truth and morality, which Descartes had tried to preserve. Again, Descartes made that attempt by linking the human mind with the Divine Mind. He did that by repeating the classical Platonic doctrine that the Divine *Logos* has its echo in the *micro-psyche*, even while rejecting the Platonic doctrine that the *macro-Cosmos* also echoed the Divine *Logos*.

For Kant, as for Descartes, 'objective' judgments about the external reality remained limited to analysis of quantitative data, especially as determined scientifically by empirical mathematical measurements. For Kant, however, such measurements were no longer knowledge of the "noumena" themselves (again, which he claimed were unknowable), but only of the subjectively experienced "phenomena." Kant called this "a posteriori knowledge," in contrast to "a priori knowledge," which he claimed was known only through the mind's categorical construction of rational order out of unordered "phenomena."

Further, for Kant, his subjective "a priori" knowledge included Ethics. He grounded his Ethics in what he called the innate "*Categorical Impera-*

---

[8] See T. K. Seung, KANT'S PLATONIC REVOLUTION IN MORAL AND POLITICAL PHILOSOPHY (Johns Hopkins University Press, 1994). In Platonic Philosophy, "noumena" – from the Greek verb *noein* meaning "to think," in turn linked to the Greek noun *nous* meaning "mind" – referred to the objective Platonic forms or ideas. By contrast, Kant's modern revision concretized their meaning yet in a manner that rendered them unknowable.

tive." Henceforth for Kant and later Kantians, morality would be grounded only subjectively in the internal categories of mind. To defend such subjectively grounded morality as universal became the great goal of the Kantian rationalist tradition. But its rationalist claim of subjective ethical universalism would prove difficult to sustain, and modern Anthropology would soon promote cultural relativism.

Again, Kant's bourgeois *psyche*, like the modernized bourgeois materialist Universe, no longer carried a spiritual dimension. Kant thus moved beyond Descartes' spiritual *psyche,* which Descartes had claimed was connected as *Res Cogitans* to the Divine Mind. In a manner acceptable to Hume's Naturalism, mind for Kant became the functioning of naturally transcendental mental categories. With Kantian knowledge now confined to human subjectivity, the Cartesian philosophical justification for Modern Psychological Spirituality disappeared.

Henceforth, Kantian-guided Western intellectual elites would be able to seek spiritual meaning only through bourgeois Romanticism, or through bourgeois Aestheticism, both of which were understood as outside the Kantian concept of reason. But such non-rational romantic or aesthetic understandings of spirituality would also prove unsustainable. (Today, within the late modern consumer culture, their symbols and myths have become *easily commodified for advertising and entertainment* by Madison Avenue and Hollywood.)

Yet, despite its abandonment of spirituality, Kantianism continued to function into the twentieth century as the philosophical support system for Liberal Protestantism. Major sectors of Liberal Protestantism, however, began to drift away from ancient orthodox Christian traditions, as Kant himself had quietly done in the eighteenth century.

In reaction, major sectors of what came to be known as "Evangelical Protestantism" reacted by rejecting both Science and modern reason from the public culture. In their place, these sectors sought religious refuge in sectarian Evangelical Fideism. Attempting to preserve Christian orthodoxy yet lacking any philosophical-scientific ground for public dialogue, such Fideism held up the Bible as the anti-historical and atomistic-mechanical (literal) source of all truth. Yet, despite Luther's claim that the Bible was its own own interpreter (*sola Scriptura*), the inevitable result was a cacophony of Evangelical interpretations and thousands of sectarian splits.

From that development, there also emerged the late modern battle between religious Evangelical Fideism on one side, and secular Scientific Materialism on the other – a tragic battle remaining counterproductive on both sides. Meanwhile, Liberal Protestantism, without a philosophical basis for spirituality and with its Kantian philosophical ground weakening, would eventually lose public cultural energy.

MARX'S & NIETZSCHE'S REJECTION OF DUALISM
FOR ATHEISM & NIHILISM

Like Descartes' seventeenth-century Catholic-Christian revision of Platonic dualism, the eighteenth-century Kantian reduction of Cartesian psychological spirituality to liberal-humanist or liberal-Protestant ethics in deontological form would also prove unsustainable.

In the nineteenth century, Kantian Liberalism came under attack from two new philosophical waves. Both new waves took a militantly radical form, with one constituting a left-wing atheist attack and the other a right-wing nihilist attack. Again, Karl Marx launched the first attack as a revolutionary and pro-worker wave. Not long after, Friedrich Nietzsche launched the second attack as a counter-revolutionary and anti-worker wave.

The full intellectual impact of Nietzsche's philosophical assault would not be felt, however, until the second half of the twentieth-century. Further, and contrary to Marx's wave of atheistic but still rationalist Materialism, the Nietzschean wave would push major strains of late modern continental European Philosophy into the anti-rationalism of voluntarist Nihilism.

Marx's Revolutionary Pro-Worker Philosophy as the Left-Wing Wave of Atheistic Materialism

Karl Marx secularized Modern Philosophy even more radically than had Kant. Despite his liberal-humanist secularization of *psyche*, Kant had sympathetically and rationally attempted throughout his philosophical career to support religion. By contrast, Marx's materialist version of Modern Philosophy – the third step in the intellectual evolution of modern continental European Philosophy – was boldly *atheistic*.

Rejecting the liberal ideology, Marx combined the early modern Epicurean Cosmology of atomistic-mechanical Materialism with Feuerbach's atheistic inversion of Hegelian idealism to construct a revolutionary dialectical-materialist vision of historical class struggle. Again, defined as Scientific Socialism, Marx's vision of a left-wing, revolutionary, and pro-worker movement of historical-dialectical Materialism became the radical nineteenth-century philosophical alternative to Kant's eighteenth-century liberal-humanist vision, as well as to Hegel's historically idealist Philosophy.

In Engels' definition of Marxism as "Scientific Socialism," the word "Scientific" referred to Marx's embrace of Newtonian Mechanics, and ultimately to its cosmological grounding in Epicurean atomistic-mechanical Materialism. (Again, Marx had written his doctoral dissertation as a comparison of the atomism of Democritus and Epicurus, with praise for Epicurus.). Marx thus synthesized Epicurean Materialism with the Feuerbachian historical-materialist dialectic. He then applied that synthesis to modern industrial class-conflict, in support of social justice as the revolutionary emancipation of the industrial working class.

Within the evolving class conflict, Marx predicted that, once the liberal-capitalist mode of production had reached its historical fulfillment, the 'scientifically guided' working-class struggle would lead first to a more rationally "socialist" form of industrial society, and finally to a libertarian society that he called "Pure Communism." According to Marx's world-historical vision, after the socialistically rationalized battle for industrial production to overcome economic scarcity was complete, there would emerge a utopian "Pure Communism" in which the instrumentally rational state would "wither away," and every human being would be able to become a truly autonomous individual.

The liberal ideology had proclaimed that Liberal Capitalism was the only path for achieving Libertarianism as the normative and final form of human society. But Marx argued that revolutionary class struggle would eventually move society beyond Liberal Capitalism – again, first toward "Scientific Socialism" and finally toward "Pure Communism." Through his radically atheistic yet still rationalist form of historical-dialectical Materialism, Marx projected a purely communist libertarian utopian future, following the socialist stage, and beyond what he saw as the pre-socialist stage of Liberal Capitalism.

In the late nineteenth century, with the Erfurt Declaration of 1891, the Marxian movement in Germany (its then strongest national base) split on one side into what became revolutionary and dictatorial Communism and on the other side into what became the evolutionary and democratic form of Socialism, known as "Democratic Socialism" or "Social Democracy."

Later, during the early twentieth century, Marx's historical-dialectical vision of atheistic-materialist rationalism became further radicalized when Russian Bolsheviks, the dictatorial-communist school of Russian Marxism, defeated the democratic-socialist school of the Russian Mensheviks.

The Bolsheviks had merged Marx's Philosophy with Vladimir Lenin's violent and dictatorial program, partly rooted in Russian Nihilism. Beginning with the Bolshevik's capture of the Russian Revolution of 1917 and continuing today with the dictatorial communist government of China and of other communist countries, the violent and dictatorial revolutionary synthesis known as "Marxism-Leninism" became, in competition with Liberalism, the second powerful world-historical ideology attempting to shape bourgeois global modernization.

While Marxism-Leninism constituted a radically atheistic ideological alternative to Liberalism, it nonetheless remained a modern *bourgeois* doctrine. For, like Liberal Capitalism, its ultimate goal was to emancipate humans as autonomous individuals to pursue their autonomous individual desires. Further, based on the materialist cosmological foundation of Modern Philosophy and Modern Science, Marxism remained grounded in Epicurean atomism. For Marx metaphorically interpreted each human being as an autonomous societal "atom," initially to be massified for class conflict, yet ultimately to be liberated for autonomous individualism.

In terms of the division of Marxism into two separate streams, Western European Democratic Socialism achieved major societal reforms, but it also adapted itself to Modern Industrial Capitalism. Meanwhile, Marxist-Leninist Communism pursued its totalitarian statist path (in effect, State Capitalism), again as seen first in the former Soviet Union and still today in communist China (in combination with Maoism), as well as in other communist countries. All these dictatorial communist countries constructed militantly atheistic states.

By contrast, Democratic Socialism has not been militantly atheistic. For example, during the second half of the twentieth century, Western European democratic-socialist political parties sometimes cooperated with Western European Catholic-inspired Christian-democratic parties. Even so, Democratic Socialism, while supporting religious toleration for the private sphere, has nonetheless promoted secularization for the public sphere.

Marxism, as the third and atheistic step in the evolution of modern continental European Philosophy, rejected the Kantian attempt to support liberal versions of Christianity, which tended to reduce religion to a subjectively grounded deontological Ethics. The Marxian framework thus not only eliminated spirituality, as the Kantian framework had done, but also sought to eliminate religion – either forcefully through the dictatorial-communist path or subtly through the democratic-socialist path. In both cases, atheistic Materialism has remained the Marxian cultural path.

Nietzsche's Counter-Revolutionary Anti-Worker Philosophy as the Right-Wing Wave of Anti-Rationalist Nihilism

In the second half of the nineteenth century, Friedrich Nietzsche launched the fourth and final step in the evolution of modern continental European Philosophy.[9] He rejected what he saw as a rationalist Nihilism arising from the breakdown of Western asceticism. Yet, without using the term, he constructed *an alternative voluntarist form of Nihilism,*

---

[9] Again, for a critique of the more common "gentle" interpretation of Nietzsche, see the earlier referenced classic essay by Conor Cruise O'Brien, "The Gentle Nietzscheans." In addition, my analysis here draws on Michael Allen Gillespie's deep reading of Nietzsche. Gillespie sees Nietzsche's philosophical destruction of the modern Cartesian and Kantian objective-subjective dualism as revealing "*the hidden foundation of modern reason in [blind] will.*" In Gillespie's magisterial work, NIHILISM BEFORE NIETZSCHE (University of Chicago Press, 1995), he traces the seeds of that voluntarist Nihilism back through modern Romanticism and German idealism to Descartes' cosmological paradigm of an atomistic-mechanical and materialist Universe. Gillespie's follow-up book, THE THEOLOGICAL ORIGINS OF MODERNITY (University of Chicago Press, 2008), then traces Descartes' philosophical path further back to the Baconian and Hobbesian call to master both Nature and politics by domination through force and technology, and still further back to Luther, Florentine Humanism, Petrarch, and ultimately William of Ockham's late medieval philosophical revolution of voluntarist Nominalism. (If will and not reason is the foundation of reality, then there is indeed no such thing as rational meaning or wisdom. There is only blind will.)

which was counter-revolutionary, anti-worker, and anti-rational. Nietzsche's voluntarist form of Nihilism supports an elitist and individualist, as well militarist and domineering, model of power that holds the "masses" (Marx's industrial workers) in contempt.[10]

Especially as expressed in the posthumous book THE WILL TO POWER, and also throughout his other writings, Nietzsche claimed that his elitist, individualist, and voluntarist vision was rooted in the drive of biological life.[11] But his atomistic or individualistic understanding of biological life reveals the modern *bourgeois* character of his doctrine. For the modern bourgeois interpretation of biological life as blindly and mechanically atomistic stands as fundamentally different from the emerging postmodern understanding of life as ecologically organic (i.e., symbiotically relational) and rationally unfolding, that is, as a communitarian and co-creative process of cognitive evolution.[12]

Arguing for his elitist spirit of individual domination, Nietzsche rejected the rationalist-humanist ethics of the entire Socratic *Logos* tradition, which had flourished in various forms across late classical and medieval Christian Civilization, and then continued in modern form through Kantian secular humanism and liberal Protestantism. Yet Nietzsche rejected both the secular-humanist and liberal-Protestant forms of Kantian deontological Ethics, along with as the ancient Socratic tradi-

---

[10] On the anti-socialist and anti-worker vision of Nietzsche's project, see the insightful essay by Corey Robin, "Nietzsche's Marginal Children: On Friedrich Hayek," THE NATION, 2015-05-07, available at: *http://www.thenation.com/article/nietzsches-marginal-children-friedrich-hayek/* (accessed 2015-07-01). See also Robin's subsequent response to critics, "Nietzsche, Hayek, and the Austrians," at:
http://crookedtimber.org/2013/06/25/nietzsche-hayek-and-the-austrians-a-reply-to-my-critics (accessed 2015-07-01).

[11] This is reminiscent of Thomas Hobbes' doctrine of the self, although Nietzsche rejected Hobbes' doctrine of the state.

[12] See again Capra & Luisi, SYSTEMS VIEW OF LIFE, as well as Fritjof Capra's earlier books, THE WEB OF LIFE: A NEW SCIENTIFIC UNDERSTANDING OF LIVING SYSTEMS (Anchor, 1997) and THE HIDDEN CONNECTIONS: A SCIENCE FOR SUSTAINABLE LIVING (Anchor, 2004).

tion and its late classical, medieval, and modern Christian successors. In their place, he substituted his voluntarist and individualist paradigm, which he saw as impelled only by blind non-rational will.

Nietzsche grounded his elitist and individualist spirit of domination in his deformed retrieval of the classical hierarchical ideology of *militarist aristocratic power*. But, in so doing, he eliminated the classical aristocracy's responsibility of communitarian duties. By that deformed retrieval, Nietzsche constructed his ultramodern and voluntarist form of Nihilism, which abandoned any altruistic or rational Ethics. Again, all that remained was his individualist, blind, and selfish "Will to Power."

For Nietzsche, Kant's ethical Categorical Imperative was an absurdity. So too was the biblical ethic of altruistic concern for others, which he labeled "slave morality." Finally, his elitist and voluntarist individualism represented the very opposite of Marxian ethical support for worker solidarity (again, which constituted a secularized version of biblical Ethics). Nietzsche's voluntarist vision of Nihilism thus implicitly supports the anti-worker and ruthless form of Neoliberal Global Capitalism that emerged in the last third of the twentieth century.

From its inception, Nietzsche's late nineteenth-century voluntarist radicalization of modern continental European bourgeois Philosophy began to pull the rug out from under both the older Cartesian transcendental spirituality and the Kantian autonomously secular philosophical claims of a universally rational ethics, as well as from under the newer Marxian atheistic and class-based philosophical claims of a universally rational ethics of working-class solidarity and struggle. All that remained, Nietzsche argued, was blind voluntarist force to be exercised by individualist neo-aristocratic elites from the 'superior' minority, and in repressive domination over the 'inferior' majority.

Again, Nietzsche's anti-ethical framework became one without spiritual, humanist, or even instrumentally rational meaning. In that harsh and violent world, Nietzsche claimed that altruistic ethical guidance could no longer be accepted. That meant it could not be defined as biblical love; nor as rationally calculating Utilitarianism; nor as the rationally deontological Categorical Imperative; nor as an idealist Hegelian *geist;* nor even as an atheistic-rationalist Marxian social justice; but only as the blindly individualist, elitist, and dominating "Will to Power."

In cosmological terms, Nietzsche's framework differed in a brutal way from Epicurus' gentle quietism. As we have seen, Epicurus (in a vision that went beyond his atomistic Cosmology) had proposed living in warm sharing with close friends, moving away from the psychological stress of Roman imperial politics, and communing with Nature which he saw as beautiful, creative, and symbolically 'feminine.' By following that path, Epicurus proposed, humans could achieve psychological tranquility (*ataraxia*) within a meaningless world.

By contrast, Nietzsche – in a manner more consistent with the claim of a Universe guided only by blind will or instinct – called in a violent spirit for an arrogantly and ruthlessly individualistic version of the classical aristocratic warrior, but one uprooted from traditional communitarian bonds and 'free' to pursue selfish domination.

It was not until the late twentieth century, however (especially after the collapse of the Soviet Union) that large numbers of continental European philosophers (and philosophers elsewhere following that European tradition) would begin to embrace Nietzsche's writings. While still claiming to work in the "emancipatory" tradition of the modern European Enlightenment, those late modern philosophers implicitly rejected all forms of a rational Ethics of altruism. They then explicitly or implicitly grounded their thought in what Nietzsche had claimed was the nakedly voluntarist and nihilist reality of a Universe without spiritual, humanist, or even rational meaning.

With the direct or indirect embrace of Nietzscheism by so many late modern philosophers, the continental European form of Modern Western Philosophy completed the breakdown of its rational grounding.

That philosophical breakdown in turn signaled the breakdown of the intellectual ground for Modern Psychological Spirituality, and correlatively for Modern Industrial Civilization.

LATE MODERN WESTERN
INTELLECTUAL-SPIRITUAL BREAKDOWN

As the intellectual-spiritual crisis of Modernity grew acute beginning in the late twentieth and early twenty-first centuries, many Western intellectuals in the Liberal Arts and Social Sciences began implicitly or even explicitly to reject the traditional Western intellectual-spiritual search for deep meaning, that is, the search for wisdom (*sophia*).

Academic Descent
into Nietzschean Nihilism

In so doing, those late modern Western intellectuals entered their philosophical descent into the foundational spiritual emptiness of voluntarist Nihilism. That was especially the case in the discipline of Philosophy, as many Western philosophers abandoned the very meaning of the name of their discipline as "love of wisdom" (*philia-sophia*)

The first stage in that late modern Western intellectual descent had begun earlier in the twentieth century as an Anglo-American project that was not explicitly Nietzschean. That first stage has been known as "Analytic Philosophy." In that philosophical school, Anglo-American philosophers reduced the definition of Philosophy to the logical analysis of concepts and their formal relationships, and they rejected any access by Philosophy to deeper meaning as wisdom.

Again, that late modern Anglo-American stage explicitly abandoned Philosophy's traditional claim to search for deep meaning as wisdom. Instead, it reduced Philosophy to a technical discipline at the service of Modern Science, whose cosmological paradigm remained atomistic, mechanical, and materialist. That philosophical reduction then cleared the academic stage for the unchecked intellectual hegemony of what Whitehead called Scientific Materialism. It also prepared the philosophical ground for the later intellectual collapse into Nietzschean voluntarist Nihilism.

Again, the final step (the late modern Western philosophical embrace of the Nietzschean voluntarist Nihilism) was continental-European in origin and style. It emerged in derivative forms through various Western European philosophical schools known in the academic mainstream as Deconstructionism, 'Postmodernism,' and Post-Structuralism. More extreme schools of overtly nihilist thought have more recently appeared within the United States under the names of Posthumanism and Transhumanism.

Rightfully therefore, Saint John Paul II (earlier in life a professor of Philosophy) warned in his 1998 encyclical letter FIDES ET RATIO (Faith and Reason) about the frightening consequences of the breakdown of reason within late modern Western Philosophy:

> *As a result of the crisis of rationalism, **what has appeared finally is Nihilism**. As a philosophy of nothingness, it has a certain attraction for people of our time. Its adherents claim that the search is an end in itself, without any hope or possibility of ever attaining the goal of truth. In the nihilist interpretation, life is no more than an occasion for sensations and experiences in which the ephemeral has pride of place. Nihilism is at the root of the widespread mentality which claims that a definitive commitment should no longer be made, because everything is fleeting and provisional. (Bold font added.)*

And again:

> *Philosophy needs first of all to recover its **sapiential dimension** as a search for the ultimate and overarching meaning of life ... This sapiential dimension is all the more necessary today, because the immense expansion of humanity's technical capability demands a renewed and sharpened sense of ultimate values. [Otherwise] this*

technology ... could soon prove inhuman and even become the potential destroyer of the human race.[13] *(Again, bold font added.)*

Intellectual-Spiritual Crisis
of the Late Modern Western University

The late modern Western university has been playing a central role in the abandonment by Western Philosophy of the search for meaning as wisdom.[14] As we have seen, amidst what Guardini predicted as "The End of the Modern World," the intellectual life of many Western universities is now becoming not only globalized and secularized, but also *commodified.*

With deep meaning as intellectual-spiritual wisdom rejected, and with only empirical data accepted for institutional guidance, the language of empiricist Mathematics became inevitably *monetarized.* Money thus became the dominant public measure of value. Further, as most late modern Western universities came increasingly under neoliberal corporate control (through their boards of trustees), their institutional guidance first collapsed into the dominant empiricist paradigm of Scientific Materialism, and then began the inevitable slide toward its logical successor of Nietzschean voluntarist Nihilism.[15]

---

[13] Pars. 46 & 81. The official English version may be found at:
http://w2.vatican.va/content/john-paul-ii/en/encyclicals/documents/hf_jp-ii_enc_14091998_fides-et-ratio.html.

[14] As early as the middle of the twentieth century, the great Welsh historian and Catholic convert Christopher Dawson, first holder of the Stillman Chair of Catholic Studies at Harvard University, ominously warned of the profound threat to intellectual life within the late modern university. See the republished edition of his now classic 1961 book, THE CRISIS OF WESTERN EDUCATION (Catholic University of America Press, 2010).

[15] The American Association of University Professors (AAUP), the distinguished professorial organization co-founded in 1915 by the great American intellectuals John Dewey and Arthur O. Lovejoy, now refers regularly in its publications to what it calls the "corporate university," which through boards of trustees has come under the control of neoliberal business elites.

For a long time, apart from the alternative network of Catholic universities attempting to develop a publicly influential Aristotelian-Thomist philosophical movement (thus far a failed attempt), the modern Western university remained philosophically grounded in first Descartes' and then Kant's revisionist combinations of Platonic Idealism and Epicurean Materialism.

Thus, at the undergraduate level on the 'subjective' side, modern Western universities have dualistically offered the Bachelor of Arts degree for Descartes' spiritual-mental *Res Cogitans,* or for Kant's *a-priori* conceptual knowledge. On the 'objective' side, they have dualistically offered the Bachelor of Science degree for Descartes' materialist *Res Extensa,* or for Kant's *a-posteriori* empirical knowledge. A similar dualism of degrees has existed at the master and doctoral levels.

Today, however, there is a growing 'business-like' development that seeks to reduce, or even to eliminate, the Liberal Arts.[16] That development seeks to collapse higher education into the utilitarian-technocratic logic of Scientific Materialism, which then easily slides into late modern Nietzschean voluntarist Nihilism. Such late modern developments have precipitated for the Western university its profound late modern intellectual-spiritual crisis.

Paradoxically, there remains a residue of the older and deeper understanding of the sapiential role of Philosophy with the title of doctoral degree that is abbreviated as "Ph.D." Those letters refer to the Latin phrase, *Doctor Philosophiae,* which means "Teacher of Philosophy."

Further, since (as we have seen) the word "Philosophy" from its classical Greek roots means "love of wisdom" (*philia-sophia*), the full etymo-

---

[16] In classical Western Civilization, the "Liberal Arts" constituted the "liberal" knowledge necessary for people who were free. Also in the classical tradition, the opposite of the "Liberal Arts" was the "Servile Arts," which constituted the technical or practical knowledge for work that did not require societal freedom, and so could be done by slaves. The word "liberal" is, of course, derived etymologically from the Latin, *libertas,* which means "freedom."

logical meaning of Ph.D. is "Teacher of the Love of Wisdom." Yet most contemporary holders of the Ph.D. degree know little about Philosophy, or about Latin or Greek. As a result, they might be surprised to discover that they carry the title "teacher of the love of wisdom."

Despite the etymological meaning of their doctoral titles, many Western university professors today often unconsciously, though sometimes consciously, accept the emerging intellectual philosophical degeneration of rationalism into Scientific Materialism, and sometimes even into its anti-rational successor of voluntarist Nihilism. Again, they do so by accepting as the framework for their intellectual work late modern Anglo-American Analytic Philosophy, or continental European Deconstructionism, 'Postmodernism,' or Post-Structuralism, or perhaps even North American Posthumanism or Transhumanism.

Again, those schools indirectly, and sometimes directly, support late modern philosophical Nihilism, which is now triumphing in the wake of the philosophical collapse of first Descartes', then Kant's, and later Marx's unsustainable attempts to find universal rational meaning within what has been cosmologically seen in Modernity as a purely materialist Universe guided only by blind and meaningless force. By reducing all reality to the still rational Cosmology of Scientific Materialism, or by sliding further into Nietzsche's Cosmology of anti-rational voluntarist Nihilism, many contemporary university professors at least implicitly cast into doubt, or sometimes explicitly deny, any spiritual, humanist, or even rationalist ground for deep universal meaning as wisdom.

Meanwhile, taking advantage of the philosophical crisis of the late modern Western university, crude political ideologues now call for marginalizing or even eliminating the Liberal Arts in favor of *only technical training*. They seek to turn the late modern university into a center of formation in reductionist utilitarian-technocratic logic, free from ethical restraint by any literary, historical, or philosophical wisdom.

And again, as part of the growing hegemony of modern Scientific Materialism which reduces all knowledge to quantified empirical data, there has simultaneously emerged within many late modern universities the currently powerful neoliberal corporate-inspired drive not only to reduce university education to vocational training, but also to evaluate its worth only in terms of future monetary potential.

Thus, we have the *growing secularization, nihilization, and commodification of academic life* as the ultimate late modern intellectual-spiritual degradation. All of this, unfolding within what Guardini called the "End of the Modern World," constitutes the fundamental breakdown within the late modern university of the ancient human search for deep wisdom. It also signals the intellectual-spiritual breakdown of Modern Industrial Civilization, and correlatively of Modern Psychological Spirituality.

6

IDEOLOGICAL DEGENERATION &
CATHOLIC SOCIAL TEACHING

B efore turning to the emergence of Postmodern Ecological Spirituality, it may be helpful to explore how the breakdown of Modern
Philosophy has precipitated the late modern degeneration of the liberal-capitalist ideology in its current neoliberal global-electronic stage.
Correlatively, it may also be helpful to explore the postmodern strategic response by Catholic Social Teaching to that ideological degeneration, and to locate the response within what I call the "Three Historical
Strategies of Catholic Social Teaching" that stretch across the emergence and breakdown of Modern Industrial Civilization.

I hope that these supplementary reflections will assist us by providing
further background for the Catholic-Christian historical journey beyond Modern Psychological Spirituality toward Postmodern Ecological
Spirituality, and correlatively beyond Modern Industrial Civilization in
search of a globally regenerative Postmodern Ecological Civilization.

PHILOSOPHICAL DEGENERATION
OF THE LIBERAL-CAPITALIST IDEOLOGY

Growing out of the breakdown of Modern Philosophy (again, first into Scientific Materialism and second into Nietzschean Nihilism), two false ideological doctrines have undergirded the late modern degeneration of the liberal-capitalist ideology. The first false ideological doctrine is the *Neoliberal economic fantasy of a deified 'Free-Market.'*[1] The second false ideological doctrine is the *Neoconservative political fantasy of a deified 'National Security State.'* Both false doctrines constitute the two deified but crumbling pillars of late modern Liberal Capitalism's ideological degeneration.

Neoliberal Economic Fantasy of
Deified 'Free Market'

First, on the economic side, Nietzsche's late nineteenth-century voluntarist Nihilism has implicitly fed, via the libertarian Austrian school of Economics (and later via its American acolyte the "Chicago school of Economics), into the late modern liberal-capitalist economic doctrine of Neoliberalism.[2] In the late modern stage of Global Capitalism, that neoliberal ideological revision, alternately known as the "Washington Consensus," became normative for international financial institutions and for much of late modern liberal-capitalist economic theory.

---

[1] On the deification of the 'Free Market,' see Harvey Cox, THE MARKET AS GOD (Harvard University Press, 2016).

[2] On the late modern neoliberal ideology, see the fine overview in David Harvey, A BRIEF HISTORY OF NEOLIBERALISM (Oxford University Press, 2007). On Nietzsche's relation to the neoliberal Austrian school, see again the insightful essay by Corey Robin, "Nietzsche's Marginal Children: On Friedrich Hayek," THE NATION, 2015-05-07, available at: *http://www.thenation.com/article/nietzsches-marginal-children-friedrich-hayek* (accessed 2015-07-01). See also, and again, Robin's subsequent response to critics, "Nietzsche, Hayek, and the Austrians," available at: *http://crookedtimber.org/2013/06/25/nietzsche-hayek-and-the-austrians-a-reply-to-my-critics* (accessed 2015-07-01).

Again, the false economic ideological doctrine of Neoliberalism calls for *globalization of the fantasy of a deified 'Free-Market.'* To that end, it calls for governments to dismantle the twentieth century's important social reforms. Those reforms grew out of the political struggles of broad-based social and religious movements seeking either Social Democracy or reforms of Laissez-Faire Liberalism, all of which led to creation of the mid-twentieth century's Social-Welfare State.

Neoliberalism's dismantling of the Social-Welfare State seeks to reduce, or even to eliminate, regulations of markets for the common good, pro-labor laws, progressive taxation, social insurance for medical and re-tirement needs, and government supported social-service programs for the poor. the elderly, and those suffering handicaps. To that end, Ne-oliberals call for capitalist 'privatization' of many state functions and for their conversion into 'Free-Market' commodities, so that they may become sources for private capital accumulation.[3]

Further, for the neoliberal ideological doctrine, government and its employees become the enemy (and especially teachers!), but excepting employees in state-security sectors. In addition, for that doctrine, the poor are to be 'liberated' only as autonomous individuals, and only by this fantasy of a deified 'Free Market.'[4]

---

[3] For an insightful critique of the Austrian and Chicago schools of Economics from the tradition of Catholic Social Teaching, see Angus Sibley, THE "POISONED SPRING" OF ECONOMIC LIBERTARIANISM: MENGER, MISES, HAYEK, ROTHBARD: A CRITIQUE FROM CATHOLIC SOCIAL TEACHING OF THE 'AUSTRIAN SCHOOL' OF ECONOMICS (Pax Romana, 2013); and Angus Sibley, CATHOLIC ECONOMICS: ALTERNATIVES TO THE JUNGLE (Liturgical Press, 2015). See also Andrea Tornielli & Giacomo Galeazzi, THIS ECONOMY KILLS: POPE FRANCIS ON CAPITALISM AND SOCIAL JUSTICE (Liturgical Press, 2015).

[4] Recall that, as we have seen, the 'classical' modern liberal fantasy of a 'Free Market' was philosophically constructed by applying Newtonian Mechanics, grounded in the Epicurean Cosmology of atomistic-mechanical Materialism, to the modern industrial political economy. That fantasy of a 'Free-Market' redefinition of economic life rejected the truly classical Western understanding of economic life as the "ordering of the home," which is reflected in the every name of "economics" (*oikos-nomos* in Greek). By contrast, the modern liberal redefinition claimed that economic life was rather the competition of autonomous or atomized economic actors pursuing their own autonomous (atomized)

Yet it has now become clear that such a ruthless and destructive economic ideology cannot be sustained within a participatory democratic framework. Rather, as Naomi Klein has shown in her earlier mentioned book THE SHOCK DOCTRINE, the neoliberal ideology requires for its imposition either a "managed democracy" (legally and culturally undermining broad political participation) or even a full dictatorship.[5]

Neoconservative Political Fantasy of
Deified 'National-Security State'

In addition, because the false late modern (and implicitly Nietzschean) neo-liberal *economic fantasy* of a now deified 'Free Market' works against democracy, it has become allied with the false late-modern (and implicitly Hobbesian) neoconservative *political fantasy* of a now deified 'National Security State.'[6] Further, the growing triumph of the National-Security State has required mass-psychological construction of what has been called a *"culture of fear."*[7]

Again, the alliance of the neoconservative political fantasy of a deified 'National Security State' with the neoliberal economic fantasy of a deified 'Free Market' has now become the synthesized ideological foundation for the political-economy of late modern Global Capitalism. Further, that synthesized ideology now also includes the economic integration of authoritarian Communism within the new Global Capitalism.

---

self-interests. The modern liberal economic doctrine of autonomous (atomized) individual interests is, of course, fundamentally opposed to Catholic Social Teaching, which has continued to understand economic life as called to function within "social markets," framed by a cultural vision of cooperation for the common good.

[5] See again Naomi Klein, THE SHOCK DOCTRINE: THE RISE OF DISASTER CAPITALISM (Picador, 2008).

[6] For an early and prophetic Catholic study of the late modern ideological doctrine of the National Security State in Latin America, where it first became most fully developed, see José Comblin, THE CHURCH AND THE NATIONAL SECURITY STATE (Orbis Books, 1979).

[7] On the "culture of fear," see Corey Robin's insightful book, FEAR: THE HISTORY OF A POLITICAL IDEA (Oxford University Press, 2004).

In this late modern ideological framework, there remains a strong possibility that the ideological synthesis of those two ideological fantasies could lead significant sectors of global capitalist elites to abandon democracy, and in its place to promote authoritarian or even dictatorial forms of national government. Such a dangerous combination of deified 'Free-Market' economics with anti-democratic authoritarian politics has already been modeled by the state-capitalism supported by the government of Communist China, and by the 'Free-Market capitalism supported by the post-communist authoritarian government of Russia.

Philosophical Linkage to Societal Degeneration

Despite its appearance of global triumph, the late modern ideological synthesis of the neoliberal deified 'Free Market' with the neoconservative deified 'National Security State' cannot guide the human family, or more widely life's integral ecology, into a viable future. Further, that degenerative synthesis is fundamentally opposed to the wisdom tradition of Catholic Social Teaching.

Nonetheless, we need to acknowledge that the postmodern Electronic Revolution favors development of globalized networks. We also need to acknowledge the importance of state-security in the face of global terrorist networks. Beyond those justifiable recognitions, however, the philosophical degeneration of the late modern ideology of Liberal Capitalism is legitimating *growing devastation of life's integral ecology* across our loving Creator's beloved and beauteous garden-planet Earth.

Further, that ideological synthesis legitimates both *neoliberal austerity* for economic life and *neoconservative militarization* for political life. It promotes economically, and protects politically, the increasing global concentrations of economic wealth and political power in the hands of tiny financial oligarchies of billionaires within both capitalist and communist state systems.[8] The classical name for such concentration of

---

[8] See the 2016 Oxfam report, AN ECONOMY FOR THE 1%, available at:

political-economic power is "plutocracy," which from its Greek roots means "rule of the wealthy.[9]

From a philosophical perspective, the neoliberal form of libertarian economics and the neoconservative or militarized form of politics have deep roots in the late modern intellectual triumph of Scientific Materialism and Nietzschean Nihilism. Those affinities should not be surprising, however, since (as we have seen) the Modern Mechanical Cosmology, which is rooted in the mechanical atomism of Epicurean Materialism, lies at the philosophical foundation of Modernity's ideologies of Liberal Capitalism and Scientific Socialism. That Modern Mechanical Cosmology, like its ancient Epicurean source, denies that there is any deep wisdom or ultimate spiritual meaning in the Universe. Once the Divine source of deep wisdom is denied, demonic alternatives inevitably fill the void.

The global triumph of Materialism and Nihilism across late modern industrial societies has also been advanced by the the public triumph of late modern bourgeois secularization, which is undermining our human family's rich and vast spiritual heritage. For that culturally degenerative process, the monetarized quantifications of Finance Capitalism are now becoming the only public guiding values. As Karl Marx once famously wrote, "All that is solid turns into air." To that we might add: all that remains is the materialist and nihilist financial commoditization of everything.

---

https://www.oxfam.org/en/research/economy-1 (accessed 2016-01-19). Subtitled "How privilege and power in the economy drive extreme inequality and how this can be stopped," the report states:

> *The global inequality is reaching new extremes. The richest 1% now have more wealth than the rest of the world combined. Power and privilege is being used to skew the economic system to increase the gap between the richest and the rest. A global network of tax havens enables the richest individuals to hide $7.6 trillion.* (p. 2)

[9] See Chrystia Freeland, Plutocrats: The Rise of the New Global Super-Rich and the Fall of Everyone Else (Penguin Press, 2012).

THIRD HISTORICAL-STRUCTURAL STAGE OF
MODERN INDUSTRIAL CAPITALISM

As has been noted earlier, these degenerative ideological developments constitute a third ideal-type stage in the evolution of liberal-capitalist political economy for the industrial-center countries.

- *In technological terms*, the Electronic Revolution has precipitated the new stage of Global Capitalism, which follows the earlier stage of National Capitalism (precipitated by the Machine Revolution) and the still earlier stage of Local Capitalism (precipitated by the Factory Revolution).

- *In economic terms*, the new stage may be called "Neoliberal Global Capitalism."

- *In political terms*, the new form of liberal government is the National-Security State, which follows the second and reformed liberal form of government known as the Social-Welfare State, and which in turn had followed the first and 'classical' liberal form of government known as the Laissez-Faire State.

While this is not the place to offer a full social analysis of these three political-economic stages, the chart on the following page provides a visual overview for ideal-types of their evolving historical structures within the industrial-center countries.[10]

---

[10] For the original version of this chart, see Joe Holland & Peter Henriot, SOCIAL ANALYSIS: LINKING FAITH & JUSTICE (Orbis Books, 1980), p. 66. For more on these three stages, see Joe Holland, "The Crisis of Family and Unions in Late Modern Capitalism," JOURNAL OF CATHOLIC SOCIAL THOUGHT," Vol. 9, Issue 1, Winter 2012, pp. 43-58. My forthcoming book, SOCIAL ANALYSIS II – END OF THE MODERN WORLD, will more fully explore these three historical-structural stages of Modern Industrial Capitalism.

HISTORICAL STAGES			
STRUCTURES	STAGE I LOCAL CAPITALISM (1760-1870)	STAGE II NATIONAL CAPITALISM (1870-1970)	STAGE III GLOBAL CAPITALISM (1970 ...)
Deep Structures			
CAPITAL:	Local Family Firm *(Entrepreneurial)*	National Corporation *(Managerial)*	Global Conglomerate *(Strategic)*
TECHNOLOGY:	Factory Revolution (Labor-Intensive)	Machine Revolution (Capital-Labor Balance)	Electronic Revolution (Capital Intensive)
Surface Structures			
ECONOMIC:	'Classical' Liberalism *(Poverty & Exploitation for Labor)*	Reformed Liberalism *(Social Contract with Labor & Growing Prosperity)*	Neoliberalism *(Austerity for Labor & Marginalization)*
POLITICAL:	Laissez-Faire State	Social-Welfare State	National-Security State
CULTURAL:	'Classical' Stage of Liberal Ideology *(Liberty)*	Social Reform of Liberal Ideology *(Opportunity)*	Degeneration of Liberal Ideology *(Security)*

Late Modern Spiritual Pathologies

Again, while Western Civilization moves into the end of its modern industrial form, Modern Western Philosophy collapses into Scientific Materialism and Nietzschean Nihilism. Further, since the continental European branch of Modern Western Philosophy intellectually underlies the West's Modern Psychological Spirituality, the late modern breakdown of that philosophical tradition inevitably undermines the intellectual foundation for Modern Psychological Spirituality.

That undermining has unfolded through the philosophical reduction of human spiritual consciousness first to a privatized, next to a secularized, and finally to a nihilized *psyche.* In addition, the late modern intellectual degeneration of the ideology of Liberal Capitalism (reflecting the late modern philosophical breakdown) culturally undermines Modern Psychological Spirituality. In that process, any healthy and publicly creative version of Modern Psychological Spirituality becomes *unsustainable.*

Yet, faced with the late modern breakdown of the intellectual foundation for Modern Psychological Spirituality, some religious leaders have been attempting in a reactionary manner to restore that now undermined modern bourgeois form of the spirituality of interiority. We may call that attempt part of the *strategy of restoration.*

By attempting to restore and perpetuate the modern bourgeois form of the spirituality of interiority beyond its historical time, such reactionary religious leaders instead produce a late modern pathology of the spirituality of interiority. That pathological form is an *anti-intellectual and voluntarist Fideism,* meaning faith without an intellectual dimension. That fideist spiritual pathology expresses itself in two dysfunctional ways, with one being interior and psychological and the other being exterior and sociological.

- *Interior Psychological Narcissism.* First, with the interior psychological dimension, anti-intellectual Fideism often retreats into an inner-directed pseudo-spirituality of psychological narcissism. That narcissism then tends to abandon ethical responsibility for other human beings, and especially for the poor, as well as for the rest of our loving Creator's beloved and beauteous creation.

- *Exterior Sociological Resentment.* Correlatively, on the exterior societal side, anti-intellectual Fideism often projects an outer-directed and religiously grounded sociological resentment. That resentful sociological pattern often legitimates global ecological plundering of Nature, global political violence through constant warfare, and global economic abandonment of the poor.

Outside the West, we have seen examples of such outer directed religious resentment in fanatical versions of Islamist Fideism that support violent terrorism, and in the United States especially with the 2001 attack on the Twin Towers of the World Trade Center. But we have also seen within the United States a fanatically terrorist form of Christianist Fideism with the 1995 bombing of the U.S. Federal Building in Oklahoma City.

A more general Christianist form, however, has been documented in 2009 by the Pew Research Center's project on "Religion and Public Life." Within the United States and particularly for white-Anglo Catholic and Evangelical Christians, the Pew research showed that the more people attended Christian churches, the more they supported torture. Such a late modern reactionary form of Christianity – attempting to preserve modern bourgeois society by violent means – abandons the non-violent Gospel of Jesus.[11]

STRATEGIC RESPONSE BY
POSTMODERN CATHOLIC SOCIAL TEACHING

Meanwhile, a regenerative global Catholic-Christian response, which is seen here as authentically postmodern, has been arising from what I have called "Postmodern Catholic Social Teaching" (as well as from other intellectual-spiritual sources).

For more than half a century now, the social-magisterial tradition of papal encyclical letters has been officially declaring the failure of both

---

[11] The Pew studies also linked that correlation to political-party affiliation, with 64% of Republicans reportedly supporting torture and 36% of Democrats reportedly supporting it. Of course, the majority of white-anglo Evangelical Christians are Republican, and very many white-anglo Catholics, once largely Democrats, have migrated to the Republican Party. See Pew reports at: *http://www.pewforum.org/2009/04/29/the-religious-dimensions-of-the-torture-debate* and *http://www.pewforum.org/2009/05/07/the-torture-debate-a-closer-look*.

dominant ideologies of Modern Industrial Civilization, and of their underlying Modern Philosophy of Materialism and Nihilism. At the same time, Postmodern Catholic Social Teaching has been calling globally for a new social order, in effect a new form of civilization beyond failures of modern ideologies.[12] In the emergence of this postmodern global stage of Catholic Social Teaching, we can discern three distinct phases thus far.

Saint John XXIII: First Postmodern Phase

Postmodern Catholic Social Teaching's recognition of the need for a new social order began with the prophetic papal vision of Saint John XXIII (again, Bishop of Rome from 1958-1963). Beginning with his prophetic 1961 encyclical letter MATER ET MAGISTRA, John became the first Catholic-Christian Bishop of Rome to argue that both dominant modern ideologies had failed.[13]

Prior to John's papacy and beginning with Pope Leo XIII (elected in 1871), the earlier social-magisterial stage known as "Modern Catholic Social Teaching" had also pointed out the erroneous philosophical foundations of the dominant modern ideologies of Materialism (again, Liberal Capitalism and Scientific Socialism). But, while the Leonine stage had rejected Scientific Socialism because of its explicit atheism, it had called for philosophical and social reform of Liberal Capitalism.

Yet Leo had insisted that the long-term success of his practical program of *social reform* depended on the success of his theoretical program of

---

[12] As noted earlier, in my analysis authentically postmodern phenomena are found only within the historical-cultural framework of the emerging Postmodern Ecological Cosmology, which goes beyond the receding Modern Mechanical Cosmology originally established by Descartes and Newton. By contrast, what is often called "postmodern" in dominant academic circles, I prefer to describe as "late modern," since it is only a radicalization of the receding Modern Mechanical Cosmology.

[13] See MATER ET MAGISTRA, Part IV, especially Pars. 212-217. For the English text, see: *http://w2.vatican.va/content/john-xxiii/en/encyclicals/documents/hf_j-xxiii_enc_15051961_mater.html* (accessed 2017-01-05).

philosophical reform, which called for a modern revival of the medieval neo-Aristotelian philosophy of Saint Thomas Aquinas (1225-1274). But Leo's attempt to create a neo-Aristotelian Thomist philosophical foundation for modern liberal societies failed. The Thomist revival never achieved a broad intellectual acceptance among mainstream Western philosophers. Instead, despite Leo's wider hopes, it has remained confined to a Catholic-Christian intellectual sub-culture.

In the second half of the twentieth century, Saint John XXIII became the first Catholic pope to recognize that a new strategy of Catholic Social Teaching was called for, beyond the Leonine strategy. John proposed a radical advance for Catholic Social Teaching, one that called for deeper transformation and on a global scale. By so doing, John became the prophetic founder of a new global strategic stage, which I have named "Postmodern Catholic Social Teaching."

Soon after MATER ET MAGISTRA and in response to the infamous Cuban Missile Crisis of October 1962, John issued his still celebrated 1963 encyclical letter PACEM IN TERRIS (prepared even as he was dying).[14] In the Cuban Missile Crisis, the American and Russian superpowers – each promoting one of the two dominant modern scientific-materialist ideologies – came perilously close to destroying by thermo-nuclear war much of life on planet Earth.

Recognizing the historical bankruptcy of the two dominant modern ideologies embodied in the two dominant modern superpowers, John's PACEM IN TERRIS boldly declared the urgent global need for a *"new social order"* (the practical side) that would be grounded in philosophical *"truth"* (the theoretical side).

---

[14] See the English version of PACEM IN TERRIS at: *http://w2.vatican.va/content/john-xxiii/en/encyclicals/documents/hf_j-xxiii_enc_11041963_pacem.htm* (accessed 2015-07-01). See also and again, Dubois & Klee, PACEM IN TERRIS: ITS RELEVANCE, as well as Joe Holland, PACEM IN TERRIS: SUMMARY & COMMENTARY FOR THE 50TH ANNIVERSARY OF THE FAMOUS ENCYCLICAL LETTER OF POPE JOHN XXIII ON WORLD PEACE (Pacem in Terris Press, 2012). Again, both books were prepared in relation to a fiftieth-anniversary conference on Pacem in Terris held at the United Nations in New York City.

To guide the new social order at the global level, John called for "global governance" – implicitly based on his retrieval of the ancient Stoic philosophy which had celebrated the rational "order" of the Cosmos. That ancient Stoic philosophy, which so influenced the *Logos* tradition of early Christianity, had argued that the human social order needs to reflect the astronomical order of the Cosmos.

In PACEM IN TERRIS, John was thus expanding the ancient Stoic call for rational "order" up to the new global level. In addition, through his call for a new social "order" based on "truth," John was implicitly rejecting the Modern Mechanical Cosmology (again, rooted in the atomistic-mechanical Philosophy of Epicurean Materialism), which has under-girded Modernity's Hobbesian tendency to understand geopolitics purely in terms of material "force."

Through PACEM IN TERRIS, John also urged the human family to search globally for a new social order that would be truly *human*. Since the emerging global community encompasses many religions. John moved beyond the ancient Constantinian concept of "Christian Civilization," Even so, John urged disciples of Jesus to bring "Christian inspiration" to what he hoped would be a new *humanistic* "social order." Further, John's earlier MATER ET MAGISTRA had called for a new *cooperative* form of human society that would remain *rurally rooted*. In summary, John implicitly called for a new global civilization of rational global govern-ance that would be grounded in "truth" and that would be humanistic, cooperative, and agroecological, and that would at least in part be shaped by Christian inspiration.

Let us now jump ahead to reflect on the social teachings of Saint John Paul II. This means jumping over the important social teachings of Blessed Paul VI (Bishop of Rome from 1963 to 1978). The reason is that, rather than constituting a new phase in Postmodern Catholic Social Teaching, Paul's social teachings continued and intensified John's orig-inal vision.

Saint John Paul II: Second Postmodern Phase

While Saint John XXIII's two great social-encyclical letters raised opti-
mistic hopes across the human family, the future proved more complex. During the late twentieth century, "Real Socialism" became the
first of the two modern ideologies of Scientific Materialism to break
down, at least within the Russian orbit and for the Marxist-Leninist
side of the scientific-socialist tradition. In 1991, the leadership of Union
of Soviet Socialist Republics (USSR) officially declared its termination.

The collapse of the USSR then led to what some naively assumed was
the definitive global triumph of Modern Industrial Capitalism. That
apparent triumph arose from the new global mobility of finance capital, made feasible by the Electronic Revolution and legitimated by the
neoliberal ideological degeneration. As noted, the apparent neoliberal
triumph was intellectually grounded in the so-called Austrian and Chicago schools of Economics, which had developed a late modern ideology of selfish individualistic Materialism, which is fundamentally opposed to Catholic Social Teaching.[15]

Playing a significant role in the move beyond Soviet Communism,
Saint John Paul II (again, Bishop of Rome from 1978 to 2005) initiated
the second phase of Postmodern Catholic Social Teaching.[16] His second
phase expanded in two ways the claim of Saint John XXIII that both
dominant modern ideologies of Scientific Materialism had failed.

- *Culture of Death.* First, while others were proclaiming the utopian
  triumph of Liberal Capitalism, John Paul, in his 1995 encyclical letter EVANGELIUM VITAE (Gospel of Life), instead stated that we were

---

[15] Again, on the Austrian school of Economics, see Sibley, "POISONED SPRING" OF
ECONOMIC LIBERTARIANISM, and Sibley, CATHOLIC ECONOMICS.

[16] For more on Saint John Paul II as postmodern, see my essay, "The Cultural Vision of
Pope John Paul II: Toward a Conservative/Liberal Dialogue," in David Ray Griffin,
William A. Beardslee, & Joe Holland, Editors, VARIETIES OF POSTMODERN THEOLOGY
(State University of New York Press, 1989).

210

living in a late modern *"culture of death."*[17] That culture of death, he proposed, was unleashing a global attack on human life, especially on unborn humans, but also in many other ways. (Recall that John Paul had personally lived amidst the violent killings of World War II and Nazism, including the Holocaust, as well as under the violent oppression of Russian Communism.) Further, in his earlier 1990 World Day of Peace Message, John Paul had decried the global devastation of ecological life across our garden-planet Earth.[18]

- *Collapse into Nihilism.* Second, in his 1998 encyclical letter FIDES ET RATIO (again, Faith and Reason), John Paul traced the foundational cause for the breakdown of Modernity's scientific-materialist ideologies to the fact that so many modern Western philosophers had abandoned the deep and rational search for wisdom, and instead had collapsed philosophically into anti-rational and voluntarist Nihilism.[19] Again, that meant they had abandoned the discipline's very purpose, since (as noted) the word "Philosophy" means from its Greek roots the "love of wisdom" (*philia-sophia*).

In FIDES ET RATIO, John Paul confirmed what we saw in the prior chapter, namely, the intellectual breakdown of the modern continental European philosophical tradition. The emergence and degeneration of that tradition had traveled the long philosophical road from Descartes

---

[17] On the "culture of death," see especially EVANGELIUM VITAE's Par. 24 at: *http://w2.vatican.va/content/john-paul-ii/en/encyclicals/documents/hf_jp-ii_enc_25031995_evangelium-vitae.html* (accessed 2015-07-01). See also John's pre-papal text, SIGN OF CONTRADICTION (Seabury, 1979).

[18] His 1990 World Day of Peace Message, "Peace with God the Creator, Peace with All of Creation" was the first extended papal statement on ecology. The text is available at: *https://w2.vatican.va/content/john-paul-ii/en/messages/peace/documents/hf_jp-ii_mes_19891208_xxiii-world-day-for-peace.html* (accessed 2017-02-21). In addition, in 1979 John Paul had proclaimed Saint Francis of Assisi as "the heavenly patron of all of those who promote ecology." (Apostolic Letter, "*Inter Sanctos,*" ACTA APOSTOLICAE SEDIS, 71,1509f.

[19] See again *http://w2.vatican.va/content/john-paul-ii/en/encyclicals/documents/hf_jp-ii_enc_14091998_fides-et-ratio.html (accessed 2017-02-21).*

to Kant to Marx to Nietzsche. The final societal result of that philosophical breakdown has now become the late modern scientific-technological path of Nietzschean voluntarist Nihilism, misguided by the two bankrupt ideologies of Scientific Materialism.

Those bankrupt paths are now globally *undermining* the natural, human, and spiritual reproduction of the integral ecology of life, throughout its interwoven natural, human, and spiritual fabric across our loving Creator's beloved and beauteous garden-planet Earth.

Let us now turn to Pope Francis and his already famous encyclical letter on ecology, LAUDATO SI'. This means once more jumping over the prior pope, this time Benedict XVI. As in the case of Paul VI, the social teachings of Benedict also remain important. But, despite his having a philosophical framework that is more Platonic-Augustinian than Aristotelian-Thomist, Benedict' contributions built on those of John Paul, with both forming a single phase.

Pope Francis: Third Postmodern Phase

Pope Francis (again, beginning in 2013 as Bishop of Rome), through his 2015 encyclical letter LAUDATO SI' - ON CARE FOR OUR COMMON HOME, advanced Postmodern Catholic Social Teaching to its fully ecological phase. That ecological orientation had been implicit in Saint John XXIII's call for a balanced global development that would sustain and dignify traditional rural life with its organic roots in Nature. Saint John Paul had then strengthened the ecological dimension of the Postmodern Johannine Strategy with several important statements on ecology.

Yet, until Francis, no pope had emphasized ecology in such a central way for Catholic Social Teaching. Where Paul VI had introduced for global society the helpful phrase "integral [holistic] development,", Francis moved ecology to center stage for the Postmodern Johannine Strategy by calling for a global society rooted in "integral ecology."

This is not the place to provide a full summary of LAUDATO SI, and many excellent summaries already exist. But, in order to highlight the central role that Francis has given to ecology, let us repeat here one quote from his landmark encyclical letter.

Doomsday predictions can no longer be met with irony or distain. We may well be leaving to coming generations debris, desolation, and filth. The pace of consumption, waste, and environmental change has so stretched the planet's capacity that our contemporary lifestyle, unsustainable as it is, can only precipitate catastrophes.[20]

More on John as Prophetic Founder of the Postmodern Strategy

As mentioned in the Introduction, before deciding to write this book I had been finishing a different manuscript, one on the prophetic global vision of Saint John XXIII. Yet, as noted, two unexpected sequential thoughts suddenly began to haunt me. Together those two thoughts said that, before publishing the manuscript on John, I should first write and publish *two additional books!*

Strange as those thoughts seemed, I obeyed them. Again, this current book on "Postmodern Ecological Spirituality" is the first of three interrelated books (again, with the remaining two to be published soon). Yet why such an unexpected interruption of the original project?

To answer that question, we first need to explore more deeply the historic significance of the prophetic global and implicitly ecological vision of Saint John XXIII within what I call the "Three Historical Strate-

---

[20] The quotation is from Par. 161. Again, for the official English text of the entire encyclical letter, see: *http://w2.vatican.va/content/francesco/en/encyclicals/documents/papa-francesco_20150524_enciclica-laudato-si.html.* (Accessed 2015-07-15.).

Note that, in the following paragraph (162), the text uses the word "postmodern," but in the way that it is more commonly used today, but which I prefer to describe as "late modern."

gies of Catholic Social Teaching." These three strategies have evolved since the first mechanically printed papal encyclical appeared in 1740.[21]

That original manuscript on John – again, tentatively titled THE PROPHETIC GLOBAL VISION OF SAINT JOHN XXIII – explains how he stands out as the radical-traditional founder of the postmodern global strategic stage of Catholic Social Teaching.[22] As we have seen, in his foundational social encyclicals MATER ET MAGISTRA (1961) and PACEM IN TERRIS (1963), John boldly called for a transformative new global social order that would be humanistic, cooperative, agroecological, and at least in part Christian-inspired. Again, for shorthand, I have called Saint John XXIII's new global stage of Catholic Social Teaching the "Postmodern Johannine Strategy."

The still unfolding Postmodern Johannine Strategy builds on, and yet goes beyond, what I have called the tradition's "Modern Leonine Strategy," founded by Pope Leo XIII (again, elected in 1878). As we have seen, Leo proposed his earlier modern strategy as a Catholic-inspired reform of the liberal-capitalist side of Modern Industrial Civilization (at the time, beginning the second stage of the Industrial Revolution), and as a rejection of the its scientific-socialist side. Yet, as we have also seen,

---

[21] For the three-part historical framework of what I call the Anti-Modern Pre-Leonine Strategy, the Modern Leonine Strategy, and the Postmodern Johannine Strategy, I am endebted to the profound analysis of Michael Schuck in his pioneering book, THAT THEY ALL MAY BE ONE: THE SOCIAL TEACHING OF THE PAPAL ENCYCLICALS 1740-1989 (Georgetown University Press, 1991). Michael Schuck's study, however, uses the phrases of the "Pre-Leonine Period," the "Leonine Period," and the "Post-Leonine Period."

For more on these three ecclesial strategies of Catholic Social Teaching and on their correlation with the three societal stages of Modern Industrial Capitalism, see the Introduction to my earlier book, MODERN CATHOLIC SOCIAL TEACHING: THE POPES CONFRONT THE INDUSTRIAL AGE 1740-1958 (Paulist Press, 2003). See also my earlier mentioned article. "The Crisis of Family and Unions in Late Modern Global Capitalism."

[22] John's vision is described here as "implicitly postmodern," since he did not explicitly use the word "postmodern." Indeed, that word had not yet come into vogue. Even so, John clearly understood that what Guardini had called the "Modern World" was ending. He concluded therefore that a new and global "social order" needed to be created.

Leo insisted that his proposed modern social reform needed to be grounded in St. Thomas Aquinas' medieval Catholic adaptation of the classical organic-teleological Philosophy of Aristotle – a proposal that was ultimately rejected.

The Modern Leonine Strategy built on, and then went beyond, what I have called Catholic Social Teaching's still earlier and defensive "Anti-Modern Pre-Leonine Strategy." Again, that earlier strategy had begun in 1740 when Pope Benedict XIV inaugurated the tradition of mechanically printed papal encyclical letters by publishing through the mechanical printing press his first encyclical letter, UBI PRIMUM.

Whereas Leo XIII had launched his reforming papal strategy in response to the second stage of the modern Industrial Revolution, Benedict XIV had initiated his earlier defensive papal strategy in response to the modern European Enlightenment, which quickly flowed into the first stage of the modern Industrial Revolution. Taken as a whole, the Anti-Modern Pre-Leonine Strategy rejected the emerging bourgeois "Modern World." The Strategy tried first to defend, and later to restore, the classical aristocratic mode of Western Civilization as the societal foundation of Catholic-Christian evangelization.

By contrast and as we have seen, Saint John XXIII – implicitly referring to the Modernity's two dominant and competing materialist ideologies of Liberal Capitalism and Scientific Socialism – argued that both modern ideologies *had failed*. And again, John called on the global human family, and on the global Catholic family within it, to transcend those failed ideologies by creating a new global "social order."

These three evolving historical strategies of the print-based papal-encyclical tradition (again, Anti-Modern Pre-Leonine, Modern Leonine, and now Postmodern Johannine) correlate approximately with three historical stages of Modern Industrial Capitalism. The reason for this correlation is that each of the three papal stages has constituted a strategic ecclesial response to new spiritual challenges coming from the new contextual stage of society.

THREE PAPAL STRATEGIES[23]

CATHOLIC SOCIAL TEACHING	STAGE OF CAPITALISM	STRATEGIC CHALLENGE	PAPAL RESPONSE
ANTI-MODERN PRE-LEONINE STRATEGY: *(1740-1878)*	**STAGE I** **Laissez-Faire** **Local Capitalism** *(Factory Revolution 1760-1870)*	**New Bourgeois** **Materialist Ideologies** **of Modern European** **Enlightenment**	**Defense &** **Restoration of** **Pre-Modern** **Aristocratic Society**
MODERN LEONINE STRATEGY: *(1878-1958)*	**STAGE II** **Social-Welfare** **National Capitalism** *(Machine Revolution 1870-1960)*	**Bourgeois** **Societal Triumph** **of Modern Industrial** **Capitalism**	**Reform of** **Modern Bourgeois** **Liberal-Capitalist** **Society** *(Rejection of Marxism)*
POSTMODERN JOHANNINE STRATEGY: *(1958 ....)*	**STAGE III** **National-Security** **Global Capitalism** *(Electronic Revolution (1960 ...)*	**Degeneration of** **Modern Bourgeois** **Ideologies of** **Materialism** *(Climaxing in Crisis of Integral Ecology)*	**Creation of New** **Global Social Order** **Beyond Modern** **Materialist Ideologies** *(Ultimately grounded In Integral Ecology)*

Again, these three societal stages have been based on the three sequential technological revolutions within Modernity's Industrial Revolution, namely, the Factory Revolution, the Machine Revolution, and now the Electronic Revolution. (Yet the Electronic Revolution also carries the second and more powerful role of technologically precipitating the postmodern transformation.)

---

[23] Dates for the papal strategies are exact, but dates for the stages of Capitalism are approximate, since the decline of one stage overlaps with the emergence of the next stage.

CIVILIZATION AS DEEP LEVEL OF
CATHOLIC SOCIAL TEACHING

The evolving relationship of Catholic Social Teaching (and of its under-lying form of Catholic-Christian spirituality) to the rise and fall of historical forms of the contextual civilization constitutes *the tradition's deep level*. At this deep level, we have identified three evolving strategic responses by Catholic Social Teaching to evolving spiritual challenges from the three stages of Modern Industrial Capitalism – again, the Anti-Modern Pre-Leonine Strategy, the Modern Leonine Strategy, and the Postmodern Johannine Strategy.

It may be helpful here to offer a supplementary analysis that specifies the modalities of these three strategies of the papal encyclical tradition of Catholic Social Teaching as respectively *aristocratic, bourgeois, and ecological*. In addition, it may also be helpful to note that each strategy has carried a widening geographic scale, with the first having been *European*, the second more broadly *Western*, and the third now fully *global*.

Again, according to this deep analysis, the societal goal of the anti-modern European-aristocratic modality was initially defense and eventually *restoration of the collapsing aristocratic era*. The societal goal of the modern Western-bourgeois modality was *reform of the triumphing bourgeois society*, though only on its liberal-capitalist side. The societal goal of the postmodern global-ecological modality is now fully understood as *global regeneration of the integral ecology of life*.

Strategy I: European Aristocratic Restoration, 1740-1878

Since the rise of the Imperial Church early in the fourth century, European Catholic Christianity had embraced the aristocratic class as the mediator of evangelization. At that deep level of civilization, the Anti-Modern Pre-Leonine Strategy responded to the modern European Enlightenment, and soon also to the first stage of the modern Industrial Revolution. Again, that first stage was grounded in the social technology of the Factory Revolution, which took the societal form of Local Laissez-Faire Capitalism.

That papal strategy rejected the emerging modern bourgeois mode of Western Civilization. In doing so, it attempted first to defend, and then to restore, Western Civilization's collapsing classical European aristocratic mode. For that reason, we may describe the modality of the Antimodern Pre-Leonine Strategy as *European and aristocratic*. That means it was rooted in the collapsing European aristocratic form of Western Civilization, and that it pursued the societal goal of initially defending, and later attempting to *restore* to political power, the Western European aristocracy.

With the final defeat of Western European aristocratic state-power in the second half of the nineteenth century, the Anti-Modern Pre-Leonine Strategy collapsed. That final collapse included the loss of the Papal States (in the middle section of today's Italy), and it ended the ancient role of the pope as a political king. The papacy's long rise as a European political-economic power, which had taken on theocratic power during the eleventh century, suddenly ended late in the nineteenth century, when Pope Pius IX (1846-1878) lost his Papal States and his political kingship, and became a "prisoner of the Vatican."

Strategy II: Western Bourgeois Reform, 1878-1958

Leo XIII, elected as Bishop of Rome in 1878, established the "grand design" that became the Modern Leonine Strategy.[24] In a dramatic strategic turn, he cautiously but positively accepted the societal triumph of

---

[24] Leo laid out that philosophical program in his 1879 encyclical letter AETERNI PATRIS ("On the Restoration of Christian Philosophy"). Leo later defended workers' unions in his famous 1891 encyclical letter RERUM NOVARUM ("On Capital and Labor"). In addition, He issued an encyclical attacking socialism, another in defense of the family, plus four encyclicals on the nature of the state, and one on Freemasonry – all prior to RERUM NOVARUM. For more on these encyclicals as all together constituting his "grand design," see Chapter 5 of my earlier book, MODERN CATHOLIC SOCIAL TEACHING.

the modern bourgeois class across the Western industrializing nations. Leo thus accepted what had become the normative form of bourgeois modernization – namely, National Capitalism as the second stage of the modern Industrial Revolution (again, grounded technologically in the Machine Revolution).

As we have seen, in return for legitimating National Capitalism, Leo demanded not only societal reform but also, and more fundamentally, philosophical reform of Liberal Capitalism. At the same time, he philosophically rejected Scientific Socialism (Marxism), which as we have seen constituted an atheistic ideological variant of bourgeois modernization. Again:

- *On the philosophical side*, Leo called for an intellectual-spiritual reform of Liberal Capitalism based on a modern retrieval of Saint Thomas Aquinas's medieval Philosophy, which had constituted a Catholic-Christian adaptation of Aristotle's classical Philosophy;

- *On the societal side,* Leo called a societal reform of National Capitalism that included a regulatory state serving the common good and defense of workers' unions, as well as a major campaign against Marxism.

In accord with Leo's proposed societal reform, Western social movements eventually developed the reform of Liberalism that became National Social-Welfare Capitalism. But, while the societal side of the Leonine Strategy is better known today than its philosophical side, Leo had conceived his philosophical reform as *an indispensable and foundational requirement for his proposed societal reform*. Without that philosophical reform, he believed that the societal reform would fail.

That is indeed proving the case today within the third stage of Global Capitalism. The late modern corporatist-militarist alliance of neoliberal economics with neoconservative politics (both anti-Aristotelian and anti-Thomist) is now undermining the important social-welfare reforms achieved during the second stage of National Capitalism.

Again, we may describe the modality of the Modern Leonine Strategy as *bourgeois and Western*. Its societal goal was to reform the normative liberal-capitalist side of the Industrial Revolution's Stage II, while rejecting its atheistic scientific-socialist side. Because of the Strategy's attempt to reform Modern Industrial Civilization on its liberal-capitalist side, scholars have named the Leonine corpus of papal encyclical letters "Modern Catholic Social Teaching."

Strategy III: Global Ecological Regeneration, 1958 ...

Again, in another dramatic strategic turn, the Postmodern Johannine Strategy – beginning in 1958 with Saint John XXIII – declared that the two dominant and now globalized modern Western bourgeois ideologies of Materialism (Liberal Capitalism and Scientific Socialism) *had failed*. In their place, John called globally for a "new social order" (implicitly a new civilization), which would be *humanistic, cooperative, and agroecological*, as well as implicitly post-liberal, post-Marxian, and postmodern., as well as partly shaped by Christian inspiration.[25]

John argued that this new global social order needs to promote what his successor Pope Paul VI (1963-1978) later called "integral development." According to John's vision, this new global social order needs integrally to defend both the threatened urban poor and threatened rural farming communities, as well as the agroecological foundations of social life, and to promote worker and consumer cooperatives in both the rural and urban sectors.

Today, because of the 'advanced' global degradation of life's integral ecology, and using the language of Pope Francis' LAUDATO SI', we may now describe the modality of the still developing Postmodern Johannine Strategy as *global and ecological*.[26]

---

[25] John did not call for a global "Christian Civilization," but rather for a truly "human" civilization that Christians could help to shape through "Christian inspiration."

[26] Again, the term "ecology" is taken here as a comprehensive metaphor for the evolving creative communion of natural, human, and spiritual life.

PAPAL STRATEGY	CONTEXTUAL CIVILIZATION	STRATEGIC MODALITY	STRATEGIC SOCIAL GOAL
STRATEGY I: Anti-Modern Pre-Leonine	BREAKDOWN Premodern European-Aristocratic Civilization	ARISTOCRATIC & EUROPEAN	RESTORATION Premodern Aristocratic Political Defense
STRATEGY II: Modern Leonine	TRIUMPH Modern Western-Bourgeois Civilization	BOURGEOIS & WESTERN	REFORM Modern Bourgeois Philosophical-Social Transformation
STRATEGY III: Postmodern Johannine	BREAKDOWN Late Modern Global-Bourgeois Civilization	ECOLOGICAL & GLOBAL	REGENERATION Postmodern Transition Toward Ecological Civilization

In its present ecological fullness, the Postmodern Johannine Strategy integrates human ecology with the wider natural ecology within which human ecology is nested, as well as with what Francis has called "ecological spirituality" (again, described here as "spiritual ecology"). Within this holistic global framework, the full societal goal becomes *the integral ecological regeneration of life,* throughout its interwoven natural, human, and spiritual fabric, across our loving Creator's beauteous and beloved garden-planet Earth.

CONTRIBUTION OF GUARDINI'S BOOK
ON THE END MODERN WORLD

By calling in PACEM IN TERRIS for a global and implicitly postmodern "new social order," Saint John XXIII echoed the deep critique of Modernity published several years earlier by the distinguished Italian-German and Catholic-Christian philosopher Romano Guardini. In 1950, slightly more than a decade before John's prophetic social encyclicals, Guardini had published a radical humanistic-ecological critique of Modernity in his magisterial work DAS ENDE DER NEUZEIT (The End of the Modern World).[27]

Postmodern Catholic Social Teaching's Intellectual-Spiritual Debt to Romano Guardini

Saint John XXIII knew well Guardini's 1950 critique of Modernity. In that same year and while serving as Papal Nuncio in Paris, he had met with Guardini for an intensive three-hour conversation. Reportedly, Guardini came away from the meeting "deeply impressed" with John's intellectual depth.[28]

More than half a century later in his papal encyclical letter on ecology LAUDATO SI', Pope Francis revealed his own deep intellectual debt to Guardini's prophetic analysis of "The End of the Modern World." Decades earlier, as the young Argentinean Jesuit Jorge Mario Bergoglio, Francis had begun in Germany doctoral studies focused on Guardini's thought. Before completing his doctorate, however, Bergoglio was called back to Argentina. Decades later, as Bishop of Rome, Francis made Guardini's thought central to LAUDATO SI. As noted, in that great 2015 encyclical letter, Francis cited DAS ENDE DER NEUZEIT eight times!

Thus, beginning with Saint John XXIII and continuing through to Francis, the Catholic-Christian Bishops of Rome continued to advance Guardini's dramatic claim that *the "Modern World" is breaking down*. All of John's papal successors – Blessed Paul VI, Saint John Paul II, Benedict XVI, and now Francis – have offered their own profound insights into that breakdown, and into the papal attempt to articulate a post-

---

[27] Again, available in English as THE END OF THE MODERN WORLD (ISI Books, 2001).

[28] See Meriol Trevor, POPE JOHN BLESSED JOHN XXII (Gracewing, 2000), p. 226.

modern regenerative strategy for the human family and for Catholic-Christian evangelization.[29]

First Haunting Thought:
Need for a Book on the End of the Modern World

As already noted, while finishing the manuscript on John's prophetic vision, two thoughts began to haunt my still searching mind. Awareness of John's deep social analysis had opened my mind to the first unexpected haunting thought that, by declaring the failure of modern ideologies, John was announcing what Guardini called "The End of the Modern World."

Before publishing my manuscript on John's prophetic vision, the first haunting thought told me that I should first write and publish a book explaining "The End of the Modern World." Such a book was needed, that thought told me, because most commentators on John's encyclical letters MATER ET MAGISTRA and PACEM IN TERRIS seemed not to understand that those documents announce "The End of the Modern World."

Again, that "End" is called here the breakdown of Modern Industrial Civilization. The breakdown is revealed by its massive devastation of the integral ecology of life. That devastation flows from the modern bourgeois philosophical misunderstanding of Nature and of humanity within Nature, and from a still deeper, older, and oppressive distortion of sexual symbols and myths. Obeying that first haunting thought, I began work on a second manuscript, again tentatively titled SOCIAL ANALYSIS II – END OF THE MODERN WORLD.[30]

---

[29] In future books on these popes I hope to address these additional papal enhancements to the Postmodern Johannine Strategy.

[30] That manuscript builds on my earlier book with Peter Henriot, SOCIAL ANALYSIS: LINKING FAITH AND JUSTICE, Revised and Enlarged Edition (Orbis Books), 1983. Hence, the titled SOCIAL ANALYSIS II.

That second manuscript, now almost complete, provides a deep social-analytical background for understanding the Postmodern Johannine Strategy. It further explores the breakdown of Modern Industrial Civilization primarily within the evolving context of the four ideal-type deep eras of human history, as well as with the evolving context of the three ideal-type stages of Modern Industrial Capitalism. It also explores various scenarios for the breakdown of Modern Industrial Civilization. That breakdown could be gradual or sudden, as well as violent or peaceful. It could lead to the end of Western Civilization, or Western Civilization could prove creatively resilient and make a successful regenerative transition to a fresh postmodern form.

Even though we do not know what the future holds, we may be certain that the postmodern transition – through the breakdown of the late modern and now globalized form of Modern Industrial Civilization – will be turbulent, confusing, and dangerous. Indeed, we are already living within that turbulence, confusion, and danger. Hence, *we need a prophetic ecological spirituality* to inspire and to guide us as we journey through that turbulent, confusing, and dangerous passage in search of a regenerative postmodern Global Ecological Civilization.

Again, that projected future civilization will be technologically based in the Electronic Revolution. Also, it needs to become foundationally ecological. In addition, it needs to create an intellectual-spiritual symphony that humbly orchestrates the diverse eco-spiritual wisdom traditions of our human family's rich legacy of spiritual traditions, cultures, and civilizations.

For that to happen, intellectual-spiritual leaders across planet Earth need to develop what the Pacem in Terris Ecological Initiative has called the "*Postmodern Ecological Renaissance.*" We may rejoice that this Renaissance is already emerging in seminal form.

Second Haunting Thought:
Need for a Book on Postmodern Ecological Spirituality

As I neared completion of the second manuscript on the "End of the Modern World," a second haunting thought unexpectedly told me that, even if readers were to understand John's implicit announcement of the "End of the Modern World," such knowledge alone would not be life-giving. It could lead to immobilizing depression, or even to fatalistic resignation.

For that reason, the second haunting thought also told me that, before publishing either of the two preceding manuscripts, I should write and publish yet another book, this time one exploring *a hope-filled path of ecological spirituality for the emerging Postmodern Global Era*. Such a book, this second haunting thought told me, should try to help people to discover the regenerative energy of ecological spirituality that *the Holy Spirit is already stirring up among us in both humanistic and Christian forms*.

That second haunting thought also told me that she is stirring up this regenerative spiritual energy in order to guide our human family, and our Christian family within it, through the turbulent, confusing, and dangerous breakdown of Modern Industrial Civilization and toward a Postmodern Ecological Civilization.

NEED FOR REGENERATIVE LAY MOVEMENTS OF
POSTMODERN ECOLOGICAL SPIRITUALITY

As this chapter ends, let us recall that each time that a given historical stage of Christianity's contextual civilization begins to break down, an intellectually fresh form of spirituality begins to flow within the same history. Let us also recall that, within the historical evolution of Catholic Christianity, such fresh intellectual-spiritual energy generally comes from *the laity*.

The original Jesus-movement was lay. The late classical coenobitical movement was lay. The feudal monastic movement was originally lay. Within the medieval mendicant movement, Francis of Assisi originally understood himself and his companions as lay. With the early modern apostolic movement, Ignatius' original group of "Jesuits" was a lay band. Finally, within the modern wave of especially female apostolic communities, many such communities began as lay.

In the emerging Postmodern Era, we once again see emerging *new lay movements*. This time, however, preservation of their lay charism becomes essential to the movements' identity and mission. In addition, since the postmodern Electronic Revolution has become global, the identity and mission of these new lay movements also needs to become global. Further, these new lay movements need to seek *theoretical and practical pathways for regenerating life's integral ecology.* They need to overcome the late modern nihilistic devastation of integral ecology across the creative communion of natural, human, and spiritual life.

In the following chapter, we will explore the postmodern emergence of new lay movements as *signs of spiritual hope*. We will also explore the challenge to embrace at the deep level a globally regenerative mission centered in life's integral ecology. In the chapter after that, we will explore the significance of these new lay movements for refounding declining "apostolic religious communities" within the 'advanced' industrial regions.

Lastly (prior to a final reflection), we will explore the lay ecological vision of Peter Maurin for a "New Monasticism," which he saw as called to be rurally grounded and to plant seeds of holistic regeneration for what he called a "new society."

In all of this, let us try to listen to what I propose is the Holy Spirit's postmodern call for holistic regeneration of the creative communion of life's integral ecology, throughout its interwoven natural, human, and spiritual fabric, across our loving Creator's beauteous and beloved garden-planet Earth.

7

POSTMODERN ECOLOGICAL SPIRITUALITY
& NEW LAY MOVEMENTS

T his chapter explores the emergence of Postmodern Ecological
Spirituality and of new Catholic-Christian lay movements as fer-
tile ground for its development. The following chapter calls for an eco-
spiritual alliance between new lay movements and older but refounded
"apostolic" movements of "religious life," in service of the postmodern
regeneration of life's integral ecology. As a project for that eco-spiritual
alliance, the next and final chapter (again, prior to the Concluding Reflection) explores what I propose is the Holy Spirit's call for an ecological lay "New Monasticism" that resonates with the regenerative ecological vision of Peter Maurin's "Green Revolution."

The technological context for these possibilities is the Postmodern Electronic Revolution. Becoming strong by the year 2000, that revolution
has been making *technologically feasible* the emergence of a fresh Postmodern Ecological Civilization. As we have seen, the reason for that
feasibility is that the Electronic Revolution's holistic networking of information has been precipitating a holistic postmodern ecological-
evolutionary paradigm of Cosmology for Philosophy and Science, and
for human society at every level from the local to the global.

At the same time, the holistic networks of information flowing from Electronic Revolution have also been making *spiritually feasible* the postmodern holistic consciousness that is precipitating Postmodern Ecological Spirituality. Again, the word "ecological" refers broadly here to the evolving creative communion of life's integral ecology, throughout its interwoven natural, human, and spiritual fabric, across our loving Creator's beloved garden-planet Earth.

EMERGING POSTMODERN
CATHOLIC-CHRISTIAN ECOLOGICAL SPIRITUALITY

Old & New Dimensions of
Ecological Spirituality

The emerging Postmodern Ecological Spirituality has both new and old dimensions within human consciousness. We find *ancient yet still living human roots* for ecological spirituality in the Nature-grounded traditions of Indigenous Peoples across our garden-planet Earth. These rich eco-spiritual traditions help all of us to recall the ancient eco-spiritual tribal traditions from which we are all descended.

We also find *ancient yet still living biblical roots* for this spirituality in the cosmic spirituality of thanksgiving and praise within the Hebrew Scriptures, especially the Psalms, and in the Christian New Testament's proclamation of cosmic salvation. In addition, we find *ancient yet still living Catholic-Christian roots* in the sacramental understanding of creation, which is also found within Orthodox and Anglican Christianity.

The new dimension of Postmodern Ecological Spirituality is of course not found in those ancient roots, but rather in the still developing scientific discovery of *cosmic evolution,* including the evolution of life on our garden-planet Earth, and within it of our own human family's reflective consciousness. Yet, for the emerging ecological spirituality, evolution is not understood though the atomistic-mechanical reductionism of modern Scientific-Materialism, which has cosmologically grounded

Darwinian and Neo-Darwinian interpretations of evolution. Rather, it is found in the holistic and post-Darwinian understanding of evolution being explored by visionary scientists like Fritjof Capra and Pier Luigi Luisi,[1] as well as by mystical-prophetic figures like the late eco-spiritual visionary Thomas Berry.

Further, Postmodern Ecological Spirituality finds its grounding in mystical-prophetic consciousness of the Divine Mystery present both within and beyond creation. It finds that grounding in the mystical dimension of the evolutionary creative communion unfolding across our splendorous Cosmos, across our beauteous garden-planet Earth, across Earth's vibrant biosphere of which we are part, and within our own human family's profound reflective consciousness.

What is new in this mystical-prophetic awakening is that all created reality has evolved and is still evolving. Further, in this awakening, postmodern Christians discover that cosmic creatures are not *passive objects* of our Creator's loving creativity, but *profoundly active co-creators* with our loving Creator's own divine creativity. Hence, Postmodern Global Ecological Spirituality constitutes *a spirituality of evolving ecological co-creativity*, or alternately of evolving creative communion.

This sacred co-creativity is still holistically revealing its unfolding energy throughout the interwoven natural, human, and spiritual fabric of life's integral ecology across our garden-planet Earth and across our majestic Cosmos. Yet, on the negative side, we have also come to realize that, within this evolving evolutionary-ecological framework, *human sin* has emerged as a blasphemous and death-dealing attack on the creative communion of life's integral ecology.

In addition, as we have seen, the Catholic-Christian form of this still emerging Postmodern Ecological Spirituality is explicitly *lay*. It roots Catholic-Christian spirituality back not only into our loving Creator's wondrous creation of Nature, but also into the foundational lay nature

---

[1] See again their pioneering book, THE SYSTEMS VIEW OF LIFE.

of Christian discipleship. Supporting this lay rootedness, recent scholarship has re-emphasized Jesus' own Jewish identity as lay, and the lay character of the entire early Jesus movement.[2]

As pointed out earlier in this book, Jesus' preaching holistically proclaimed the resurrection of the body and the eschatological renewal of the "Heavens" and Earth. Jesus' holistic proclamation of a Nature-rooted spirituality stands as profoundly opposed to the modern Western drive philosophically and scientifically to de-spiritualize Nature, and technologically and economically to devastate its ecological regeneration.

Ecological Spirituality as Panentheistic

The emerging Postmodern Ecological Spirituality may be described as a form of "*Panentheism.*"[3] From its Greek roots, that word means "God is in everything" – with "*Pan*" meaning "all," *en*" meaning "in," and "*Theos*" meaning "God," and thus all together meaning "God in all."

Panentheism differs from *Pantheism*, which identifies the Divine Mystery only with creation. By contrast, Panentheism perceives the Divine Mystery both as immanently revealed within the depth of creation and as transcending all created reality. Panentheism may also be contrasted with a *purely transcendent Theism*, which perceives the Divine Mystery as revealed only beyond creation, and with a *purely immanent Materialism*, which claims there is no transcendence.

As we have seen earlier, the modern Western bourgeois project tried initially and schizophrenically to combine a purely transcendent The-

---

[2] On Jesus as a layperson, see John P. Meyer, A MARGINAL JEW: RETHINKING THE HISTORICAL JESUS, THE ROOTS OF THE PROBLEM, Volume I (Doubleday, 1991).

[3] For more on Panentheism, see the article on the topic in the STANFORD ENCYCLOPEDIA OF PHILOSOPHY at *http://plato.stanford.edu/entries/panentheism* (accessed 2016-09-11). As that article notes, Panentheism finds strong resonances in Eastern Christian Theology. For pioneering Catholic-Christian philosophical work in this area, see the article's references to Joseph A. Bracken, SJ. For pioneering Protestant-Christian philosophical work in this area, see the article's references to John Cobb and David Ray Griffin.

ism for a psychologized spiritual consciousness with a purely immanent Materialism for a reductionist philosophical-scientific understanding of the Universe. Over time, as we have also seen, such a weak psychologized bourgeois spirituality became first privatized, then secularized, and finally nihilized.

In the contemporary late modern period, that intellectual-spiritual degeneration has resulted in a triumphant culture of Scientific Materialism and even Nietzschean Nihilism. As a result, the dominant public
values promoted by the materialist-nihilist culture of the corporate
global culture industries are now *money, power, and fame*. Hence, the
urgent historical need for Postmodern Ecological Spirituality.

Visionary Projects of Ecological Spirituality

Gratefully, we are discovering within contemporary Catholic-Christianity (and elsewhere as well) hope-filled projects rooted in Postmodern Ecological Spirituality. For example, within the United States, we
see pioneering members of the Catholic Worker Movement pursuing
the agroecological vision of Peter Maurin. They are returning to the
land to embrace a rurally rooted way of life that seeks regeneration for
the creative communion of life's integral ecology.[4]

Also, some members of Catholic-Christian "religious orders," and especially women, have also become visionary pioneers in this emerging
Postmodern Ecological Spirituality. One U.S. example is the wonderful
work of Sister Miriam Therese MacGillis of the Dominican Sisters of
Caldwell. Following the ecological teachings of Thomas Berry, Sister
MacGillis has created and sustained the northern New Jersey ecological
complex called Genesis Farm.[5] Another example is the ecological re-

---

[4] See Eric Anglada, "The History and New Growth of Catholic Worker Farms," AMERICA
MAGAZINE, May 6, 2013, available at: *http://americamagazine.org/issue/taking-root*.

[5] See *http://www.genesisfarm.org*. On the teachings of Thomas Berry, see again his lyrical
early work, THE DREAM OF THE EARTH, and the book written toward the end of his life,
THE GREAT WORK.

serve known as Maryknoll Ecological Sanctuary, established in the Philippines by the Maryknoll Sisters and originally directed by Maryknoll Sister Ann Braudis.[6]

In addition, there are important Protestant-initiated examples. One creative U.S. example is the visionary project known as the Narrow Ridge Earth Literacy Center in the U.S. State of Tennessee. Grounded in the cosmological vision of Thomas Berry, it was founded by United Methodist minister Bill Nickle, in cooperation with United Methodist lay leader Dr. Macgregor Smith. Today, it is directed by Dr. Mitzi Wood-von Misener.

Celebrating in 2016 its twenty-fifth anniversary, the Narrow Ridge project has developed an ecological village that protects and cherishes more than seven hundred acres of gently rolling Appalachian hills. Encompassing lush green meadows and dark verdant forests, it provides a common ecological home for humans and myriad other creatures who live together there within Nature's vibrant family of life.[7]

Late Modern Spiritual Erosion

Encouraged by such mystical-prophetic seeds of regeneration, Western Catholic Christianity, and indeed all of global Christianity, is beginning to face the historically new strategic challenge arising from the vast late modern devastation of life's integral ecology. Again, the late modern and now globalized form of Modern Industrial Civilization is the source of that devastation.

At the same time, Western Christians are beginning to face the correlative strategic challenge arising from the breakdown of the West's Modern Psychological Spirituality. As we have seen, that Western bourgeois spirituality – schizophrenically dualist in character – has been

---

[6] See *https://maryknollsisters.org/mk-sister/sister-ann-braudis/*

[7] See *http://www.earthliteracycenter.org/about* (accessed 2016-02-11). Disclosure: my wife and I are members of the Narrow Ridge family of community land-trusts.

undermined by the privatization of religion and by the secularization of society, and it is now collapsing into Nietzschean Nihilism.

As the correlative breakdowns of the late modern Western bourgeois forms of both civilization and spirituality become clear, we find ourselves living today not only in a confusing and turbulent time, but also in a time of great danger. The reason for the danger is that so many late modern institutional leaders are still relentlessly (albeit often unknowingly) promoting the degenerative philosophical paths of Scientific Materialism and even Nietzschean Nihilism. Across our loving Creator's beloved planet Earth, those late modern institutional paths are inflicting vast planetary devastation on life's integral ecology.

Further, as we have also seen for the current late modern period, Western Catholic Christians are experiencing the breakdown of the modern industrial model of evangelization. Within that breakdown of evangelization, they are also experiencing correlative breakdowns of the modern "apostolic" model of "religious life," and of the modern "clerical"-celibate-seminary model of the presbyterate.

Those interrelated but collapsing modern Western Catholic-Christian models – for spirituality, for evangelization, for "religious life," and for the presbyterate – were developed within and for the historical context of Modern Western Industrial-Colonial Civilization. They all now face historical breakdown within the wider contextual breakdown of Modern Industrial Civilization.

Restoration, Modernization, or Regeneration?

The solution to the late modern Western Catholic-Christian breakdown is not the so-called 'conservative' Christian temptation to *restore* classical cultural-spiritual forms, nor the so-called 'progressive' (or liberal) temptation to *integrate* further with Modernity's collapsing culture.

Again, what Romano Guardini called the "Modern World" (Modern Industrial Civilization) has been breaking down for some time. Within that breakdown, any 'progressive' attempt to pursue deeper modernization often becomes pathological. In addition, the late modern breakdown has older roots in the classical cultural-spiritual forms that many 'conservatives' are attempting to restore. For that reason, such 'conservative' attempts can also become spiritually pathological.

Within the terminal crisis of Modernity, many 'conservative' Christians seek (again, in the name of "restoration") to preserve or to recover certain late classical or early modern cultural additions to Christianity. However, many such cultural additions find little or no support from the New Testament. For example, as we have seen for Catholic Christianity, neither the canonical "clerical state in life" nor the canonical "religious state in life" existed in Christianity's foundational and early stages, during which time the Christian movement was entirely lay.

Yet, authentic cultural-spiritual gifts of the past – spanning the Primal, Classical, and now receding Modern Eras – all remain valuable, and need to be integrated within the emerging Postmodern Era. To seek a postmodern future that will include authentic cultural-spiritual gifts from all past human eras, we need to allow the inspiring wisdom of the Holy Spirit to guide us in creating a life-giving synthesis. Again, that synthesis needs authentically to conserve past gifts and authentically to progress toward future possibilities.

Once again, as Modern Industrial Civilization and Modern Psychological Spirituality together go deeper and deeper into their late modern breakdowns, we are seeing a correlative decline in the modern Western Catholic-Christian industrial model of evangelization. At the same time, we are also seeing correlative declines in the modern Western Catholic-Christian "apostolic" model of special mystical-prophetic communities, and in the modern seminary-trained and clerical-celibate model of the Western Catholic-Christian presbyterate, at least within the 'advanced' industrial regions.

Within the sad turbulence and confusion of those declines, and for some religious institutions even death, we need to trust that at times of cultural and spiritual chaos, when everything seems to be falling apart, at such times the Holy Spirit seeks to guide us toward the birthing of a new era of spiritual and societal creativity.

Within the depressing and growing *spiritual emptiness* across the late modern industrialized world, prophetic visionaries are returning to the Spirit-inspired dark mystical womb of regeneration. In that mystical darkness, the human experience becomes prophetically regenerated. It then brings forth *freshly creative spiritual energy*. For this reason, Catholic Christianity is now experiencing the global emergence of new lay forms of special Catholic-Christian mystical-prophetic communities.

EMERGING POSTMODERN CATHOLIC-CHRISTIAN LAY MOVEMENTS

As we have seen, the Christian Church, as the lay gathering of Jesus' disciples, is called to drink from the life-giving waters of the Holy Spirit in order to heal, and to sanctify more deeply, the Creator's beloved, mystical, and yet also sinfully wounded, creation. In addition, as we have seen, the Holy Spirit's regenerative power of healing and deeper sanctification takes distinct historical forms.

Historical Evolution of Catholic-Christian Mystical-Prophetic Communities

Again, special Catholic-Christian mystical-prophetic communities need to drink deeply from the Holy Spirit's regenerative waters. In relation to that need, two earlier-mentioned points seem worth repeating.

- *Ecclesial Mission.* First, special Catholic-Christian mystical-prophetic communities are called to help in healing sinful woundedness within the wider gathering of disciples (that is, to assist in renewing the church's internal life), in order that a renewed

237

church may help to renew the creative communion of life's integral ecology across the wider sin-wounded world.

- *Societal Correlation.* Second, there is always an historical correlation between the historical form of society's woundedness from sin and the historical form of Catholic-Christian mystical-prophetic communities arising to renew the church for healing in the sin-wounded world. Thus, as the historical form of society's sin-filled woundedness shifts, so too we experience an historical shift in the deep historical mission of Catholic-Christian mystical-prophetic communities.

As we have seen, with the birth of a new historical era, a form of Catholic-Christian mystical-prophetic community that flourished in one historical era goes into decline and a fresh form emerges to occupy its space. But the new era need not eliminate the declining form, for that form can continue as a secondary yet still important part of the church's vast treasury of spiritual energy. The old form may thus play a continuing, albeit reduced, role in the future. In addition, with each new wave of historical transformation, the wider community of disciples learns new things from both old and new special Catholic-Christian mystical-prophetic communities. Yet leadership belongs to the new form.

Like a Flowing River
Suddenly Changing Course

We may think of a spiritual river flowing through an historical valley between two large mountains. Over centuries, the spiritual river had carved in the valley a deep channel flowing with the historical era's spiritual waters of regenerative and co-creative life. Suddenly, an earthquake causes a landslide to tumble down from the mountains. It blocks the river's channel. Quickly, the flowing waters of spiritual life back up behind the blockage.

238

Before long, however, the backed-up spiritual waters break through into another channel and again flow down into the valley. The newly flowing river of spiritual energy then begins to carve out a new and deepening spiritual channel. Soon, the living waters of spiritual energy flow powerfully down the new channel, while only a small stream continues to slip through the blocked old spiritual channel.

In the wake of the postmodern spiritual earthquake, some wish to dig out again the old blocked channel, and to force a strong flow of spiritual waters back into that old route. Yet that goal proves an impossible quest. The rubble from the historical landslide is too vast. For that reason, it is better to celebrate the new channel of life-giving spiritual waters, to drink deeply from their new course of mystical-prophetic flow, and to rejoice in the regenerative healing of those waters' spiritual strength.

Even so, and again, some spiritual water will continue to flow through the old channel. The flow of spiritual water in the older channel becomes quieter, yet its special healing grace remains. Such is the manner of transformation for the historical-cultural form of special Catholic-Christian mystical-prophetic communities within the postmodern spiritual transformation.

In terms of today, the landslide is the postmodern transition, precipitated by the technological earthquake of the Electronic Revolution. That earthquake has led to the still unfolding breakdown of the modern bourgeois and industrial-colonial form of Western Civilization, including its recent globalization, and for both of its materialist ideologies of Liberal Capitalism and Scientific Socialism. Correlatively, it has also led to the contemporary breakdown of the modern bourgeois form of the dualist spirituality of psychological interiority.

Beyond Religious Dualism

As the old modern spiritual channel shrinks, and in some places even dries up, the late modern Western Catholic Church experiences within the industrial-center countries a "vocation crisis" for the modern "apostolic" form of "religious life," which has been grounded in the now collapsing Modern Psychological Spirituality. That modern Western form had once responded powerfully and creatively to the spiritual challenges of the Modern Era. Now, however, within the industrial-center nations that form has fallen into decline.

Yet, the Holy Spirit's life-giving spiritual waters are already spreading beyond the old blocked modern channel. They are breaking through to create a new and regenerative postmodern spiritual channel. For that reason, we now see emerging *new lay forms* of Catholic Christian mystical-prophetic communities.

Again, the "apostolic" cultural-spiritual model of "religious life" within the Western Catholic Church was developed for the "Modern World" of the Western industrializing and colonizing nations. Now, it is yielding to the emergence of a postmodern lay spirituality, which this book proposes is called to become ecologically regenerative.

Beyond Hierarchical Clericalism

Again, the same shortage of "vocations" for "religious life" is also true for the modern bourgeois seminary-trained and clericalized-celibate model of the Western Catholic-Christian presbyterate.

At the Ecumenical Council of Trent (1545-1563), that modern Western model was consolidated in a manner analogous to "religious life." A decree from the Fifth Session of the Council of Trent required special schools for standardized training of future priests. Soon called "seminaries," these schools imitated monastic life. In addition, following the Council of Trent, the monastic-inspired papal law of celibacy was promoted even more intensely by Western Catholic-Christian bishops.[8] Thus, the modern Western Catholic-Christian model of the presbyterate was constructed in three historical stages.

- **Stage 1 - Imperial Clericalism.** In the fourth century, the Emperor Constantine legally 'elevated' bishops and presbyters to a 'higher' imperial class authorized to rule over the "laity," with laity then demoted below the "clergy" in the hierarchical structure of the new Imperial Church.

- **Stage 2 - Monastic Celibacy.** In the eleventh century, the papal 'Gregorian Reform,' inspired by the monastic network of Cluny, violently imposed monastic celibacy by police force on the then largely married Western diocesan bishops and presbyters, in order to support a new papal theocracy.

- **Stage 3 - Monastic Seminaries.** In the sixteenth century, the Council of Trent decreed that candidates for the diocesan presbyterate should be trained outside universities and in ecclesial segregation from the rest of the priestly *Laos*. The purpose of his segregation was to combat Protestantism's penetration into kinship networks within Catholic regions. This segregation uprooted Catholic evangelization from its traditional roots, dating back to apostolic times, in locally rooted kinship and friendship networks.

The Protestant Reformation rightfully rejected the non-evangelical papal law of monastic celibacy for Western diocesan presbyters and bish-

---

[8] As we saw in Chapter 2, in the fourth century the Catholic-Christian episcopacy and presbyterate had been clericalized by the Roman Empire's Constantinian construction of the Imperial Church. Much later, in the eleventh century, the 'Gregorian Reform' had imported its papal law of celibacy from monasticism and imposed it by police-force on the largely married Western Catholic diocesan presbyters and bishops. As also noted earlier, that monastic-inspired papal campaign was in part justified by misogynist contempt for women, and it even involved papal enslavement of presbyters' wives and children. But the deep motive seems to have been papal lust for theocratic power. Yet common-law clerical marriages continued across the West long after the so-called 'Gregorian Reform,' and long after the Council of Trent, especially in rural regions.

ops, and it successfully launched its long and still continuing wave of evangelization. The Reformation's rejection of that papal law may have been one of the major reasons for the Reformation's initial successes in Northern Europe. It may also be one of the major reasons for the still growing success in evangelization of Protestant Evangelical and Pentecostal movements throughout the world.

Further, outside Western Catholic Christianity, practically all of the other twenty-three *sui juris* Churches of the global Catholic communion never accepted monastic celibacy as mandatory law for diocesan presbyters. They still largely follow the ancient apostolic tradition of allowing married presbyters, if not bishops. Finally, the non-evangelical papal law of monastic celibacy for diocesan presbyters never existed as a broad institutional policy within the Western Church during its entire first millennium.

Today, the modern clerical-celibate-seminary model for Catholic-Christian presbyters in the Western Church is breaking down. That breakdown is revealed through the "shortage of vocations" and through the often intellectually weak and sometimes emotionally unhealthy quality of seminarians.[9]

But most of the contemporary Western Catholic-Christian bishops still resist understanding the depth of this historical-spiritual breakdown of the modern Western Catholic-Christian clerical-celibate-seminary model of the presbyterate.[10] They also still resist understanding the re-

---

[9] For a reflection on this breakdown, see the essay by Alberto Melloni, "*La messa è finita. Così dopo cinque secoli tramonta la figura del prete,*" LA REPUBBLICA (Italy), 2017-03-22, available at *http://ilsismografo.blogspot.it/2017/03/italia-la-messa-e-finita.html* (accessed 2017-03-30). For an English-language article on this essay see Robert Mickens, "Letter from Rome: The Church's Seminary Problem," COMMONWEAL MAGAZINE, 2017-03-27, available at *https://www.commonwealmagazine.org/letter-rome-117* (accessed 2017-03-30).

[10] Despite the crisis of "vocations" for the clerical-celibate-seminary model of the presbyterate, there seems to be a surplus of Western Catholic-Christian presbyters pursuing a "vocation" to the episcopate. That may be due due to the sociological disease of careerism found in all human institutions.

lationship of that historical-spiritual breakdown to the wider historical-spiritual breakdown of Catholic-Christian evangelization across the Western industrial-center countries. Again, those breakdowns form part of the wider and correlative Western breakdowns of Modern Psychological Spirituality and of Modern Industrial Civilization.

At the end of the aristocratic *Ancien Régime,* the Western European Catholic-Christian episcopacy remained imprisoned in what might be called its "aristocratic captivity." It failed to understand the deep spiritual challenges emerging from the Industrial Revolution. In major regions of Western Europe, that failure caused the massive failure of evangelization called the "loss of the working class."

Today, across the industrial center countries of Western Civilization, we see what might now be called the Western Catholic-Christian episcopacy's "bourgeois captivity." Often enmeshed in a corporate-capitalist model of leadership, many bishops remain blind to the deep spiritual challenges emerging from the Electronic Revolution. As a result, yet another great Western de-evangelization is now occurring, and this time especially across the 'advanced' English-speaking countries of Modern Industrial Civilization.

Yet there is no shortage of "vocations" for ordained ministerial leadership within the Protestant Reformation's contemporary Evangelical and Pentecostal movements.[11] The reason is that those still growing Christian movements have rejected for ministerial leadership the non-evangelical model of clericalism, as well as the non-evangelical requirement of celibacy. In their place, they have embraced the *original*

---

[11] These churches are different from the "mainline" Protestant denominations, which have maintained a deracinated professionalism for ministerial leadership. Further, the "mainlines" have by and large become culturally accommodated to Modernity, and thus often lack the counter-cultural spiritual energy found in the Evangelical and Pentecostal movements. But the "mainline" Protestant churches, at least in the United States, have a different problem. While they do not have a shortage of "vocations" for pastoral ministry, they do have a growing shortage of congregational members to serve.

lay form of ecclesial leadership. In addition, many of those pastoral leaders have embraced the Electronic Revolution as a central medium for evangelization.

More importantly, the still globally expanding Evangelical and Pentecostal movements have returned to the ancient Christian tradition of pursuing evangelization, and of discerning ecclesial leadership within evangelization, primarily through *locally-rooted lay kinship and friendship networks*. In that return, Evangelical and Pentecostal movements frequently ordain local grass-roots leaders and often allow them to stay and to minister within their local communities, as happened in the original lay movement of Jesus' disciples.

Those contemporary Reformation movements have thus rejected the deracinated and segregated clerical-celibate-seminary model for ordained leadership developed by the Catholic papacy in the late classical, medieval and modern periods. They have also often rejected the deracinated professionalized model developed for the "mainline" Protestant Churches, which sought cultural integration with Modern Philosophy and Modern Science as the intellectual foundations for Modern Industrial Civilization.

Consequently across the globe, Evangelical and Pentecostal movements, and especially Pentecostal movements which empower grass-roots women, have been dramatically expanding their evangelization. Meanwhile, within the 'advanced' industrial-center countries, the uprooted and segregated clerical-celibate-seminary model of the Catholic-Christian presbyterate collapses into ever deeper crisis, and at times in a pathological manner.

Thus, the late modern crisis of the Western Catholic-Christian presbyterate within the industrial center-countries remains inseparable from the Western Church's non-evangelical law of celibacy for diocesan presbyters and bishops. Yet changing that papal law will not of itself resolve the late modern crisis of Catholic-Christian evangelization, though such a change is surely a necessary pre-condition. To address the crisis at the deep level, however, there will also need to be a profound transformation in the grounding spirituality, as well as a return to the apostolic model of ordaining local grass-roots leaders to the presbyterate without the clerical-celibate-seminary superstructure.

Of course, voluntary evangelical celibacy constitutes an important spiritual charism for those whom the Holy Spirit calls to it. But human-made church law cannot forcibly impose the Holy Spirit's gift of a special charism on an institutional office. When that happens, there eventually occurs an anti-spiritual distortion of the very nature of that office, as well as an institutional weakening of its spiritual power.

Further, as we have seen, the postmodern cultural-spiritual transformation, in its *deep mythic-symbolic foundation,* is moving beyond classical hierarchical patriarchy and beyond modern hyper-masculinism (with both carrying undertows of misogyny), and toward an egalitarian and co-creative partnership of feminine and masculine spiritual energy. For that reason, it is now essential to create across global Catholic Christianity *regenerative postmodern paths empowering women's spiritual leadership.*

DEEP MISSION OF POSTMODERN
CATHOLIC-CHRISTIAN LAY MOVEMENTS

As this book has repeatedly proposed, the new historical-cultural context is the deep transition from the now globalized form of Modern Industrial Civilization toward the future global emergence of a Postmodern Ecological Civilization. In addition, as we have seen, correlated with this deep societal transition is the *deep spiritual transition* from Modern Psychological Spirituality which has been Western and dualistic, toward Postmodern Ecological Spirituality which is global and holistic.

Within this transitional framework, we have also seen that there is emerging a fresh Catholic-Christian spiritual wave of *postmodern lay movements.* Again, these movements are the newest historical form of special Catholic-Christian mystical-prophetic communities. This new wave follows the past waves of foundational, coenobitical, monastic, mendicant, and apostolic communities. Like those earlier waves, this new one responds to a new historical context. Thus, while the modern Western "apostolic "form of Catholic-Christian mystical-prophetic communities has been declining within the 'advanced' industrial countries, these new postmodern lay movements have been growing.

New Mission of Ecological Regeneration

Within this postmodern societal-spiritual transformation, what needs to become the *deep spiritual mission* of this fresh postmodern lay wave of special Catholic-Christian mystical-prophetic communities?

- *Classical Restoration.* Is it to *restore* the elitist and dualistic Platonic spirituality of late classical aristocratic and hierarchical-patriarchal culture?

- *Modern Integration.* Is it to *integrate* further with the now disintegrating atomistic-mechanical and materialist culture of hyper-masculine bourgeois Modernity, which has secularized Nature and society and both privatized and undermined religion?

- *Postmodern Regeneration.* Or is the mission to *regenerate* our loving Creator's evolving integral ecology of life, within a fresh postmodern framework that is holistic and global, while remaining faithfully rooted in authentic ancient Christian traditions?

If the deep spiritual mission is indeed holistic postmodern regeneration of life's integral ecology, then how should that mission be described? Again, I have proposed that the deep historical mission for the postmodern wave of new Catholic-Christian lay movements may be described as follows:

The Holy Spirit is now calling us both personally and institutionally to embody and to preach the Good News of Jesus in and through holistic regeneration of the evolving creative communion of life's integral ecology, throughout its interwoven natural, human, and spiritual fabric, and across our loving Creator's beloved garden-planet Earth.

This needs to become the *deep spiritual mission* not only for special Catholic-Christian mystical-prophetic communities, but also for the wider global communion of Catholic Christian Churches, and indeed for the entire global Christian family. Further, this deep spiritual mission needs to undergird the existing missions of all contemporary institutions within global Christianity.

Retrieving the
Regenerative Lay Model of Church

As expressly lay in identity, the new Catholic-Christian movements typically welcome women and men, celibates and marrieds, and children too. In so doing, they move beyond the mono-sexual celibate monopoly that has characterized earlier historical-cultural models for Catholic-Christian mystical-prophetic communities.

By embracing women and men, marrieds and singles, and children as well, these new lay movements are returning to the *foundational lay model of the early Jesus' movement*. They are allowing the Holy Spirit to re-root their evangelical-sacramental energy back into the original spiritual power of Jesus' foundational *Laos*.

Further, by virtue of their lay character, these communities implicitly do not follow the *world-rejecting spirituality* of many earlier forms of Catholic-Christian mystical-prophetic communities. As we have seen, much of the earlier tradition of Catholic-Christian "religious life" carried, along with its evangelical-sacramental richness, an anti-worldly legacy known in Latin as the *fuga mundi* (flight from the world). Even modern "apostolic" communities, despite magnanimously serving the "secular world" through their outer-directed "apostolates," nonetheless attempted in their inner-directed psychological spirituality of interiority to "retreat" from the world.

By contrast, postmodern Catholic-Christian lay movements, again by virtue of their self-consciousness lay character, are implicitly following a *world-affirming spirituality*. While modern "apostolic" communities have understood themselves as separate from the "secular world," postmodern lay communities find their identity and mission within their lay character and within the so-called "secular world."

Further, through their lay identity, postmodern Catholic-Christian lay movements are rediscovering the foundational nature of the lay baptismal path to holiness within the sacred realities of *family, work, and citizenship*. These realities are indeed sacred, because they co-creatively share in our loving Creator's own Divine Creativity. Many emerging postmodern lay movements have rooted their charisms in at least one of these three sacred human areas of the creative communion of life. Again, these are family, work, and citizenship. That is where their charism of lay spirituality takes practical root.

Contemporary examples of these lay movements include multiple new creations. Movements favored by Catholic popes in the late twentieth century have tended to be so-called 'conservative' in character, yet they embrace a world-affirming spirituality. One such example is Opus Dei, which roots its spirituality in the sacred task of *human work*. Additional examples include communities of the Charismatic Renewal and Focolare, both of which stress the sacred task of *family*. Still another example is Communion and Liberation, which emphasizes Christian education for societal life, which we might describe as linked to the sacred task of *citizenship*.

There are also so-called 'progressive' lay movements like the Catholic Worker, L'Arche, the Jesuit-linked Christian Life Communities,

Maryknoll Lay Missionaries and Affiliates, Pax Christi, Pax Romana, San Egidio, 'Secular' Franciscans, etc. Many of these 'progressive' movements stress the post-Vatican II themes of "justice and peace," and many have recently added the theme of ecology. By and large, we may interpret these 'progressive' emphases as related to the sacred lay task of *citizenship*. These 'progressive' movements seem weaker, however, in their spiritual celebration of the sacred character of family and work.

BEYOND DEFICIENCIES,
ONE-SIDEDNESS, & POLARIZATION

Historically, new movements of Catholic-Christian mystical-prophetic communities have in their initial forms often carried deficiencies. For example, Saint Francis of Assisi did not invent the medieval Italian model of devotion to the poor by becoming poor Catholic-Christian beggars (mendicants). During Francis' time, there had already been formed within Italy diverse bands of Christian beggars known as the *poverelli* (the poor ones). Reportedly, however, some of them had the unfortunate practice of assassinating Western Catholic-Christian bishops addicted to aristocratic opulence and power. Francis purified that already existing mendicant model by promoting non-violence and peace. His purified peaceful model then flourished, while the violent model did not.

A late modern deficiency appears within some contemporary Catholic-Christian lay movements when their leaders pursue only a one-sided 'conservative' strategy of premodern *restoration,* or a one-sided 'progressive' strategy of modern *integration*, rather than a holistic ecological strategy of postmodern *regeneration*.[12]

---

[12] For an earlier and preliminary exploration of these three strategies of restoration, modernization, and regeneration, see Anne Barsanti & Joe Holland, AMERICAN AND CATHOLIC: THE NEW DEBATE (Pillar Books, 1987).

When that happens, such leaders become partially trapped in one or the other poles of the *tragic late modern polarization*. They become at least partially trapped either within the reactionary late-modern restoration strategy, or within the disintegrating late-modern integration strategy. When that happens, members at both dysfunctional poles can easily slide into fear, resentment, and even hatred toward those following the other partially dysfunctional pole. Such bitter polarization then becomes the opposite of Jesus' call to unity in love.

Further, there is also a problem in the way that many new postmodern lay movements celebrate the sacred lay spiritual co-creativity expressed through family, work, and citizenship. In so doing, they rightfully become counter-cultural in relation to the collapsing late modern bourgeois model of civilization. Yet they often become counter-cultural only in a one-sided manner. While counter-culturally criticizing one pole of degenerative late-modern bourgeois consciousness, they can remain imprisoned within its opposite pole.

Thus, for Western Catholic-Christian movements on the so-called 'conservative' side, their counter-cultural spiritual energy appears typically devoted to challenging the psychologically oriented *expressive individualism* of late modern bourgeois culture, and especially in the psycho-sexual area. This 'conservative' side criticizes what Robert Bellah and his colleagues, in their sociological classic HABITS OF THE HEART, have called Modernity's "*therapeutic ethos*."[13]

Meanwhile, for Western Catholic-Christian movements on the 'progressive' side, their counter-cultural energy appears typically devoted to challenging the technologically oriented *instrumental individualism* of the late modern bourgeois political economy. This 'progressive' side criticizes what Robert Bellah and his colleagues in HABITS OF THE HEART have called Modernity's "*managerial ethos*."

---

[13] See again Robert Bellah *et al.* HABITS OF THE HEART.

As a result, across Western Catholic Christianity, these 'conservative' and 'progressive' one-sided limitations often prevent Catholic-Christian lay movements from becoming fully postmodern, and from fully serving the regeneration of life's integral ecology.

In rejecting bourgeois Modernity's psychologically oriented expressive individualism, the late modern 'conservative' wing emphasizes subordination of the psychological self to disciplined institutional structures and traditions. It is therefore more effective at organizing power on an institutional basis within both church and society. Yet, since the 'conservative' wing typically lacks a prophetic critique of technologically oriented instrumental individualism, it tends to resist Catholic Social Teaching's sociological and ecological critiques of Liberal Capitalism.

In contrast, the late modern 'progressive' wing, while rejecting technologically oriented instrumental individualism, often lacks the skills of structural discipline and frequently fails to organize successfully on an institutional basis within both church and society. Further, because it is more sympathetic to the psycho-sexual dimension of expressive individualism, it often downplays bioethical issues like abortion, embryonic stem-cell research, and euthanasia, even while it remains strong in defense of the poor, peace, and ecology. As a result, although supporting the sociological and ecological critiques of Liberal Capitalism by Catholic Social Teaching, it often fails to engage with the concerns of Catholic Bio-Ethics.

Thus, while many Western Catholic-Christian lay movements appear to be counter-culturally prophetic, many nonetheless limit their counter-cultural critique to only one side or the other of late modern bourgeois breakdown. As a result, each one-sided partiality of the emerging postmodern lay Catholic-Christian wave carries a *residual late modern bourgeois limitation,* which is either 'conservative' or 'progressive.'

Yet again, as a result of these late modern bourgeois limitations, some followers of either strategy collapse into fear, resentment, and hatred toward the other side, rather than opening in loving dialogue to hope, compassion, and joy. Those who cultivate such polarization tragically abandon Jesus' Gospel of love. They block the Holy Spirit's postmodern call for prophetic-mystical regeneration of life's integral ecology.

Two Equal & Co-Creative Images
of the Divine Mystery

At the *deep mythic-symbolic level*, many late modern Western Catholic-Christian proponents of either the 'conservative' restoration strategy or the 'progressive' integration strategy sometimes seem tempted to celebrate only one side of what GENESIS 1:27 teaches us are the two equal images of the Divine Mystery.

The 'conservative' side of the current late modern Western societal and ecclesial polarization typically celebrates *the Classical Era's masculine transcendent symbols of the Divine Mystery*. But it typically forgets *the Primal Era's feminine immanent symbols of the Divine Mystery*, which still flourish within the profound consciousness of the Holy Spirit across the Eastern Orthodox and Eastern Catholic Churches.[14] That 'conservative' one-sided strategy then often pursues one-sided and misguided psychological and sociological tactics.

- *Psychologically*, the 'conservative' side often holds up against Modernity's expressive individualism a reactionary attempt at resistance by retrieving *deformed hierarchical-patriarchal symbols* from classical European aristocratic culture. Indeed, the classical deformed-masculine aristocratic-patriarchal metaphor of "hierarchy" is still widely used as a name for the Catholic bishops. Yet we do not find that metaphor in the New Testament, since it expresses the reverse of Jesus's preaching about humble servant-leadership.

---

[14] Again, for more on the Primal, Classical, Modern, and Postmodern Eras in the human journey, including their spiritual forms, see my forthcoming book from Pacem in Terris Press, SOCIAL ANALYSIS II – END OF THE MODERN WORLD.

- *Sociologically*, the 'conservative' side often supports – again, contrary to Catholic Social Ethics – the modern materialist ideology of Liberal Capitalism, with its underlying *deformed hyper-masculine symbols* from modern bourgeois culture. In so doing, the 'conservative side often rejects social-welfare functions for the state, despite Saint John XXIII's important declaration in MATER ET MAGISTRA that such examples of "socialization" are praised by Catholic Social Teaching.[15]

Both tactics – one psychological as well as classical and patriarchal-hierarchical, and the other sociological as well as modern and hyper-masculine – draw on dysfunctional distortions of the masculine symbol-system.

In addition, and in a distorted and even pathological masculine manner, some lay Catholic-Christian 'conservatives' within the United States have even embraced the destructive call for *constant warfare,* and for dramatic increases in funding for the national-security function of the state with its growing "military-industrial complex," all of which Catholic Social Teaching critiques. Such a call for constant military warfare represents a pathological spiritual deformation of the noble-warrior tradition.

Further, such 'conservative' calls are often joined with calls for constant "cultural warfare." That warring spirit then poisons the spirituality of its proponents with the hyper-masculine and culturally militarist infection of the late nineteenth-century Prussian *Kulturkampf* (meaning "culture-struggle").

Meanwhile, the 'progressive' side of the late modern Western societal-ecclesial polarization often creatively retrieves the Primal Era's feminine immanent image of God. By so doing, the 'progressive' side chal-

---

[15] Recall also the prophetic teachings of the Hebrew Scriptures that the king should be the defender of orphans and widows. When the king abandons that role, he becomes idolatrous.

lenges the one-sided hegemony of the distorted and dysfunctional masculine symbol-system held up by many 'conservative' movements. Yet the 'progressive' side is often tempted to forget the deep-masculine symbol of the Divine Mystery as "Father."

Paradoxically, many on the 'progressive' side also often ignore or even reject the powerful Pentecostal movement still expanding across global Christianity. Yet currently, as the most dynamic global form of Christianity, Pentecostalism is spreading rapidly across planet Earth. Perhaps the reason for such dramatic growth is that the Pentecostal movement reveals at the deep-symbolic level the charismatic power of Holy Spirit as the feminine image of the Divine Mystery.

In addition and as mentioned, many on the 'progressive' side typically downplay importance for defense of the life of unborn humans, including embryonic human life, as well as defense of life for elderly and handicapped persons threatened by euthanasia. In so doing, they downplay Catholic Bio-Ethics. Similarly, many 'progressives' also appear to be unaware of the continuing bioethical threat of Eugenics, including from movements supporting bio-engineering of human nature (as with "Posthumanism" and "Transhumanism").

In contrast to these mirror-opposite partialities, this book proposes that the Holy Spirit is revealing the feminine symbolic face of the Divine Mystery, and is calling Catholic-Christians, as well as all Christians, and indeed the entire human family, to become open to the fullness of authentic postmodern spiritual energy. According to the vision proposed here, this spiritual energy celebrates *the egalitarian and co-creative partnership of the feminine and masculine symbols of the Divine Mystery.*

According to the vision of this book, the Holy Spirit is calling us to leave behind the classically aristocratic-patriarchal distortion of authority as elite male hierarchical domination. She is also calling us to leave behind the modern bourgeois hyper-masculine distortion of authority as elite male uprooting and fragmenting managerial manipulation. She is thus calling us to resist the spiritual deformation from both sides of the late modern societal-ecclesial polarization, and instead to synthesize the authentic spiritual gifts of both sides.

The deep solution to what Guardini called "The End of the Modern World" cannot be simply to restore classical hierarchical-patriarchal discipline and order on the turbulent surface of late modern bourgeois society's integral-ecological degeneration. Neither can it be to continue to lose spiritual energy within the degenerative secularization and nihilization of late modern bourgeois Materialism.

Rather, holistic regeneration of the creative communion of the life's integral ecology requires re-awakening to the sacred character of the Cosmos, to the sacred character of our garden-planet Earth, to the sacred character of all of Earth's life, and especially to the sacred character of our human family's egalitarian and co-creative partnership between women and men.

Again, this book proposes that the Holy Spirit is calling postmodern Catholic-Christian lay movements, from both 'conservative' and 'progressive' sides, as well as "religious communities" and "clerical" bishops, presbyters, and deacons, to resist the late modern societal-ecclesial polarization. That polarization spreads the demonic infections of fear, resentment, and even hatred on both 'conservative' and 'progressive' sides. It undermines both the postmodern societal common good and postmodern ecclesial evangelization.

The ultimate loser in the late modern polarized divorce between Western Catholic Christianity's 'conservative' and 'progressive' wings is postmodern evangelization. A Church sinfully wounded by internal division cannot be credible as the carrier of regenerative healing to late modern polarized society. Its own festering and sinful wound of polarization blocks its regenerative communication of the Good News as healing and joyful love. Thus, the current 'conservative' versus 'progressive' polarization undermines the loving truth of Jesus' Gospel of life. That is why, at the Last Supper, Jesus prayed to the Father: "that they may be one in us, that the world may believe." (John 17:21b).

Let us hope and pray that postmodern ecological development of Catholic-Christian lay movements, along with postmodern ecological refounding of some Catholic-Christian "apostolic" communities, will lead to a co-creative partnership of solidarity seeking a regenerative conservative-progressive synthesis. Surely, the distinctly 'progressive' and 'conservative' emphases in spirituality need not be hostile opposites. Surely, there must be a creative path for their loving embrace in a fruitful life-generating manner.

Let us hope and pray that we will all hear the call of the Holy Spirit urging us to join together to seek regeneration for the evolving creative communion of life's integral ecology, throughout its interwoven natural, human, and spiritual fabric, across our loving Creator's beloved garden-planet Earth.

AWAKENING TO
POSTMODERN ECOLOGICAL SPIRITUALITY

As we are journey through the spiritual "Dark Night" of Modern Industrial Civilization, we are called to awaken to the Holy Spirit's loving invitation to embrace Postmodern Ecological Spirituality. In that awakening, we are called to long prayerfully for the regenerative "Dawn" of Postmodern Ecological Civilization.

Again, as we have learned from recent discoveries in Science, our mystical Cosmos (and everything within it) is not simply being sustained. Rather, it is all still *evolving ecologically*. Hence, our emerging postmodern eco-spiritual consciousness realizes that our loving Creator is still lovingly continuing to create our mystical Cosmos. Further, within our evolving and mystical Cosmos, all of our loving Creators' beloved creatures are co-creatively contributing to the evolving cosmic expression of our loving Creator's Divine Creativity.

Wherever prayerful longing for global ecological regeneration arises, the living waters of Postmodern Ecological Spirituality are already beginning to flow – though so far only as a small and often unnoticed stream, and not yet as a great flowing river. Even so, when we drink from *its life-giving waters,* we become prophetically and mystically refreshed, so that we may seek regenerative pathways out of the late modern global degeneration of the sacred creative communion of life's integral ecology.

For that reason, this book urges both newer Catholic-Christian lay movements and older Catholic-Christian "religious" movements, as well as "clerical" deacons, presbyters, and bishops, and indeed the entire global Christian family, to listen prayerfully to the Holy Spirit's loving invitation to drink from the living and regenerative waters of the emerging Postmodern Ecological Spirituality.

Again, this means awakening – both mystically and prophetically – to our deep spiritual grounding in the sacred and still evolving co-creativity of the Cosmos, to our deep spiritual grounding in the sacred and still evolving co-creativity of Earth's planetary ecosystem, and to our sacred and still evolving grounding in our human family's co-creativity within Earth's biosphere.

Most importantly, in Christian form it means re-awakening – again, both mystically and prophetically – to the Sacred Trinity's loving co-creativity. That is the ultimate source and goal of the sacred creative communion of life's still evolving integral ecology within our sacred and still evolving mystical Cosmos.

In addition, through this awakening, mystical-prophetic streams within the late modern Western Christian Churches, both Protestant and Catholic, are now beginning to learn again from the rich and ancient Christian cosmic spiritual tradition that the Eastern Christian Churches, both Orthodox and Catholic, have constantly celebrated through songs of praise and thanksgiving to our loving Creator. Ancient Eastern Christian liturgies constantly and beautifully sing joyful songs of praise and thanksgiving in gratitude for the beauty and goodness of our loving Creator's beloved creation.

Again, this book proposes that the Holy Spirit is urgently inviting all Christian churches across planet Earth – Orthodox and Protestant and Catholic, East and West and North and South – to further develop the ancient Christian cosmic spiritual consciousness,. In that development, we need to celebrate in prayerful and joyous song our still evolving and sacred cosmic creation as the *primary revelation* of the beauty, goodness, and truth of our loving Creator.

So full of goodness and beauty and truth is our loving Creator's sacred creation that ancient theologians like Saint Augustine of Hippo called the "*Book of Nature*" the first book of divine revelation. This first book of revelation needs to be read as the horizon and ground for our loving Creator's second book of revelation, which is of course the Bible.

Again, some mystical-prophetic individuals and communities within the Western Christian churches are already drinking deeply from the Holy Spirit's regenerative waters of the emerging Postmodern Ecological Spirituality. These individuals and communities are already awakening to the evolutionary creative communion of life's integral ecology, which is revealed throughout the co-creative evolution of our loving Creator's vast and majestic Cosmos.

Yet the Holy Spirit's Postmodern Ecological Spirituality has not yet found a comprehensive and integrated understanding within the Western Christian churches. So how can we help to develop such a profound mystical-prophetic consciousness, and (for this book's purposes) especially within Catholic Christianity? It is that question which the remaining chapters try to address.

8

REFOUNDING "RELIGIOUS LIFE"
AS LAY ECOLOGICAL REGENERATION

A s new Catholic-Christian lay movements emerge and grow, not only does the question arise of how will they develop, but also the question of how older movements of "religious life," particularly modern "apostolic" forms, will relate to the new development. Will the new lay movements simply retreat into the sterile strategy of "restoration"? And will modern "apostolic religious movements" simple retreat to the margins of history with little hope for an influential future?

Or might both join hands in co-creative response to the late modern breakdown of the now globalized form of Modern Industrial Civilization? Might both join hands to co-creatively seek the guidance of the Holy Spirit in nurturing the emerging seeds of Postmodern Ecological Spirituality and of a fresh Postmodern Ecological Civilization?

In response to these questions, this book proposes that the Holy Spirit is calling both older and newer Catholic-Christian mystical-prophetic communities, one lay and the other "religious," as well as the wider Catholic-Christian communion of Churches, the wider Christian family, and indeed our entire human family, to seek deep grounding in Postmodern Ecological Spirituality. Further, this book proposes that the Holy Spirit is calling us to do so in a way that synthesizes the prior authentic gifts of Christian and wider human spiritualities.

INCOMPLETE LATE MODERN TRANSFORMATION
OF LAY & RELIGIOUS MOVEMENTS

As we have seen, Western Catholic-Christian commitment to ecological ethics and the beginnings of an ecological spirituality seem to be found more in the 'progressive' behavior of some 'progressive' "apostolic-religious" communities, especially some women's communities. In addition, as we have also seen, some women in these "religious communities" have been creatively retrieving the Primal Era's *spirituality of feminine immanence*. As stated earlier, this ancient spirituality cherishes the feminine image of the Divine Mystery as announced in GENESIS 1:27.

By contrast, many emerging postmodern Catholic-Christian new lay movements on the 'conservative' side do not yet seem to have developed an ecological ethics or spirituality. Rather, many appear to cultivate only a human-oriented ethics and spirituality uprooted from ecology. Further, and as noted, some in the still early wave of these new lay movements even defend the Classical Era's problematic aristocratic spirituality of defining transcendence as hierarchical and patriarchal.

As a result, it sometimes seems as if 'conservative' sectors of the postmodern new lay movements, by virtue of their lay nature, are creating postmodern organizational structures, but simultaneously attempt to restore classical spiritual consciousness. Meanwhile, it also sometimes seems as if sectors in the 'progressive' "religious" communities are exploring postmodern ecological-spiritual consciousness, but simultaneously clinging to classical organizational structures. Perhaps this contrast is the Holy Spirit's way of provoking dialogue between new and old waves. So important is this contrast that we need to reflect further on it.

Some "apostolic-religious" communities appear to be trying to become more relevant to the modern "secular" world. Yet this attempt paradoxically does not fully open their "religious" structures at an equal level to "secular" lay membership, which would include both sexes, singles and marrieds, and children. At the same time, with equal paradox, some new lay movements (as noted) seem to be yearning nostalgically for a restoration of the authoritarian hierarchical-patriarchal values of classical aristocratic male understanding transcendence, even while they retrieve of the egalitarian lay identity of the original Jesus-movement.

In both cases, we have the double paradox of some "religious" 'progressives' clinging to a classically dualist organizational structure while pursuing holistic postmodern eco-spiritual consciousness, and some lay 'conservatives' creating a holistic postmodern organizational structure while restoring classically dualist hierarchical-patriarchal consciousness. Lurking somewhere in the future, there is hopefully a *co-creative 'conservative-progressive' synthesis* that will integrate postmodern holistic consciousness and postmodern holistic structures, and also integrate the emerging Catholic-Christian Postmodern Ecological Spirituality with older Catholic-Christian spiritual traditions.

In response to the above paradox, this book proposes that some modern "apostolic-religious" forms of Catholic-Christian mystical-prophetic communities" consider linking with the postmodern lay spiritual energy. The birth of postmodern lay spiritual energy would thus provide the opportunity for an *ecological and lay-oriented refounding* by some modern "apostolic-religious" communities, if the Holy Spirit indeed is calling those communities to such a challenging path.

In a moment, we will reflect more on such refounding. But first let us look at three competing historical-strategic paths, as institutional choices available to modern "apostolic-religious" communities facing decline and in some cases even death.

THREE COMPETING STRATEGIC PATHS
FOR APOSTOLIC-RELIGIOUS COMMUNITIES

Within the modern-to-postmodern transition, I propose that *three distinct strategic paths* are available to declining modern Western "apostolic religious" communities within 'advanced' industrial societies. Each of these three strategic paths is legitimate, and the choice of one or another belongs only to the communities themselves in their discernment of the Holy Spirit's call.

Path I
Survival by Premodern Restoration

Path I faithfully continues the original mission of the founder of a "religious" community, and it preserves certain cultural artifacts from its original style – for example, a "religious habit." While within the 'advanced' industrial world some of the "apostolic-religious" communities which follow that path may perish, others will survive and may even grow modestly by attracting new 'conservative' members.

Yet such surviving institutions will become less central in Catholic-Christianity's emerging postmodern lay ecological strategy. They will not provide transformative mystical-prophetic leadership for the emerging Postmodern Ecological Era. Even so, their spiritual gifts will remain important. Again, the 'conservative' path will always remain a legitimate option that we need to cherish. The "apostolic-religious" communities which chose this path will continue to play a secondary role, just as coenobitical, monastic, and mendicant communities continued on a smaller scale beyond their age of historical dominance.

Path II
Ambiguity from Late Modern Integration

Path II positions itself ambiguously between premodern restoration and postmodern regeneration. It appears that this path of ambiguity is a common one for many "apostolic-religious" communities presently in decline within the 'advanced' industrial-center countries. Because this path appears so common, it may be helpful to reflect soon at some length on two dimensions of its ambiguity, with one on the external side of "apostolates" to the "secular world," and the other on the internal side of "religious" spirituality and structure. In a moment, we will examine this ambiguity in greater detail. But, first, let us identify the third path of refounding, which this book sees as the most fruitful one.

Path III
Refounding as Postmodern Regeneration

Path III explores a refounding alliance with, and partial embrace of, the postmodern lay ecological form and spirituality. In earlier stages of the tradition, some hermits became partial "monastics" ("cenobites"), as later some monastics became partial "mendicants," and still later as some mendicants became partial "apostolics." In such an alliance, some modern "apostolic" communities may embrace, at least partially, the new postmodern lay form and spirituality. Experiments in this embrace could become vital for the Western Church's postmodern regeneration.

Later in this chapter, we will explore further this postmodern path of refounding. Before doing so, however, let us first explore a bit more the problematic strategy of ambiguity.

REFLECTIONS ON LATE MODERN PATH
OF STRATEGIC AMBIGUITY

Again, there are two sides to this ambiguity, one on the external side of "apostolates" to the "secular world," and the other on the internal side of "religious" spirituality and structure.

Integration of External "Religious Apostolates"
with Neoliberal Corporate Capitalism

First, there is the problem of ambiguity on the side of external "apostolates." One example of this occurs when some "religious communities" sponsoring Catholic-Christian hospitals allow their hospitals to imitate for-profit secular hospitals in the neoliberal 'Free-Market' fantasy by blocking their own employees from organizing themselves into a democratic union.

When that happens, such "apostolates" accept the currently unjust model of the *neoliberal corporate-capitalist healthcare system,* which carries the same fundamental philosophical errors as the dominant modern Western bourgeois cosmological paradigm of Scientific Materialism for Philosophy and Science.

Such unfortunate developments may be called the "neoliberal capitalist corporatization" of some late modern "religious apostolates" for healthcare ministry. In such cases, their "apostolates" are *integrating with neoliberal secular modernization.* When that strategy is chosen, it is usually the result of the "religious" community having turned institutional guidance for the "apostolate" over to presumably well-meaning lay trustees and administrators, who are often recruited from the leadership of 'Free-Market' capitalist corporations.

Such developments, however, can block the Holy Spirit from opening the prophetic imagination of sponsoring "apostolic-religious" communities to explore authentically postmodern co-creativity in healthcare. Authentic postmodern exploration in healthcare needs to be grounded in the emerging postmodern ecological paradigm of Cosmology for Philosophy and Science.

But that ecological paradigm is generally unknown to the presumably well-meaning neoliberal corporate-capitalist elites typically serving as trustees and administrators for Catholic healthcare institutions. Knowledge of the ecological paradigm is also not generally found within most members of the contemporary medical profession, since the academic teaching of Biology still remains largely imprisoned within the modern cosmological paradigm of Scientific Materialism.

When some "religious communities" sponsoring Catholic healthcare "apostolates" pursue neoliberal corporate-capitalist integration, they probably will not attract young candidates who are searching for a postmodern ecological future. Nor will they probably attract young candidates who seek to preserve traditional values from the classical past. As a result, recruitment of new members for such "religious communities" will probably fail because of the late modern ambiguity.

A similar case occurs when some "religious communities" sponsoring Catholic-Christian universities allow their schools to become both organizationally and academically like late modern "secular" universities. These too are increasingly being "corporatized" by presumably well-meaning business-based trustees and administrators, who typically follow the late modern neoliberal capitalist model, and who often implicitly accept that ideology's underlying Cosmology of Scientific Materialism.

Despite having a chaplain, a chapel, and a Theology program, such Catholic-Christian universities can often fail to explore *across all academic disciplines and in their institutional life* the Holy Spirit's countercultural call to challenge the late modern bourgeois intellectual-spiritual degeneration of truth and wisdom, and the wider late modern bourgeois economic-technological devastation of life's integral ecology.

Instead, they can often collapse into the dysfunctional posture of so many late modern institutions operating within the now globalized stage of Modern Industrial Civilization. In that collapse, they can often allow (no doubt unconsciously, but nonetheless relentlessly) their non-theological curricula to teach the secularist, relativist, and sometimes even nihilist doctrines of the late modern Western intellectual-spiritual breakdown.

In addition, some Catholic-Christian schools, like their parallel Catholic-Christian healthcare institutions, often resist by managerial and legal means the desire of many of their employees to form themselves into a democratic union. Acting in the manipulative manner that Robert Bellah and his colleagues have called the "managerial ethos" of "instrumental individualism," those business-based trustees and senior managers can often in effect deny both the truth and the justice of the human right of employees to organize themselves into a democratic union.

Further, they can then frequently define such employee's unions as "outside third-parties," which denies that a union is a democratic organization of the employees themselves. They can then often hypocritically hire outside law-firms and management consultants (in fact, highly expensive "third parties") to lead them in an immoral battle against the truth and justice of the human rights of their own employees.

In such cases, by pursuing the *integrating strategy of neoliberal corporate capitalist integration*, such trustees and senior management of such universities can often unconsciously block the Holy Spirit from opening their hearts and minds to explore regenerative postmodern co-creativity in education.

Again, such a postmodern exploration would need to be grounded not in the dominant and degenerative intellectual legacy of Scientific Materialism, but rather in the regenerative vision of the Postmodern Ecological Cosmology and in the regenerative energy of Postmodern Ecological Spirituality.

In both cases, one for healthcare and the other for education, some trustees and senior administrators of some Catholic-Christian institutions can sometimes cruelly reject Catholic Social Teaching's indisputable support for the human right of employees to form themselves into a democratic union.

Whenever they make such a rejection, such trustees and senior managers would commit *an objective social sin* against the regenerative inspiration of the Holy Spirit and against the life-giving Gospel of Jesus. When that happens, we might describe their tragic situation as the late modern "bourgeois captivity" of so many trustees and senior administrators of Catholic-Christian educational and healthcare "apostolates."

Perpetuation of Internal Spiritual-Structural Dualism

The other side of the late modern path of ambiguity for some "religious communities" is internal. It can often be found in the *dualistic spirituality* that typically undergirds the *dualistic organizational structure*. This second problematic of modernizing ambiguity can occur even though some "apostolic communities" try to become more "relevant" to Modernity by adopting "secular" dress, by being more active in "the world," and even by embracing postmodern ecological consciousness.

The ambiguity can arise because some "religious communities," despite trying to be externally relevant, do not transform their internal dualist spirituality, which is expressed in its internal dualist structure. That means that such "religious community" do not grow beyond Modern Psychological Spirituality, or beyond what may be called the institutional structure of a "religious" mono-sexual monopoly.

In so doing, such a community continues to exclude from core membership one sex, as well as married people and children. Again, in such cases the members are adopting 'progressive' consciousness, yet preserving a 'conservative' spirituality and structure. They are thereby not opening themselves fully to the Holy Spirit's call to explore postmodern lay possibilities.

Again, the problem here can be that the path's mixed message impedes recruitment. Those who are attracted to the 'progressive' consciousness of the community's behavior may not be drawn to its 'conservative' structure. Those who are attracted to its 'conservative' structure may not be drawn to its 'progressive' consciousness. As a result, the path of ambiguity may lead to a community's decline, and for some even death. Yet, in the mystery of our loving Creator's Divine Providence, life-giving creativity still arises even out of such a loss.

ECOLOGICAL REFOUNDING THROUGH
ISLANDS OF REGENERATIVE CO-CREATIVITY

Within the strategic framework of Path III, what might be the regenerative path of deep transformation for re-founding an "apostolic religious community" on Postmodern Ecological Spirituality and the postmodern lay ecological-spiritual model, while maintaining living roots in past traditions?

The New Zealand Marist priest and anthropologist Gerald Arbuckle has argued that re-founding requires embracing the myth of regeneration by entering into a *death-life cycle of transformation*. According to Arbuckle, this cycle entails three stages.[1]

- *Foundation.* This is the original stage of *birth and growth*, flowing directly from the founder's original spiritual energy and with the founder's original vision, mission, and structure.

- *Crisis.* Later, there comes the stage of *decline and chaos*, which so many "apostolic-religious" communities have now experienced within 'advanced' industrial societies (beginning in the closing decades of the twentieth century). Institutionally, this represents for those institutions their spiritual "Dark Night." Yet this "Dark Night" can also become the dark womb of regenerative creativity. From within that dark womb, there can grow renewed life.

- *Regeneration.* If there is *new birth*, then the community enters into regeneration, fed by a transformed vision, mission, and structure. Today, I have proposed, this means embracing the postmodern lay ecological form of spirituality and membership structure.

---

[1] See Gerald Arbuckle, STRATEGIES FOR GROWTH IN RELIGIOUS LIFE (Alba House, 1986). See also his OUT OF CHAOS: REFOUNDING RELIGIOUS CONGREGATIONS (Paulist Press, 1988), and FROM CHAOS TO MISSION: REFOUNDING RELIGIOUS LIFE FORMATION (Liturgical Press, 1997)

Yet regeneration requires *new founders*. The transformed vision, mission, and structure will not first come from committees or chapters. Rather, as Gerald Arbuckle and also Mary Jo Leddy have both proposed, it will first appear in visionary individuals.[2] If "religious communities" wish to pursue the path of postmodern transformation, they first need to discern the identity of their re-founding persons.

Communities pursing the path of postmodern regeneration could then support re-founding persons in what might be called "*islands of regenerative co-creativity.*" These could be small experiments in lay-centered ways of integral-ecological living as a postmodern Catholic Christian mystical-prophetic community, outside the main structure of the traditional institutions yet in close dialogue with those institutions. Such islands of co-creativity would use cooperative capital and ecological technologies, and they would be guided by the egalitarian partnership of both feminine and masculine spiritual energies.

Such islands of regenerative co-creativity could gather women and men, singles and marrieds, and children as well, in *experimental ecovillages* for a return to ecological communion with our wounded Earth, to social communion with the marginalized poor, and to spiritual communion with the Divine Mystery as revealed in Nature.[3]

Further, these islands of regenerative co-creativity could ground themselves in natural, human, and spiritual ecology, in a spirit of extended family, and in a spirituality of the co-creativity of the feminine and masculine faces of the Divine Mystery. They could thus provide a life-

---

[2] See Mary Jo Leddy, REWEAVING RELIGIOUS LIFE: BEYOND THE LIBERAL MODEL (Twenty Third Publications, 1990).

[3] For more on ecovillages, see the next chapter. Such ecovillages, however, should not been conceived as stand-alone projects, but rather as experimental centers of postmodern ecological vision and spiritual energy humbly serving the regeneration of rural life in the surrounding bioregion. For more on this wider regional regeneration of rural life, see the brilliant and pioneering book by Anthony Flaccavento, BUILDING A HEALTHY ECONOMY FROM THE BOTTOM UP: HARNESSING REAL-WORLD EXPERIENCE FOR TRANSFORMATIVE CHANGE (University of Kentucky Press, 2016).

bearing sacramental sign for regeneration of the sacred creative communion of life's integral ecology. Further,, these islands of regenerative co-creativity could seek to heal what Saint John Paul II called the "culture of death"[4]

Such islands of regenerative creativity could build bridges between their new experiments and the older community's traditional institutions – bridges of mutual sharing and dialogue. Over time, and as a result of dialogue between the two poles, traditional "religious" institutions could begin to be transformed into postmodern institutional forms serving regeneration of life's integral ecology.

Such transformed institutions could give witness to the the regenerative power of the Holy Spirit and life-giving Gospel of Jesus for our wider society. They could show how we can all together regenerate the sacred and evolving creative communion of life throughout its interwoven natural, human, and spiritual fabric. Such transformed institutions could then become witnessing places where Earth is healed, where families are healed, and where the deep psychological wounds of the late modern individuals are healed – all in the warm embrace of the Holy Spirit.

In service of that mission, such postmodern islands of creativity could seek to become pioneering Catholic-Christian mystical-prophetic servants of the regeneration of life's evolving integral ecology. They could humbly seek to serve our loving Creator's beloved family of creatures, including our loving Creator's beloved human family.

ECOLOGICAL REVISION OF VOWS
AS SPIRITUAL PROMISES OF REGENERATION

Let us now explore the question of how might the traditional "religious vows" of *poverty, chastity, and obedience* become regenerated for "reli-

---

[4]Again, John Paul used this phrase in EVANGELIUM VITAE, Par. 12.

gious communities" that chose to seek refounding through the lay transformation of Postmodern Ecological Spirituality?

As part of addressing this question, let us now in a lay style rename these "religious vows" as "spiritual promises." But then what might these spiritual promises mean? To answer this question, we need to be guided by the *deep spiritual mission* of regenerative postmodern mystical-prophetic communities. Once again, the proposed deep spiritual mission of postmodern global lay communities is as follows:

> *The Holy Spirit is now calling us, both personally and institutionally, to embody and to preach the Good News of Jesus in and through holistic regeneration of the evolving creative communion of life's integral ecology, throughout its interwoven natural, human, and spiritual fabric, across our loving Creator's beloved garden-planet Earth.*

That also implies helping to create a Postmodern Ecological Civilization, which will serve the regeneration of life's integral ecology at every level from the womb to the planet. In this way, such regenerative communities would provide a life-giving regenerative alternative to what Saint John Paul II called the late modern "culture of death."

Postmodern Spiritual Promise of Poverty

In the postmodern lay ecological-spiritual refounding, the spiritual promise of poverty would not mean contempt for material creation, but rather the loving embrace of it. In this sense, poverty would mean owning few things, yet belonging in relationship to everything. In imitating the lilies of the field and the birds of the air, those making this promise would seek to become more consciously united with all of life on our garden-planet Earth.

This loving embrace would not be possessive, for the desire to expand controlling ownership has produced the *modern active-aggressive bourgeois-technological plundering of the material world*. That modern plundering is the mirror-opposite of the *classical passive-aggressive aristocratic-ascetical despising of the material world*. It is also the modern anti-ecological outcome of that classical anti-material despising.

Again, the classical aristocratic-ascetical contempt for matter and the modern bourgeois-technological addiction to its plunder are sequential anti-spiritual rejections of our loving Creator's self-revelation in and through the beauty and goodness of creation. The final result of modern consumerist Materialism is not love of matter, but rather its *integral-ecological devastation*.

Again, the loving embrace of material creation would be neither an act of contemptuous rejection nor one of possessive control. It would be a conscious expression of *loving communion* with all the species (including our human species) within our garden-planet Earth, and with the entire Cosmos. It would mean celebrating our rooted and relational participation in material creation, while being free of the desire to "subdue" it.[5]

Such a postmodern spiritual promise of poverty would be grounded in the theological affirmation that all material creation constitutes the "primary revelation," as Thomas Berry reminded us concerning the first and fundamental disclosure of the Divine Mystery in and through Nature.[6] Also and again, another and ancient way of expressing this truth is Saint Augustine's classical teaching that the "Book of Nature" is the first book of Divine revelation.

---

[5] The translation into English as "subdue" from the original Hebrew word in GENESIS 1:28, may be the result of subsequent patriarchal interpretations of early Hebrew narratives. One does not "subdue" a garden (Garden of Eden). Rather, one cares for it. See David K. Goodin, "Understanding Humankind's Role in Creation: Alternative Exegesis on the Hebrew Word *Kabash* and the Command to Subdue the Earth," STUDIES IN SCIENCE AND THEOLOGY, Vol. 10: STREAMS OF WISDOM? SCIENCE, THEOLOGY, AND CULTURAL DYNAMICS, ed. Hubert Meisinger, William B. Drees, and Zbigniew Liana (Lund, Sweden: Lund University Press, 2005), pp. 293-311.

[6] See Thomas Berry & Mary Evelyn Tucker, THE SACRED UNIVERSE: EARTH, SPIRITUALITY, AND RELIGION IN THE TWENTY-FIRST CENTURY (Columbia University Press, 2009).

This postmodern spiritual promise of poverty rejects the classical spiritual "*fuga mundi*" (flight from the world). For this postmodern promise, material creation becomes the *foundational natural sacrament*, the first and fundamental expression of the Creator's loving *Logos* and *Eros*, revealed in the beauteous Cosmos of evolution's creative communion.

This postmodern spiritual promise of poverty would require a life-long commitment to the regeneration of life's integral ecology, throughout its interwoven natural, human, and spiritual fabric, across our loving Creator's beloved garden-planet Earth. Those who make this commitment would also commit themselves to feeling deeply the pain of the late modern degeneration of life's integral ecology, and to feel it as spiritual pain.

In addition, they would promise to devote themselves, both personally and institutionally, to the regenerative healing of the deep ecological wounds increasingly inflicted on our loving Creator's beloved garden-planet Earth and on our loving Creator's beloved and myriad creatures of Earth, including our loving Creator's beloved human family.

This postmodern spiritual promise of poverty would also mean a life-long commitment to the solidarity of human ecology with people who are poor, to defense of the special dignity human life at every stage, including not yet born humans, and to the struggle for justice and peace everywhere.

The promisors would try to live in close life-style and friendship with people who suffer from oppressive poverty – partly out of humble compassion, yet also out of the desire to learn from the profound traditional wisdom of many marginalized communities. Especially important for this commitment would be learning from *the rich wisdom-traditions of Indigenous Peoples,* many of who have remained close to our human family's ancient roots. For these peoples are living heirs to our human family's ancient and healing eco-spiritual resources.

In such transformed postmodern Catholic-Christian mystical-prophetic communities, both single and married people would make the spiritual promise of poverty. In turn, the work of the members, many of whom would presumably be engaged in "secular" employment and not necessarily in church "ministries," could generate funds for the community.

Further, this promise, in terms of belonging to a particular community, could be for a lifetime or for a limited term, and so it would not be absolute. For such belonging is not a sacrament. As Jesus told his critics, the Creator made the Sabbath for humans, not humans for the Sabbath.

In sum, the postmodern promise of poverty would be a spiritual affirmation of the sacred and evolving integral-ecological life of our loving Creator's beloved creation. It would also be an act of spiritual solidarity with the regeneration of life's integral ecology, across our sacred garden-planet Earth, including the preferential option for the poor and in defense of the special dignity of human life at all stages.

Postmodern Spiritual Promise of Chastity

While the traditional vow of chastity was frequently interpreted as the Platonic goal of escaping from our human body and our sexuality, the postmodern spiritual promise of chastity would be grounded in the sacred character of our body and of our sacred sexual energy of *Eros*. Further, this postmodern promise would counter the late modern trivialization of sexuality into a means of self-gratification within the commodity-fetish of the Liberal Capitalism's consumer society.

The modern consumerist trivialization of human sexuality is the active-aggressive counterpart to the classical Platonic passive-aggressive fantasy of escaping from the body. Thus, the postmodern spiritual promise of chastity would challenge in counter-cultural form both the modern reduction of sexuality to trivial self-gratification and the classically ascetical demeaning of sexuality as anti-spiritual. Instead, it would honor sexual energy as both deep and sacred, because it carries the regenerative energy of life. The postmodern spiritual promise of chastity would oblige its promisor to reverence sexuality's sacred depth and to channel its regenerative energy into life-giving paths.

This would mean honoring our sacred body as our first and fundamental participation in the natural sacrament of the sacred Cosmos. To be cared for through diet and exercise, our sacred body would then become our first and basic means of prayer, with that prayer expressed through word and gesture as well as in song and dance, and both individually and communally. For in our body, we have our deepest personal experience of God's loving self-manifestation through creation.

As the vast majority of the human race has always recognized, the basic life-giving channeling of our body's sexual energy occurs through the primal institution of family. Yet family is more than immediate spouses and children, for it embraces kinship across time and space, including both ancestors and those not yet born. Further, in its magnanimity it embraces friends through adoptive familial bonding, as in the Latin *compadrazco* relationship.

Ultimately, there are no final human boundaries to human families, except the human race itself. Further, our wider biological relationships include not only our human family with its rich diversity of cultures, but also all of our garden-planet Earth's other creatures, whom St. Francis of Assisi called his "sisters and brothers."

This diversity embraces the plants and animals who give up their organic lives as food for our human family, and who thus provide the constantly recycling material of our living human bodies. Similarly, the water that makes up so much of our bodies is billions of years old, and remains a flowing part of the ancient yet continuing recycling of Earth's great hydrological cycle that includes clouds, oceans, rivers, and streams. Further, our extended kinship extends even to the Cosmos, for in the material of our bodies we find a gift from the carbon of exploded stars. Cosmos and Earth flow within us, and we with within Cosmos and Earth.

The spiritual promise of chastity would thus be a commitment to celebrate our bodily participation in our wider human family, in our wider family of all creatures within planet Earth, and in our vast cosmic family of creation. In addition, it would be a promise locally to help regenerative familial communities to grow, and globally to help to network these familial communities in support of the global regeneration of life's integral ecology.

Again, this postmodern spiritual promise of chastity would represent a Catholic-Christian mystical-prophetic witness against the modern trivialization of sexuality, as well as against the classical demeaning of it, by an authentically postmodern spirituality that celebrates the human body and human sexuality's co-creative life-giving energy as a profound expression of the co-creative life-giving energy of the entire Cosmos, and ultimately of its loving Creator.

Postmodern Spiritual Promise of Obedience

Late modern bourgeois society propagandizes the consumer culture's expressive individualism, and as a result it often portrays obedience with a negative image. It tends to identify obedience with authoritarianism and repression. That is partly because in the Classical Era hierarchical-patriarchal male aristocratic elites often demanded unquestioning obedience and often exercised authoritarian control over subordinates. Modern emancipatory social movements rightly rebelled against that deformation of authentic obedience. One of greatest gifts of bourgeois Modernity has been to defend the individual person as carrying an inviolable integrity of freedom.

Yet bourgeois Modernity, following the Epicurean atomism of its cosmological foundation, wrongly defined the individual as *autonomous*, that is, as free from any bonds of obligation except those of legal contracts. Then, following the ultimately non-rational voluntarism of Epicurean Philosophy, Modernity wrongly defined human freedom as *arbitrary choice*, with no substantive or spiritual meaning.[7]

For those reasons, a recovery of meaningful obedience can become a healing step toward *postmodern communitarianism*, which honors the dignity and freedom of the human person, and also understands that the human person is nested within the wider ecological community of life, at once holistically natural, human, and spiritual.

In particular, modern Anglo-American legal theory and social theory have wrongly understood the individual as preceding community, with the community supposedly formed only by contracts of autonomous individuals. In fact, the opposite is true. The individual grows out of family and its wider community, and the individual remains an organic part of the integrally ecological community of life that is at once natural, human, and spiritual.

If, however, the human person indeed becomes atomized and uprooted, as the erroneous anthropological-cosmological paradigm of Modern Philosophy and Modern Science has wrongly imagined, the human person can experience great difficulty in the search for happiness and community. Again, it is not individuals who create community, but community that creates individuals. Individuals emerge in and through relationships, beginning with family relationships and expanding through friendships and wider networks of community.

The brilliant Catholic eco-philosopher Charlene Spretnak has persuasively argued that cultivation of relationship is an especially *feminine gift*. She has also argued that women's role in recovering relationality in all aspects of life needs to become a central part of healing the devasta-

---

[7] It is perhaps not surprising that, in the movement promoting so-called "reproductive rights," the word "choice" (versus the word "life") becomes the core strategic theme.

tion of natural and social ecology by contemporary "ultra-modern" (and hyper-masculine) society.[8]

Again, the Classical Era laid an authoritarian and often repressive superstructure on the Primal Era's organic and egalitarian character of community, while the Modern Era rightfully rebelled against that repressive domination. From its emancipatory rebellion, Modernity then gave birth to the great wave of democracy that is still sweeping across planet Earth. Yet Modernity also began to uproot and fragment individual persons from the duties of legitimate communitarian obedience within the evolving creative communion of life's natural, human, and spiritual ecology.

Our postmodern task is to find regenerative integration for the rights of the human person with co-creative duties to communitarian solidarity. Regenerative obedience would seek integrating pathways that would simultaneously nurture personal integrity and communitarian solidarity. On the one hand, such pathways would avoid the Classical Era's authoritarian repression. On the other hand, they would avoid the Modern Era's uprooting fragmentation. Postmodern obedience as process would seek to synthesize person and community, while postmodern obedience as substance would seek to follow the call of holistic regeneration.

Within such a holistic communitarian style, the Catholic-Christian postmodern spiritual promise of obedience would find its deepest spiritual center in the promise to be obedient to the Holy Spirit's healing call for the regeneration of life's integral ecology, throughout its interwoven natural, human, and spiritual fabric, across our loving Creator's beloved garden-planet Earth.

Having reviewed the still emerging postmodern lay spiritual energy and its deep ecological challenge for "apostolic-religious" communities,

---

[8] See again her pioneering book mentioned earlier, RELATIONAL REALITY.

we will in the next chapter explore the regenerative and integrally eco-logical strategic program of Peter Maurin.

Peter was a prophetic lay Catholic-Christian visionary who proposed a regenerative path that would take us toward what has been called here a Postmodern Ecological Civilization. Such a civilization would include retrieving our human family's ancient and regenerative rootedness in rural life. Of course, writing during the first half of the twentieth century, Peter did not use the words "postmodern" or "ecology," since such language was not yet in vogue. But he did call for a "new society."

Peter's prophetic vision, I propose, could serve as a regenerative program of eco-spiritual refounding for Catholic-Christian "apostolic-religious" communities, for eco-spiritual deepening of Catholic-Christian new lay movements, and indeed eco-spiritual deepening of all Christians who seek to journey beyond the breakdown of Modern Industrial Civilization.

Peter's prophetic vision could help to guide us all in the local-global regeneration of the sacred creative communion of life's evolving integral ecology, throughout its interwoven natural, human, and spiritual fabric, across our loving Creator's beloved garden-planet Earth.

9

PETER MAURIN'S

NEW LAY ECOLOGICAL MONASTICISM[1]

ALASDAIR MACINTYRE'S CALL FOR
A NEW MONASTICISM

At the end of the first edition of his profound book AFTER VIRTUE, philosopher Alasdair Macintyre, a Scottish former Marxist turned Aristotelian and later Catholic-Christian Thomist, prophetically called for a new yet different Saint Benedict.

> [For] our own age in Europe and North America and the epoch in which the Roman empire declined into the Dark Ages ... certain parallels are there ... This time however the barbarians are not waiting beyond the frontiers; they have already been governing us for some time ... We are waiting not for Godot, but for another – doubtless very different – St. Benedict.[2]

Later, in his Prologue to the Third Edition of that book, Professor Macintyre continued his theme.

---

[1] An earlier version of this chapter was published as PETER MAURIN'S ECOLOGICAL LAY NEW MONASTICISM: A CATHOLIC GREEN REVOLUTION DEVELOPING RURAL ECOVILLAGES, URBAN HOUSES OF HOSPITALITY, & ECO-UNIVERSITIES FOR A NEW CIVILIZATION (Pacem in Terris Press, 2015)

[2] Alasdair Macintyre, AFTER VIRTUE: A STUDY OF MORAL THEORY, Third Edition (University of Notre Dame Press, 2007), p. 263.

Benedict's greatness lay in making possible a quite new kind of insti-
tution, that of the monastery of prayer, learning, and labor, in which
and around which communities could not only survive, but flourish
in a period of social and cultural darkness ... Ours too is a time of
waiting for new and unpredictable possibilities of renewal. It is also a
time for resisting as prudently and courageously and justly and tem-
perately as possible the dominant social, economic, and political order
of advanced modernity[3]

Professor Macintyre's call points toward what I have called a lay ecological "New Monasticism." Yet once again, allow me to cite what I
have proposed as the deep spiritual mission of the new monasticism:

The Holy Spirit is now calling us, both personally and institu-
tionally, to embody and to preach the Good News of Jesus in
and through holistic regeneration of the evolving creative
communion of life's integral ecology, throughout its interwo-
ven natural, human, and spiritual fabric, across our loving
Creator's beloved garden-planet Earth.

In response to that call of the Holy Spirit, this chapter explores the prophetic and radical-traditional vision of a lay ecological New Monasticism as proposed by Peter Maurin (1887-1949),[4] co-founder with Dorothy Day of the Catholic Worker. This book holds up Peter's vision as a
prophetic project for new new lay movements, for "apostolic-religious"
communities seeking lay ecological "refounding," and for all Christian
movements across our global human family.

---

[3] AFTER VIRTUE, p. xvi. Note, however, that Macintyre, though himself apparently of
Keltic ancestry, seems not to have realized that it was Irish-Keltic monasticism and not
Benedictine-Latin monasticism that laid the new intellectual and spiritual foundation for
Western Civilization. Benedictine monasticism built on that powerful Irish-Keltic
intellectual-spiritual foundation. (See the earlier section in this book on monasticism.)

[4] On the life and "green" teachings of Peter Maurin, see Dorothy Day and Francis J.
Sicius, PETER MAURIN: APOSTLE TO THE WORLD (Orbis Books, 2004). On Peter's own
writings, see Peter Maurin, EASY ESSAYS. Catholic Worker Reprint (Wipf and Stock
Publishers, 2003). On the Catholic Worker movement, see *www.catholicworker.org.*

PETER'S LAY ECOLOGICAL NEW MONASTICISM
AS A THREE-PART GREEN REVOLUTION

Writing during the first half of the twentieth century, Peter issued what I have described as an early postmodern prophetic call for a lay New Monasticism of integral-ecological regeneration. As we face breakdown of the integral ecology of life within the globalized yet terminal phase of Modern Industrial Civilization, Peter's vision of integral ecological regeneration still calls to us today, and even more powerfully than when he first proclaimed it.

Peter understood his prophetic vision as a contemporary reenactment of the heroic work by Irish-Keltic missionary monks, whom he preferred to call "scholars," following the fall of the Western Roman Empire.[5] Fluent in both Greek and Latin and well versed in the classical literature of both traditions, as well as in the literature of the early Catholic-Christian theological tradition, those highly educated "scholars" successfully evangelized and educated leaders of the migrating 'barbarian' German tribes. Then, together with the new 'barbarian' Catholic-Christian leaders, they co-created a regenerative Catholic-Christian intellectual-spiritual foundation for Western Civilization.[6]

A millennium and a half later during the Great Depression of the 1930's and referring to the collapse of "modern empires," Peter called for

---

[5] For his knowledge of the contribution of the early medieval Irish-Keltic scholars, Peter drew on the earlier mentioned research by Benedict Fitzpatrick in his magisterial book IRELAND AND FOUNDATIONS OF EUROPE. Again, Fitzpatrick's related book, IRELAND AND THE MAKING OF GREAT BRITAIN, was originally the first part of his vast study of the evangelizing work of the Irish-Keltic mission. As mentioned, the Irish-Keltic evangelization of the migrating German tribes succeeded, whereas earlier Latin attempts had failed, probably because the Irish-Keltic missionaries also came from tribal traditions, with their leaders typically from royal or aristocratic tribal families. Also, Peter's name of "scholars" rather than 'monks" came from his lay vision of monasticism.

[6] The great Welsh Catholic-Christian historian, Christopher Dawson, insisted in several of his books that the rich cultural dynamism of medieval Europe was due historically to fresh cultural energy from the migrating tribes.

"planting seeds for a new society" with rural roots. Again, amplifying and updating Peter's prophetic call, this book has described his "new society" as a future *Postmodern Ecological Civilization.*[7]

Peter repeatedly stated that he took his three-part program of a "Green Revolution" (which he contrasted with the communist "Red Revolution") from the missionary program of those ancient Irish-Keltic "scholars." His three-point program included what he called *"rural communes"* and urban *"houses of hospitality,"* with both linked to what he called *"agronomic universities."*

Today, we might describe Peter's program of "rural communes" as a Catholic-Christian expression of the global movement creating "ecological villages," or more simply *"ecovillages."*[8] We might also today describe his vision of "agronomic universities" as "agroecological univer-

---

[7] Again, this book see this new global civilization as based technologically on the Electronic Revolution. There have been some in the Catholic Worker Movement, however, who have rejected technological advances as foreign to Peter's vision, and particularly postmodern electronic technologies. Yet that assumption is incorrect, for Peter in his time embraced modern mechanical technologies like the printing press (then a massive technology) and even arranged for modern phonographic recordings of his "Easy Essays." (Thanks to Dr. Francis J. Sicius and Tom Cornell for information on the recordings.) Certainly, Peter – with his embrace of the printing press and phonographic recordings, as well as his constant use of trains and buses – was not anti-technological.

Such critics of technology within the Catholic Worker movement appear to have been influenced by the famous work of Jacques Ellul, THE TECHNOLOGICAL SOCIETY (Vintage Books, 1967). In that book, Ellul offered a powerful critique of Modernity's technological utilitarianism. But technology need not be limited to its modern utilitarian form. Indeed, the Greek word *techne* means "art," and so there can be degenerative art or regenerative art. For example, modern fossil-fuel technologies (employed as the basic energy system of modern utilitarian society) have become a degenerative *techne* destroying life's integral ecology. By contrast, postmodern renewable energy systems can become a regenerative *techne.*

[8] On the ecovillages movement around the world, see the website of Global Ecovillage Network at *www.gen.ecovillage.org.* See also Hildur Jackson & Karen Svensson, ECOVILLAGE LIVING: RESTORING THE EARTH AND HER PEOPLE (UIT Cambridge, 2002) and Diana Leafe Christian, CREATING A LIFE TOGETHER: PRACTICAL TOOLS TO GROW ECOVILLAGES AND INTENTIONAL COMMUNITIES (New Society Publishers, 2003).

sities," and alternately as "ecological universities" or more simply as *"eco-universities."* Thus, in today's language, we might rename the three points of Peter's program for his lay ecological "New Monasticism" in the following manner:

1. *Rural Ecovillages*, agroecological in character and planting seeds for a post-capitalist, post-Marxian, and postmodern ecological society, yet one with ancient communitarian roots in rural bioregions;[9]

2. **Urban Houses of Hospitality**, ministering to people marginalized by the breakdown of Modern Industrial Civilization;

3. *Integrating Eco-universities*, seeking intellectual-spiritual clarification of thought to guide the transition to the "new society."

Again, Peter described his three-part program as a re-enactment of the Irish-Keltic monastic and scholarly evangelization of the migrating 'barbarian' German tribes after the collapse of the Western Roman Empire. In the free verse of his "Easy Essays," Peter wrote the following description of his program. (In quotations below from Peter's "Easy Essays," I have placed key phrases in bold font.)

> *When the barbarians invaded*
> *the decaying Roman Empire,*
> *Irish missionaries went all over Europe*
> *and laid the foundations of medieval Europe.*
> *Through the establishment of **cultural centers**,*

---

[9] On the growing development of Catholic Worker "rural communes," see Eric Anglada, "The History and New Growth of Catholic Worker Farms," AMERICA MAGAZINE, May 6, 2013, available at: *http://americamagazine.org/issue/taking-root*. On one moving example, the "Peter Maurin Farm" managed by Tom and Monica Cornell (two long-time Catholic Worker members), see "Farmer Sees Fresh Catholic Worker Energy," NATIONAL CATHOLIC REPORTER, 9 Nov. 2013, at: *http://ncronline.org/news/peace-justice/farmer-sees-fresh-catholic-worker-energy*. On the concept of Agroecology, see *www.agroecology.org*, as well as Miguel A. Altieri, AGROECOLOGY: THE SCIENCE OF SUSTAINABLE AGRICULTURE (Westview Press, 1995).

*that is to say, **Round-Table Discussions**,*
they brought thought to the people.

*Through **free guest houses**,*
*that is to say, **Houses of Hospitality**,*
they popularized the divine virtue of charity.

*Through **farming colonies**,*
*that is to say, **Agronomic Universities**,*
they emphasized voluntary poverty.

It was on the basis of
personal charity and voluntary poverty
that Irish missionaries
*laid the **foundations of the social order**.*[10]

Describing his program in another essay, Peter wrote of "bringing thought to the people" by establishing "Centers of Thought." Again, in describing the intellectual work of the Irish-Keltic monks, Peter (himself once a member of a Catholic religious order) preferred in lay fashion to call them "scholars."

*When the Irish **scholars***
decided to lay the foundations
of medieval Europe,
they established:

Centers of Thought
in all the cities of Europe
as far as Constantinople,
where people could look for thought
so they could have light;

Houses of Hospitality
where Christian Charity was exemplified;

---

[10] Peter Maurin, EASY ESSAYS (Franciscan Herald Press, 1961, 1977, 1984), p. 17.

Agricultural Centers

where they combined:

a. *Cult – that is to say,* **Liturgy**

b. *with Culture – that is to say,* **Literature**

c. *with Cultivation – that is to say,* **Agriculture.**[11]

Once more drawing on the Irish-Keltic mission and writing about the "people who built the Cathedral of Chartres," Peter linked the third part of his program, "Culture," with "Philosophy."

People who built the Cathedral of Chartres
knew how to combine
cult, that is to say **Liturgy**
with culture, that is to say **Philosophy,**
and cultivation, that is to say **Agriculture.**[12]

In yet another essay, which indicates that he saw the intellectual task as central, Peter called his entire program the "*Catholic Workers' School.*"[13]

The program of the **Catholic Worker School**
is a three-point program:

1. **Round-table Discussions**
2. **Houses of Hospitality**
3. **Farming Communes** *[i.e., farming villages]*[14]

Having grown up in France where the word "commune" means "village," Peter' was referring in his third point to the creation of *farming villages*, which had been implicitly ecological from time immemorial. In an interview with Arthur Sheehan, Peter clearly had identified these "communes" as "villages." Referring to the U.S. homesteading move-

---

[11] EASY ESSAYS, p. 142.

[12] EASY ESSAYS, p. 28.

[13] EASY ESSAYS, p. 36.

[14] EASY ESSAYS, p. 36.

ment, he stated that "here in America people ... forgot the village idea, which was in Europe, but went off by themselves."[15]

Further, although Peter constantly wrote in his "Easy Essays" of "thought," "scholars," and "universities," in this interview he also spoke of "folk schools where children would learn folk dances and folk songs." Hence, for Peter, the folk-art dimension was to be an important part of his intellectual vision." [16]

PETER'S VISION OF BUILDING A NEW SOCIETY WITHIN THE SHELL OF THE OLD

In these farming villages, Peter called for integration of scholarship and labor, with both aimed at creating a "new society within the shell of the old," and he linked scholarship and labor with the unemployed.

> *We need Communes*
> *to help **the unemployed***
> *to help themselves.*
>
> *We need Communes*
> *to **make scholars out of workers***
> ***and workers out of scholars** ...*
>
> *We need Communes*
> *to **create a new society***
> *within the shell of the old.*[17]

---

[15] Again, thanks to Dr. Francis J. Sicius for this insight.

[16] The interview was printed serially in the CATHOLIC WORKER, July, May, June, and July-August, 1943. Thanks yet again to Dr. Francis J. Sicius for bringing this interview to my attention.

[17] EASY ESSAYS, pp. 36-37. During the time when Peter was writing, there was already beginning a Catholic-Christian movement to regenerate ecovillages. See Dr. Tobias Lanz et al., FLEE TO THE FIELDS: THE FOUNDING OF THE CATHOLIC LAND MOVEMENT (IHS Press, 2003). See also Fr. Vincent McNabb, THE CHURCH AND THE LAND (IHS Press, 2003), originally published in 1925.

Again, while writing during the Great Depression of the 1930's, Peter emphasized the unemployment of college graduates.

> *On Farming Communes*
> **unemployed college graduates**
> *will be taught*
> *how to build their houses,*
> *how to gather their fuel,*
> *how to raise their food,*
> *how to make their furniture;*
> *that is to say, how to employ themselves ...*
>
> *[They] will learn to use*
> *both their hands and their heads.*[18]

In calling for this "new society" Peter anticipated what this book calls the still emerging postmodern ecological strategy of Catholic Social Teaching.

Decades later, Saint John XXIII – launching that new strategy with his two great encyclical letters MATER ET MAGISTRA (1961) and PACEM IN TERRIS (1963) – officially rejected modern ideologies. Instead, he called globally for "a new social order" that would retain its rural roots. Later, but similarly, Saint John Paul II frequently wrote of moving beyond modern ideologies, and especially in his great encyclical LABOREM EXERCENS (1981). More recently, Pope Francis, in his great encyclical LAUDATO SI' (2015) on ecology, also rejected modern ideologies. To overcome them, he called for "ecological spirituality," "ecological education," and a "bold cultural revolution."

Yet decades before these popes began to reject both of Modernity's two dominant materialistic ideologies, Peter anticipated those rejections. At that time, he wrote with bold clarity:

---

[18] EASY ESSAYS, pp. 92-93.

The Catholic social philosophy
is the philosophy of the Common Good ...
Christianity has nothing to do
with either modern capitalism or modern communism ...

The capitalists, or accumulators of labor,
[treat labor] not as a gift, but as a commodity ...
But the buyers of labor ...
are nothing but commercializers of labor ...

[Further] as some people used to think
that we need a good honest war to end all wars,
Karl Marx used to think
that we need a gigantic class-struggle
to bring about a classless society.[19]

Instead of the "Bolshevik Red Revolution," Peter – again ahead of his time – called for a "*Green Revolution.*" Implicitly ecological, his Green Revolution was to bring people back to the land. Thus, he wrote:

The only way to prevent a Red Revolution
is to promote a **Green Revolution.**
... to make them look up
to Green Ireland of the seventh century.[20]

PETER'S CALL TO JOURNEY BEYOND
THE END OF MODERN EMPIRES

In yet another Easy Essay and quoting a "Father Gillis,"[21] Peter said that his three-point program was necessary because "this age is very much

---

[19] Easy Essays, pp. 37, 15, 31.

[20] EASY ESSAYS, p. 71.

[21] Peter was referring to James Martin Gillis, CSP, a Catholic Paulist priest who from 1922-1948 served as Editor the Paulist review CATHOLIC WORLD. During that time, he was one of the most publicly known Catholic priests in the United States.

like the age of the fall of Rome."[22] He identified the contemporary Western period with the fall of the classical Western Roman Empire. In so doing (as noted earlier), Peter anticipated what at mid-twentieth century Romano Guardini had described as "The End of the Modern World,"[23]

Despairing of contemporary ecclesial leadership and academic institutions,[24] Peter launched his own intellectual-spiritual *ressourcement*. In response to what he called "the fall of modern empires," Peter proposed retrieving what he saw as the three-part program of the "Irish scholars" of the seventh century. Again, he wrote:

> *In order to lay the foundations of medieval Europe,*
> *the Irish scholars established* **Salons de Culture**.
>
> *In all the cities of Europe as far as Constantinople,*
> *the Irish scholars established* **free guest houses**.
>
> *The Irish scholars established* **agricultural centers**
> *all over Europe ...*
>
> *What was done by Irish missionaries*
> *after the fall of the Roman Empire*
> *can be done today*
> *during and after* **the fall of modern empires**.[25]

---

[22] EASY ESSAYS, p. 12.

[23] Again, that phrase is the English translation of the title of Guardini's 1950 masterwork, DAS ENDE DER NEUZEIT, 9TH edition (Würtzburg, 1965). See also and again the English translation, THE END OF THE MODERN WORLD (ISI Books, 1998). As also noted earlier, Pope Francis, while still a young Jesuit, had done doctoral studies on Guardini's thought. Decades later, in his great 2015 ecology encyclical LAUDATO SI', Francis cited Guardini's book *eight times*. Peter reportedly had read Guardini's earlier writings.

[24] EASY ESSAYS, p. 21.

[25] EASY ESSAYS, pp. 205-206.

SUMMARY OF PETER'S HOLISTIC VISION OF
INTEGRAL ECOLOGICAL REGENERATION

In summary, Peter proposed a radical and prophetic, yet also traditional and ecologically "green" vision of regenerating the human family's
millennia-old experience of living in *rural ecovillages* ("farming communes"). He also linked that tradition with caring for marginalized urban people (*"houses of hospitality"*) and with regeneration of society's
intellectual foundations (*"agronomic universities"*).

In his search for his "new society," Peter centered his regenerative vision in an Earth-rooted intellectual-spiritual process of scholarship and
education ("cultural centers," "round-table discussions," "salons de culture," "centers of thought," and "agronomic universities"). For that intellectual task, he especially drew on the Catholic Social Teaching of his
time, and he prophetically anticipated the postmodern ecological strategy of Catholic Social Teaching that Saint John XXIII inaugurated early
in the second half of the twentieth century.[26]

Finally, Peter sought integration for the life of work with the intellectual life ("workers shall become scholars and scholars shall become workers"), and in a manner that would be grounded in spirituality ("cult"),
in agriculture ("cultivation"), and in "culture" ("literature," "philosophy," and "folk culture").

QUESTIONS FOR
A REGENERATIVE POSTMODERN FUTURE

Today, at the "End of the Modern World," can contemporary Catholic-
Christian visionary pioneers humbly and prayerfully advance Peter's
new lay ecological "New Monasticism" in a way that integrates postmodern electronic technologies (e.g., solar energy, computers, etc.)
with Peter's radical, traditional, and regenerative three-point program?

---

[26] See this book's Appendix of Postmodern Catholic Social Teaching.

Can contemporary visionary Catholic-Christian pioneers humbly and prayerfully plant postmodern seeds for regenerating the creative and evolutionary communion of life's integral ecology, throughout its interwoven natural, human, and spiritual fabric, across our loving Creator's beloved garden-planet Earth?

Can contemporary visionary Catholic-Christian pioneers thus humbly and prayerfully begin to heal the late modern global devastation of the integral ecology of life?

Can Catholic-Christian modern "apostolic-religious" communities and postmodern new lay movements, perhaps in an ecological alliance with each other, humbly and prayerfully create small islands of regenerative co-creativity to embody Peter's prophetic vision, and thereby plant seeds – across our loving Creator's beloved garden-planet Earth – for a regenerative Postmodern Ecological Civilization and a regenerative Postmodern Ecological Church?

Finally, is not all of this not only a prophetic message for Catholic Christians, but also for all Christians, and even for the entire human family?

10

CONCLUDING REFLECTION

At the end of this exploration, let us again recall the distinctive deep spiritual missions of the evolving waves of Catholic-Christian mystical-prophetic communities from their past foundational, classical, and feudal waves, through to the now declining modern wave, and into the emerging postmodern wave. As we have seen, there are six historical long waves of these communities (counting the one now emerging), with each having a distinct historical mission.

- *Foundational Lay Communities.* The deep spiritual mission of the foundational early church, which was completely lay, was *to witness to the messianic message of Jesus,* largely from within the idolatrous, oppressive, and often persecuting Roman Empire.

- *Classical Coenobitic Communities.* The deep spiritual mission of the classical coenobites was *to keep alive the witness of the Cross of Jesus in their own spiritual martyrdom,* and to do so in prophetic counterpoint to the compromise with the Roman Empire by the hierarchical-patriarchal "clergy" of the urban Imperial Church. In addition, by befriending plants and animals, those coenobites tried *to live a prophetic life of eschatological return to an ecological Paradise,* like the biblical Garden of Eden.

- *Feudal Monastic Communities.* The deep spiritual mission of the feudal monastics – beginning with the great missionary project of the Irish-Keltic Monks and later taken over by Latin-Roman Bene-dictine monks allied with papal centralization – was, after the col-lapse of the Western Roman Empire, *to welcome, evangelize, and edu-cate the migrating German tribes into the life-giving community of Jesus' disciples, and with their royal and aristocratic tribal leaders to regenerate Western Christian Civilization.*

- *Medieval Mendicant Communities.* The deep spiritual mission of the mendicants (again, meaning beggars) of the medieval bour-geois cities was evangelically to witness to the Gospel of Jesus by *challenging seminal bourgeois spiritual errors planted within medieval bourgeois culture by themselves living in poverty and embracing the poor, the natural world, human rights, education, and democracy.*

- *Modern Apostolic Communities.* The deep spiritual mission of "apostolic religious" communities of Modern Industrial Civilization was *to witness to the Gospel of Jesus by serving the new industrial work-ing class, as well as immigrants, rural farming families, and colonized peoples, through modern social-welfare apostolates of health, education, and social welfare.*

- *Postmodern Lay Movements.* This book proposes that the fresh deep spiritual mission of emerging postmodern lay movements, and of "apostolic-religious communities exploring "refounding," is *to witness to the Gospel of Jesus by seeking holistic regeneration for the evolving creative communion of life's integral ecology, throughout its in-terwoven natural, human, and spiritual dimensions, across our loving Creator's beloved garden-planet Earth.*

The historical challenge faced by the new lay movements, and also refounding "apostolic-religious" communities, is the breakdown of the now globalized Modern Industrial Civilization and of its collapsing Modern Psychological Spirituality, with that breakdown and collapse revealed in the the growing global devastation of life's integral ecology.

In the vision of this book, emerging postmodern lay movements are called to ground their particular charisms, and what may be called their surface missions, in this deep spiritual mission for the great post-modern transition. This means deep seeking deep grounding in the emerging Postmodern Ecological Spirituality, and planting seeds for a Postmodern Ecological Civilization.

A special emphasis in this book has been the recent and sudden decline of the modern "apostolic" form of "religious life," and the parallel emergence and growth of the postmodern lay movements. Within that emphasis, the book has proposed a possible refounding of some "apos-tolic religious communities," or at least of some sectors that would function as "islands of co-creative regeneration." Again, such refound-ing would seek deep grounding in the emerging Postmodern Ecologi-cal Spirituality, and humbly work with others to seek a Postmodern Ecological Civilization.

This book has also proposed that growing postmodern lay movements and declining modern "apostolic-religious" communities cooperate with each other in an *eco-spiritual alliance* seeking to help regenerate rural life by planting *new lay ecological monasteries* in the form of *ecovillages*, and as humble focal points for regenerating rural life.

Finally, the book has proposed that we can learn about that lay ecologi-cal "*New Monasticism*" from Peter Maurin's prophetic vision of his three part "Green Revolution – rephrased here as co-creating rural ecovillages, urban houses of hospitality, and ecological universities.

This book has called for that eco-spiritual alliance partly out of the fear that, if we lose the creative energy of so many declining "apostolic-religious" communities, and if the growing new lay movements do not drink deeply from the emerging Postmodern Ecological Spirituality, then the Western Catholic Church's evangelization will become weaker still, and may even become partly pathological – at least in the 'advanced' industrialized areas already experiencing the spiritual "Dark Night" of Modern Industrial Civilization.

Further, the book has proposed that, within the postmodern historical transition, the emerging fresh Catholic-Christian form of Postmodern Ecological Spirituality needs to synthesize the gifts of past forms of Catholic-Christian spiritual energy, as well as other human forms of spiritual energy. To that end, we need to pray to the Holy Spirit that she may guide us beyond the increasingly anti-poor, anti-life, pro-war, and anti-ecological breakdown of Modern Industrial Civilization.

In addition, the book has proposed that we need to ask the Holy Spirit to guide us into regenerative, inclusive, and peaceful pathways toward a Postmodern Ecological Civilization. Such a fresh civilization is called to seek the holistic regeneration of life's integral ecology, and at every level from the human womb to our entire garden-planet.

If, however, the new Catholic-Christian lay movements develop without an eco-spiritual alliance with their earlier "religious" predecessors, then these new global lay movements could collapse into the 'conservative' cultural-spiritual temptation of late modern *restoration*. If that were to happen, they would fail to give birth to the mystical-prophetic creativity necessary to seek globally authentic ecological, social, and spiritual *regeneration*.

Without such an eco-spiritual alliance, the important heritage of traditional "apostolic-religious" communities would presumably continue to decline, at least in the 'advanced' industrial regions. Then, the Western Catholic evangelization would continue to weaken before the anti-spiritual triumph of the anti-poor, anti-life, pro-war, and anti-ecological Modern Mechanical Cosmology of Scientific Materialism, and still worse of demonic Nietzschean Nihilism.

It is not this book's place to say which declining "apostolic-religious" communities may be called by the Holy Spirit to seek transformation through embracing the emerging lay-rooted Postmodern Ecological

Spirituality. Nor is it this book's place to say which growing new post-modern lay movements should seek an eco-spiritual alliance with the rich legacy of declining "apostolic-religious" communities, in order to promote the Peter Maurin's regenerative "Green Revolution."

Nonetheless, this book predicts that older modern "apostolic religious communities" and newer postmodern lay movements – if they chose to drink together from the living waters of the emerging Postmodern Eco-logical Spirituality – could together become co-creative partners in the local-global regeneration of life's integral ecology. Such co-creative partners could then become loving sources of healing for our global Christian family, for our wider global human family, and for the still wider and evolving creative communion of life across our loving Crea-tor's beloved garden-planet Earth.

Thus far, however, the seeds of hope are few and scattered. So, we will conclude on a somber note by repeating the profound warning from Francis of Rome:

> *Doomsday predictions can no longer be met with irony or distain. We may well be leaving to coming generations debris, desolation, and filth. The pace of consumption, waste, and environmental change has so stretched the planet's capacity that our contemporary lifestyle, unsustainable as it is, can only precipitate catastrophes, such as those which even now periodically occur in different areas of the world. The effects of the present imbalance can only be reduced by our decisive action, here and now.*

LAUDATO SI'
ON CARE FOR OUR COMMON HOME
(Par. 161)

PACEM IN TERRIS
ECOLOGICAL DECLARATION

A humble and prayerful encouragement, at the end of the Modern World,
for ecologically concerned Christians and other concerned spiritual seekers
to advance the Postmodern Ecological Renaissance,
which we believe the Holy Spirit is calling forth
within our loving Creator's beloved human family
across our loving Creator's beloved garden-planet Earth.

Revision of 1 September 2016
World Day of Prayer for the Care of Creation

A Working Paper issued by
PACEM IN TERRIS ECOLOGICAL INITIATIVE
which is the core project of
PAX ROMANA / CMICA-USA
1025 Connecticut Avenue NW, Suite 1000, Washington DC 20036 USA
www.paceminterris.net | office@paceminterris.net

*When you send forth your spirit, they are created,
and you renew the face of the Earth.*

Psalm 104: 30

T his Declaration, issued by the Pacem in Terris Ecological Initiative and
serving as its guide, is included at the end of this book because Pacem
in Terris Press (which has published this book) is part of the Initiative. Still
in development, the Initiative is a project of Pax Romana / Catholic Movement for Intellectual Affairs - USA (CMICA-USA), which is based in Washington DC. The Initiative includes this Declaration, Pacem in Terris Press, and
Pacem in Terris Ecovillages Project.

This Declaration promotes what it calls the "Postmodern Ecological Renaissance." Looking beyond the "End of the Modern World," this Renaissance
seeks holistic regeneration for the evolving creative communion of life's integral ecology, throughout its interwoven natural, human, and spiritual
fabric, across our loving Creator's beloved garden-planet Earth.

In the Initiative's name, the phrase "Pacem in Terris" (Peace on Earth) is
taken from the title of the famous 1963 encyclical letter by Saint John XXIII
on world peace. The phrase "The End of the Modern World" is taken from
the title of the ground-breaking 1950 book by the late and distinguished
Italian-German and Catholic-Christian philosopher, Romano Guardini.

Within the Declaration, the phrase "integral ecology" is taken from the great
papal encyclical letter LAUDATO SI', issued in 2015 by Pope Francis. "Integral
ecology" connects natural ecology with human ecology, since human ecology is nested within the wider system of natural ecology and remains part of
it. In addition, integral ecology is supported by ecological spirituality,
which is also described here as mystical-prophetic "spiritual ecology."

To mark the inauguration of the Pacem in Terris Ecological Initiative, this
Declaration was first issued on 19 January 2012 by Pax Romana / CMICA-
USA as a Working Paper under the name of the "Washington Declaration."
This current version, still a Working Paper and now re-named the "Pacem
in Terris Ecological Declaration," is dated 1 September 2016, which was
the World Day of Prayer for the Care of Creation.

We live today amidst the global integral-ecological breakdown of
MODERN INDUSTRIAL CIVILIZATION.
Within late modern neoliberal globalization,
that breakdown is now devastating life's integral ecology,
throughout its evolving and interwoven natural, human, and spiritual fabric,
across our loving Creator's beloved garden-planet Earth.

Despite Modernity's important and abiding contributions,
its late modern global ecological devastation
is the outcome of deeply anti-ecological errors,
embedded within Western Modernity's philosophical-scientific Cosmology,
and within Western Modernity's deeper symbolic-mythic foundations.

WESTERN MODERNITY'S PHILOSOPHICAL-SCIENTIFIC COSMOLOGY
has wrongly imagined that humans are not organically part of Nature.
In turn, it has wrongly imagined that Nature itself is not organic,
but rather atomistic, mechanical, and materialist,
and thus has no spiritual meaning.

WESTERN MODERNITY'S SYMBOLIC-MYTHIC FOUNDATIONS,
lodged at a deeper level of human consciousness than Cosmology,
have wrongly imagined that modernization should be guided
primarily by a pathological hyper-masculine and anti-feminine degradation
of the ancient archetype of the noble warrior.

Because of Western Modernity's materialist Cosmology
and because of its deformed masculine and anti-feminine symbolic-mythic foundations,
modernizing elites across the globe have wrongly imagined
that they should conquer and exploit Nature without limit,
that that should constantly pursue economic, political, and even cultural warfare,
and that they should conquer, exploit, marginalize, and even eliminate certain humans,
as if all were only utilitarian commodities without spiritual meaning,
and available for individualistic utilitarian manipulation.

Those modern Western cosmological and symbolic-mythic errors
have in turn misguided Modernity's two dominant ideologies of Materialism,
which we know as "Liberal Capitalism" and "Scientific Socialism."
Despite their abiding and complementary societal insights,
those materialistic ideologies have erroneously misdirected late modern societies
into the global devastation of life's integral ecology.

In the now acute stage of late modern global ecological devastation,
democratic liberal states promoting late modern neoliberal globalization
have entered into economic alliance with dictatorial communist states.
Both have been jointly supporting an anti-ecological global industrial system
that has unleashed ancient and demonic idolatries of
money, power, exploitation, inequality, and violence.
Those idolatries are being unconsciously promoted across planet Earth
by late modern neoliberal networks of
global financial institutions, global cultural industries,
and even globalized universities.

To heal the contemporary global devastation of life's integral ecology,
we believe that the Holy Spirit is now calling all of us across
our loving Creator's beloved human family
to undertake the turbulent, confusing, and dangerous journey beyond
MODERN INDUSTRIAL CIVILIZATION,
since it has now become globally destructive of integral ecology,
and spiritually bankrupt.

To assist with this historic global journey,
we also believe that the Holy Spirit is inspiring
eco-spiritual leaders across our global human family
to plant humble seeds for global regeneration of life's integral ecology.

We further believe that the Holy Spirit is calling our entire human family
to develop those seeds of regeneration into an emerging
POSTMODERN ECOLOGICAL CIVILIZATION,
which needs to be nourished by the vast and deep ecological wisdom
of our human family's rich and diverse spiritual traditions.

To help in planting seeds for global regeneration of life's integral ecology,
we humbly and prayerfully encourage
our concerned Catholic, Orthodox, and Protestant sisters and brothers,
including members of all twenty-four "sui juris" Catholic Churches,
as well as all concerned spiritual seekers,
to promote what we call the emerging
POSTMODERN ECOLOGICAL RENAISSANCE.

As humble and prayerful disciples seeking
to follow the loving and life-giving Way of Jesus,
we rejoice that visionary Christian individuals and movements,
across our loving Creator's beloved human family,
as well as other visionary and concerned spiritual seekers,
are already advancing this Renaissance.

To further advance this Renaissance,
we encourage concerned Christians and other concerned spiritual seekers,
across our loving Creator's beloved garden-planet Earth,
to gather in small eco-spiritual communities
for prayer, study, and dialogue,
and there to read what Jesus called the "Signs of the Times,"
and to employ the "See-Judge-Act" method of praxis.

To support the task of study by these eco-spiritual communities,
Pax Romana / CMICA-USA offers the humble services of this still developing
PACEM IN TERRIS ECOLOGICAL INITIATIVE.
The Initiative recommends that these small eco-spiritual communities
undertake a long-term study of the following intellectual-spiritual resources
for postmodern global regeneration of life's integral ecology:

First,
OUR HUMAN FAMILY'S ECOLOGICAL WISDOM TRADITIONS,
including the traditional ecological wisdom of indigenous peoples,
the traditional ecological wisdom of world religions and philosophies,
the traditional ecological wisdom of rural communities,
and the traditional ecological wisdom of women;

Second,
THE BIBLICAL SPIRITUALITY OF CREATION,
which, according to Eastern Christian traditions,
proclaims that we humans are "priests of creation,"
called to care for our loving Creator's beloved human family,
and for our loving Creator's beloved family of all creatures,
and to do so with constant and joyful prayers of praise and thanksgiving;

Third,
THE BOOK OF NATURE & THE BOOK OF THE BIBLE,
which, according to ancient Eastern and Western Christian traditions,
constitute the two complementary books of Divine revelation,
with the first read though eyes of art, reason, and science,
and the second read though eyes of liturgy, faith, and theology,
and with both revealing our loving Creator of the Cosmos;

Fourth,
POSTMODERN GLOBAL CHRISTIAN ECOLOGICAL TEACHING,
including the ecological teachings of the Eastern Churches,
particularly the ecological messages of
the Greek Orthodox "Green Patriarch" Bartholomew I,
along with ecological statements from the World Council of Churches,
and ecological statements by national Protestant denominations,
as well as Catholic papal and national ecological statements,
and especially Pope Francis' great ecological encyclical LAUDATO SI';

Fifth,
THE POSTMODERN PHILOSOPHICAL-SCIENTIFIC "NEW COSMOLOGY,"
which goes beyond Modernity's atomistic, mechanical, and materialist "Old Cosmology,"
which celebrates a co-creative and (for some) a mystical understanding of evolution,
and which for postmodern eco-spiritual Christians find its Alpha and Omega
in the endlessly overflowing and co-creative love of the Holy Trinity.

Most importantly,
we humbly and prayerfully encourage eco-spiritual communities
to ask the Holy Spirit to guide all of us in planting seeds
for regenerating the evolving creative communion of life's integral ecology,
throughout its interwoven natural, human, and spiritual fabric,
across our loving Creator's beloved garden-planet Earth.

We also ask for constant prayer that the Holy Spirit guide our
PACEM IN TERRIS ECOLOGICAL INITIATIVE,
so that it may humbly and prayerfully help to advance the emerging
POSTMODERN ECOLOGICAL RENAISSANCE,
and so that it may humbly and prayerfully encourage more concerned Christians,
as well as more concerned seekers from other spiritual traditions
to plant postmodern seeds for the global regeneration of life's integral ecology.

We have published this Declaration
in hope that concerned Christians and other concerned spiritual seekers
will become inspired to search for visionary and co-creative paths
for the postmodern global regeneration of life's integral ecology.

We have also published this Declaration
for the sake of our children and our children's children,
and for the sake of the present and future children of all living creatures
across our loving Creator's beauteous but threatened Biosphere.

We humbly and prayerfully dedicate this Declaration
to Africa's late great feminine ecological leader from Kenya,
WANGARI MAATHAI,
and to the Native-American Nature-mystic and Lilly of the Mohawks,
SAINT KATERI TEKAWITHA,
as well as to
ALL ECO-SPIRITUAL YOUNG WOMEN AND YOUNG MEN,
who are working to plant seeds of regeneration
for the evolving creative communion of life's integral ecology,
throughout its interwoven natural, human, and spiritual fabric,
across our loving Creator's beloved and beauteous garden-planet Earth.

Let us constantly pray that together we may help to bring forth
a regenerative postmodern integral-ecological future
for our global Christian family,
for our global human family,
and for our global family of all creatures,
across our loving Creator's beauteous and beloved
garden-planet Earth.

ACKNOWLEDGEMENTS

T this book has been developed in part from a background paper that I originally prepared a long time ago for the 1990 Annual Assembly of the U.S. Conference of Major Superiors of Men, held at Salve Regina College in Newport, Rhode Island. My gratitude goes to the Conference leaders at that time for the opportunity to develop the six-stage analysis of the historical long waves of these communities, as found in found in Chapter 2 of this book. I also did an expansion of that paper in 2009 and another in 2014.

For making that original paper and ultimately this book possible, I particularly thank Sister Pat Chaffee, O.P., Ph.D., a member of the Racine Dominican Sisters and a prophetic human-rights activist. During my years at the Center of Concern, Sister Pat Chaffee, with the support of her Racine Dominican community, did most helpful research on the history of "religious life." I would also like to thank Sister Rosaire Lucassen who, in her role then as the President of the Racine Dominicans, proposed that Sister Pat Chaffee volunteer at the Center of Concern.

A special thank-you goes also to Sister Ginny Sylvestri, a Sister of the American Province of the Servants of Mary, for inviting me, again many years ago, to do a video-program on that background paper. That experience helped to advance the analysis presented in this book.

More recently, I owe a debt of gratitude to Sister Maria Homberg and to Sister Peg Donovan, both members of the Maryknoll Sisters and sequential Directors of the Maryknoll Sisters Mission Institute, for inviting me to lead an Institute Seminar in 2014. That experience helped to bring closure to this book's development.

I would also like to thank a dear old friend from Ireland, John Sweeney, who first introduced me to the Irish-Keltic monastic tradition by bringing me to the ancient Irish-Keltic monastic site of Glendalough. That Irish-Keltic monastery, founded by Saint Kevin in the sixth century and nestled in a lush green valley within the gentle Wicklow Mountains, was once one of Ireland's great centers of learning for scholars from all across Europe. John also made it possible for me to visit Ireland many times as a guest lecturer, but in a situation where I was happily more learner than teacher.

In addition, I would like to thank the Pontifical Council for Justice and Peace, the United Nations International Labor Organization, and Caritas Internationalis, for the opportunity to deliver a paper at their jointly sponsored "global seminar" held in Rome in May 2016. The full title of that seminar was "Sustainable Development and the Future of Work in the Context of the Jubilee of Mercy." The seminar provided an opportunity to further develop my understanding of the prophetic vision of Peter Maurin.

Most importantly, for the ecological "New Cosmology" perspective underlying this book, I especially thank the late Catholic-Christian cultural historian Thomas Berry, and his close colleague the mathematical cosmologist Bryan Swimme.

In that same vein, I also thank my academic colleagues from St. Thomas University in Miami Gardens, Florida, and especially Dr. Elisabetta Ferrero and Dr. Joseph Iannone, for teaching me so much about the New Cosmology and about the contributions of Tom Berry and Brian Swimme. Also, a special thanks to my St. Thomas colleague Dr. Francis Sicius for all that he taught me about Peter Maurin, and to Prof. Art Kane for proof-reading so many revisions this manuscript, as well as for suggestions for improvement and for his wisdom and vision.

Lastly, warm thanks to my sister and experienced editor, Maureen Holland, to my sister-in-law and former English professor, Rosario Biascoechea, and to my former research assistant, Nick Klumack, for proof-reading early versions of the manuscript. In addition, I especially thank my former student, colleague, and friend, Dr. Cristóbal Serrán-Pagán y Fuentes, not only for proof-reading many sections of the manuscript, but also for his insightful recommendations on how to improve it. Finally, I thank my daughter Natanya Holland Allan for helping me with the clarity of a lawyer's eyes to simplify the earlier complicated title (if not the subtitle) of this still complicated book.

Of course, none of the above good persons is responsible for any errors, limitations, or other problems found in this book. That responsibility is entirely my own.

BIBLIOGRAPHY

Agnès Sinaï. 2015. "*Guerre totale contre la nature.*" LE MONDE DIPLOMATIQUE, September. *http://www.monde-diplomatique.fr/2015/09/SINAI/53706.* Accessed 2015-08-15.

Altieri, Miguel A. 1995. AGROECOLOGY: THE SCIENCE OF SUSTAINABLE AGRICULTURE, Second Edition. Westview Press.

Anglada, Eric. 2013. "The History and New Growth of Catholic Worker Farms," AMERICA MAGAZINE, May 6.

Arbuckle, Gerald. 1986. STRATEGIES FOR GROWTH IN RELIGIOUS LIFE. Alba House.

Arbuckle, Gerald. 1997. FROM CHAOS TO MISSION: REFOUNDING RELIGIOUS LIFE FORMATION. Liturgical Press.

Arbuckle, Gerald. 1998. OUT OF CHAOS: REFOUNDING RELIGIOUS CONGREGATIONS. Paulist Press.

Barstow, Anne Llewellyn. 1982. MARRIED PRIESTS AND THE REFORMING PAPACY: THE 11TH CENTURY DEBATES. Edwin Mellen.

Bartholomew I & John Chryssavgis. 2009. COSMIC GRACE + HUMBLE PRAYER: THE ECOLOGICAL VISION OF THE GREEN PATRIARCH BARTHOLOMEW I, second edition. Wm. B. Eerdmans.

Beggiani, Msgr. Seely J. 1983. EARLY SYRIAC THEOLOGY WITH SPECIAL REFERENCE TO THE MARONITE TRADITION. University of America Press.

Bell, Daniel. 1976. THE COMING OF POST-INDUSTRIAL SOCIETY: A VENTURE IN SOCIAL FORECASTING. Basic Books.

Bellah, Robert & Richard Madsen, William M. Sullivan, Ann Swidler, Stephen M. Tipton. 2007. HABITS OF THE HEART: INDIVIDUALISM AND COMMITMENT IN AMERICAN LIFE, New Preface Edition. University of California Press.

Berdyaev, Nicolas. 1934. BOURGEOIS MIND AND OTHER ESSAYS, Facsimile Edition. Ayer.

Berry, Thomas & Brian Swimme. 1994. THE UNIVERSE STORY: FROM THE PRIMAL FLARING FORTH TO THE ECOZOIC ERA – A CELEBRATION OF THE UNFOLDING OF THE COSMOS, Reprint Edition. HarperOne.

Berry, Thomas & Mary Evelyn Tucker. 2009. THE SACRED UNIVERSE: EARTH SPIRITUALITY AND RELIGION IN THE TWENTY-FIRST CENTURY. Columbia University Press.

Berry, Thomas. 1998. THE DREAM OF THE EARTH. Sierra Club.

Berry, Thomas. 1999. THE GREAT WORK: OUR WAY INTO THE FUTURE. Bell Tower Random House.

Black, Edwin. 2012. WAR AGAINST THE WEAK: EUGENICS AND AMERICA'S CAMPAIGN TO CREATE A MASTER RACE. Expanded Edition. Dialog Press.

Bossy, John. 1970. "The Counter Reformation and the People of Catholic Europe," THE PAST AND PRESENT SOCIETY, Number 47. Oxford University Press.

Boswell, John. 2005. CHRISTIANITY, SOCIAL TOLERANCE, AND HOMOSEXUALITY: GAY PEOPLE IN WESTERN EUROPE FROM THE BEGINNING OF THE CHRISTIAN ERA TO THE FOURTEENTH CENTURY. University of Chicago Press.

Braidotti, Rosi. 2013. THE POSTHUMAN. Polity.

Budde, Michael L. 1998. THE MAGIC KINGDOM OF GOD: CHRISTIANITY AND GLOBAL CULTURE INDUSTRIES. Westview Press.

Burgess, Stanley M. 1989. THE HOLY SPIRIT: EASTERN CHRISTIAN TRADITIONS. Baker Academic.

Cahill, Thomas. 1996. HOW THE IRISH SAVED CIVILIZATION: THE STORY OF IRELAND'S HEROIC ROLE FROM THE FALL OF ROME TO THE RISE OF MEDIEVAL EUROPE. Anchor.

Capra, Fritjof. 1997. THE WEB OF LIFE: A NEW SCIENTIFIC UNDERSTANDING OF LIVING SYSTEMS. Anchor.

Capra, Fritjof. 2002. THE HIDDEN CONNECTIONS: A SCIENCE FOR SUSTAINABLE LIVING. ANCHOR BOOKS RANDOM HOUSE.

Capra, Fritjof & Pier Luisi. 2014. THE SYSTEMS VIEW OF LIFE: A UNIFYING VISION. Cambridge University Press.

Catta, Lawrence & Raymond Fitz, Gertrude Foley, Thomas Giordino, Carol Lynchburg. 1985. SHAPING THE COMING AGE OF RELIGIOUS LIFE. Seabury Press.

Christian, Diana Leafe. 2003. CREATING A LIFE TOGETHER: PRACTICAL TOOLS TO GROW ECOVILLAGES AND INTENTIONAL COMMUNITIES. New Society Publishers.

Clinebell, Howard. 1996. ECOTHERAPY: HEALING OURSELVES, HEALING THE EARTH. Routledge.

Cort, John. 1998. CHRISTIAN SOCIALISM: AN INFORMAL HISTORY. Orbis Books.

Costanza, Robert & *et al.* 2014. AN INTRODUCTION TO ECOLOGICAL ECONOMICS. Second Edition. CRC Press.

Cox, Harvey. 2016. THE MARKET AS GOD. Harvard University Press.

Culp, John. 2013. "Panentheism," Stanford Encyclopedia of Philosophy at *http://plato.stanford.edu/entries/panentheism.* Accessed 2016-09-11.

Davis, Mike. 2006. PLANET OF SLUMS. Verso.

Dawson, Christopher. 2010. THE CRISIS OF WESTERN EDUCATION. Catholic University of America. (Original published 1961.)

Dawson, Jonathan. 2006. ECOVILLAGES: NEW FRONTIERS FOR SUSTAINABILITY. Schumacher Briefings Series. UIT Cambridge.

Day, Dorothy & Francis J. Sicius. 2004. PETER MAURIN: APOSTLE TO THE WORLD. Orbis Books, 2004.

de las Casas, Bartolomé. 1992. THE DEVASTATION OF THE INDIES: A BRIEF ACCOUNT. Translated Herma Briffault. Johns Hopkins University Press. (Original published 1552.)

DeConick, April D. 2011. HOLY MISOGYNY: WHY SEX AND GENDER CONFLICTS IN THE EARLY CHURCH STILL MATTER. Continuum.

Deignan, Kathleen. 2009. "The Spirituality of the Earth: Reflections on an Essay by Thomas Berry," in Mary Evelyn Tucker & John Grim, eds. LIVING COSMOLOGY: CHRISTIAN RESPONSES TO THE JOURNEY OF THE UNIVERSE. Orbis Books.

Drucker, Peter. 1994. POST-CAPITALIST SOCIETY. HarperBusiness.

Dubois, Francis & Josef Klee, Editors. 2013. PACEM IN TERRIS: ITS CONTINUING RELEVANCE FOR THE TWENTY-FIRST CENTURY. Pacem in Terris Press.

Eco, Umberto. 2014. THE NAME OF THE ROSE. Reprint Edition. Mariner Books.

Ellul, Jacques. 1967. THE TECHNOLOGICAL SOCIETY. Vintage Books.

Engels, Friedrich. 1972. SOCIALISM SCIENTIFIC AND UTOPIAN. Trans. Edward Aveling. International Publishers. (Original published 1883.)

Eusebius. EUSEBIUS: THE CHURCH HISTORY. 2007. Transl. Paul L. Maier. Kraeger Academic and Professional. (Original published c. 340 AD)

Felknor, Lori. 1989. CRISIS IN RELIGIOUS VOCATION. Paulist Press.

Feuherd, Ben. 2013. "Farmer Sees Fresh Catholic Worker Energy," NATIONAL CATHOLIC REPORTER, 9 Nov.

Fitzpatrick, Benedict. 1922. IRELAND AND THE MAKING OF BRITAIN. Funk & Wagnalls.

Fitzpatrick, Benedict. 1927. IRELAND AND THE FOUNDATIONS OF EUROPE. Funk & Wagnalls.

Flaccavento, Anthony. 2016. BUILDING A HEALTHY ECONOMY FROM THE BOTTOM UP: HARNESSING REAL-WORLD EXPERIENCE FOR TRANSFORMATIVE CHANGE. University of Kentucky Press.

Francis, Pope. LAUDATO SI', 2015. papal encyclical letter. *http://w2.vatican.va/content/francesco/en/encyclicals/documents/papa-francesco_20150524_enciclica-laudato-si.html.* Accessed 2016-07-15.

Freitas, Donna. 2013. THE END OF SEX: HOW HOOKUP CULTURE IS LEAVING A GENERATION UNHAPPY, SEXUALLY UNFULFILLED, AND CONFUSED ABOUT INTIMACY. Basic Books.

Fukuyama, Francis. 2002. OUR POSTHUMAN FUTURE. Farrar, Straus, & Giroux.

Gelpi SJ, Donald. 1984. THE DIVINE MOTHER. University of America Press.

Gillespie, Michael Allen. 1995. NIHILISM BEFORE NIETZSCHE. University of Chicago Press.

Gillespie, Michael Allen. 2008. THE THEOLOGICAL ORIGINS OF MODERNITY. University of Chicago Press.

Goldblatt, Stephen. 2012. THE SWERVE: HOW THE WORLD BECAME MODERN. W.W. Norton.

González Fernández, Antonio. 2012. GOD'S REIGN AND THE END OF EMPIRES Convivium Press,2012.

Goodin, David K. 2005. "Understanding Humankind's Role in Creation: Alternative Exegesis on the Hebrew Word *Kabash* and the Command to Subdue the Earth," STUDIES IN SCIENCE AND THEOLOGY, Vol. 10: STREAMS OF WISDOM? SCIENCE, THEOLOGY, AND CULTURAL DYNAMICS, ed. Hubert Meisinger, William B. Drees, and Zbigniew Liana Lund. Sweden: Lund University Press, pp. 293-311.

Guardini, Romero. 1965. DAS ENDE DER NEUZEIT, 9ᵀᴴ edition. Wŭrtzburg. (Original published 1950.)

Guardini, Romero. 2001. THE END OF THE MODERN WORLD. ISI Books.

Gutiérrez, Gustavo. 1993. LAS CASAS: IN SEARCH OF THE POOR OF JESUS CHRIST. Trans. Robert R. Barr. Orbis Books.

Harvey, David. 2007. A BRIEF HISTORY OF NEOLIBERALISM. Oxford University Press.

Holland, Joe & Peter Henriot. 1983. SOCIAL ANALYSIS: LINKING FAITH AND JUSTICE. Revised and Enlarged Edition. Orbis Books.

Holland, Joe & Anne Barsanti. 1987. AMERICAN AND CATHOLIC: THE NEW DEBATE. Pillar Books.

Holland, Joe. 1979. FLAG, FAMILY, FAITH: ROOTING THE LEFT IN EVERYDAY EXPERIENCE. New Patriot Alliance.

Holland, Joe. 1989. CREATIVE COMMUNION: TOWARD A SPIRITUALITY OF WORK. Paulist Press.

Holland, Joe. 2003. MODERN CATHOLIC SOCIAL TEACHING: THE POPES CONFRONT THE INDUSTRIAL AGE 1740-1958. Paulist Press.

Holland, Joe. 2012. 100 YEARS OF CATHOLIC SOCIAL TEACHING DEFENDING WORKERS AND THEIR UNIONS. Pacem in Terris Press.

Holland, Joe. 2012. PACEM IN TERRIS: SUMMARY & COMMENTARY FOR THE 50ᵗʰ ANNIVERSARY OF THE FAMOUS ENCYCLICAL LETTER OF POPE JOHN XXIII ON WORLD PEACE. Pacem in Terris Press.

Holland, Joe. 2012. "The Crisis of Family and Unions in Late Modern Capitalism." JOURNAL OF CATHOLIC SOCIAL THOUGHT" Vol. 9, Issue 1, 43-58.

Holland, Joe. 2015. "See-Judge-Act: A Praxis Method for Catholic Practical Theology," Keynote address to Iannone Conference II, St. Thomas University School of Theology & Ministry, Miami Gardens, Florida, 2 May.

Holland, Joe. 2016. PETER MAURIN'S ECOLOGICAL LAY NEW MONASTICISM: A CATHOLIC GREEN REVOLUTION DEVELOPING RURAL ECOVILLAGES, URBAN HOUSES OF HOSPITALITY, & ECO-UNIVERSITIES FOR A NEW CIVILIZATION. Pacem in Terris Press.

Hopkins, Gerard Manley. 1985. GERARD MANLEY HOPKINS: POEMS AND PROSE Penguin Classics. (Written in 1887.)

Humphrey, Nicholas. A HISTORY OF THE MIND Simon & Schuster, 1992.

Institute for Research. 1983. NEW BEGINNINGS, RELIGIOUS LIFE EVOLVES. Lumen Vitae.

Jackson, Hildur & Karen Svensson. 2002. ECOVILLAGE LIVING: RESTORING THE EARTH AND HER PEOPLE. UIT Cambridge.

Jenkins, Willis. 2008. ECOLOGIES OF GRACE: ENVIRONMENTAL ETHICS AND CHRISTIAN THEOLOGY. Oxford University Press.

John Paul II, Saint. 1995. EVANGELIUM VITAE. Papal encyclical letter. *http://w2.vatican.va/content/john-paul-ii/en/encyclicals/documents/hf_jp-ii_enc_25031995_evangelium-vitae.html.* Accessed 2015-07-01.

John Paul II, Saint. 2003. MESSAGE ON CHRISTIAN HUMANISM IN THE THIRD MIL-LENNIUM. *https://w2.vatican.va/content/john-paul-ii/en /speeches/2003/september/documents/hf_jp-ii_spe_20030929_congresso-tomista.html.* Accessed 2016-07-15.

John XXIII, Saint. PACEM IN TERRIS, 1963. Papal encyclical letter. *http://w2.vatican.va/content/john-xxiii/en/encyclicals/documents/hf_j-xxiii_enc_11041963_pacem.htm.* Accessed 2015-07-01.

Kaser, Tim. 2002. THE HIGH PRICE OF MATERIALISM. MIT Press.

Kaufman, Walter. 2013. NIETZSCHE: PHILOSOPHER, PSYCHOLOGIST, ANTICHRIST. Princeton Classics, Princeton University Press. Original published 1950.

Klein, Naomi. 2008. THE SHOCK DOCTRINE: THE RISE OF DISASTER CAPITALISM. Picador.

Klein, Naomi. 2014. THIS CHANGES EVERYTHING: CAPITALISM VS. THE CLIMATE. Simon & Schuster.

Kolbert, Elisabeth. 2015. THE SIXTH EXTINCTION: AN UNNATURAL HISTORY. Reprint Edition. Picador.

Kuhn, Thomas. 2015. THE STRUCTURE OF SCIENTIFIC REVOLUTIONS: FIFTIETH ANNIVERSARY EDITION. Fourth Edition. University of Chicago Press. Original published 1962.

Kureethadam, Joshtrom. 2014. CREATION IN CRISIS: SCIENCE, THEOLOGY, AND ETHICS. Orbis Books.

Lanz, Tobias Lanz. 2003. FLEE TO THE FIELDS: THE FOUNDING OF THE CATHOLIC LAND MOVEMENT. IHS Press.

Lea, Henry C. 2003. HISTORY OF SACERDOTAL CELIBACY IN THE CHRISTIAN CHURCH. Kessinger Publishing. (Original published 1867.)

Leddy, Mary Jo. "1989. Beyond the Liberal Model of Religious Life," THE WAY. Summer.

Leddy, Mary Jo. 1990. REWEAVING RELIGIOUS LIFE: BEYOND THE LIBERAL MODEL. Twenty Third Publications.

Lovejoy, Arthur O. 1936. THE GREAT CHAIN OF BEING: A STUDY OF THE HISTORY OF AN IDEA. Harvard University Press.

Macintyre, Alasdair. 2007. AFTER VIRTUE: A STUDY OF MORAL THEORY. Third Edition. University of Notre Dame Press.

Macpherson, C. B. (2011) THE POLITICAL PROCESS OF POLITICAL INDIVIDUALISM: HOBBES TO LOCKE. Oxford University Press Reprint Edition.

Markoff, John. 2015 MACHINES OF LOVING GRACE: THE QUEST FOR COMMON GROUND BETWEEN HUMANS AND ROBOTS. Harper Collins.

Maurin, Peter. 2003. EASY ESSAYS. Catholic Worker Reprint. Wipf and Stock Publishers.

McGrath, Alister. 2002. THE REENCHANTMENT OF NATURE: THE DENIAL OF RELIGION. Doubleday/Galilee, 2002.

McNabb, Vincent. 2003. THE CHURCH AND THE LAND. IHS Press. (Original published 1925.)

Menn, Stephen. 2003. DESCARTES AND AUGUSTINE Cambridge University Press.

Merchant, Carolyn. 1990. THE DEATH OF NATURE: WOMEN, ECOLOGY, AND THE SCIENTIFIC REVOLUTION. Reprint Edition. HarperOne. (Original published 1983.)

Merchant, Carolyn. 2006. "The Scientific Revolution and *The Death of Nature*." ISIS, 97:513-533.

Meyer, John P. 1991. A MARGINAL JEW: RETHINKING THE HISTORICAL JESUS, THE ROOTS OF THE PROBLEM. Volume I. Doubleday.

Mollenkott, Virginia Ramey. 1987. THE DIVINE FEMININE: THE BIBLICAL IMAGERY OF GOD AS FEMALE. Crossroad.

Morewood, Michael. 2004. PRAYING A NEW STORY Orbis.

Munkelt, Richard A. 2017. "Religious Evolution and Revolution in the Triumph of *Homo Economicus*." In John C. Rao, Editor, LUTHER AND HIS PROGENY: 500 YEARS OF PROTESTANTISM & ITS CONSEQUENCES FOR CHURCH, STATE, AND SOCIETY (Angelico Press, 2017), pp. 143-174.

Nader, Ralph. 2012. THE SEVENTEEN SOLUTIONS: BOLD IDEAS FOR OUR AMERICAN FUTURE. Harper.

Nagel, Thomas. 2012. MIND & COSMOS: WHY THE MATERIALIST NEO-DARWINIAN CONCEPTION OF NATURE IS ALMOST CERTAINLY FALSE. Oxford University Press.

No Author Listed. "Peter Maurin" WIKIPEDIA, at: *https://en.wikipedia.org/wiki/Peter_Maurin*. Accessed 2016-11-18.

Noble, David. 1993, A WORLD WITHOUT WOMEN: THE CLERICAL ORIGIN OF WESTERN SCIENCE. Oxford University Press.

Orestes, Naomi & Erik M. Conway. 2014. THE COLLAPSE OF WESTERN CIVILIZATION. Columbia University Press.

Orren, Karen. 1992. BELATED FEUDALISM: LABOR, THE LAW, AND LIBERAL DEVELOPMENT IN THE UNITED STATE Cambridge University Press.

Oxfam. 2016. AN ECONOMY FOR THE 1%: HOW PRIVILEGE AND POWER IN THE ECON-
OMY DRIVE EXTREME INEQUALITY AND HOW THIS CAN BE STOPPED.
https://www.oxfam.org/en/research/economy-1. Accessed 2016-01-19.

Parker, Rebecca Ann & Rita Nakashima Brock. 2009. SAVING PARADISE: HOW
CHRISTIANITY TRADED LOVE OF THIS WORLD FOR EMPIRE AND CRUCIFIXION.
Beacon Press.

Pew Research Center / Religion & Public Life. 2009a.THE RELIGIOUS DIMENSIONS
OF THE TORTURE DEBATE. *http://www.pewforum.org/2009/04/29/the-religious-
dimensions-of-the-torture-debate.* Accessed 2016-07-15.

Pew Research Center / Religion & Public Life. THE TORTURE DEBATE: A CLOSER
LOOK. 2009b. *http://www.pewforum.org/2009/04/29/the-religious-dimensions-of-
the-torture-debate.* Accessed 2016-07-15.

Pius XI, Pope. QUADRAGESIMO ANNO,1931 papal encyclical letter, at:
*https://w2.vatican.va/content/pius-xi/en/encyclicals/documents/hf_p-
xi_enc_19310515_quadragesimo-anno.html.*

Polanyi, Karl. 1944. THE GREAT TRANSFORMATION. Farrer & Rinehart.

Rao, John C., Editor. 2017. LUTHER AND HIS PROGENY: 500 YEARS OF
PROTESTANTISM & ITS CONSEQUENCES FOR CHURCH, STATE, AND SOCIETY. Angelico Press, 2017.

Robin, Corey. 2004. FEAR: THE HISTORY OF A POLITICAL IDEA. Oxford University
Press.

Robin, Corey. 2011. THE REACTIONARY MIND: CONSERVATISM FROM EDMUND
BURKE TO SARAH PALIN. Oxford University Press.

Robin, Corey. 2013. "Nietzsche, Hayek, and the Austrians."
*http://crookedtimber.org/2013/06/25/nietzsche-hayek-and-the-austrians-a-reply-
to-my-critics.* Accessed 2015-07-01.

Robin, Corey. 2015. "Nietzsche's Marginal Children: On Friedrich Hayek," THE
NATION, 05-07. *http://www.thenation.com/article/nietzsches-marginal-children-
friedrich-hayek/.* Accessed 2015-07-01.

Rodriguez-Picavea, Enrique. 2008. LOS MONJES GUERREROS EN LOS REINOS
HISPÁNICOS: LAS ORDENES MILITA RES EN LA PENÍNSULA IBÉRICA DURANTE LA
EDAD MEDIA. La Esfera de los Libros.

Rubenstein, Richard E. 2004. ARISTOTLE'S CHILDREN: HOW CHRISTIANS, MUSLIMS,
AND JEWS REDISCOVERED ANCIENT WISDOM AND ILLUMINATED THE MIDDLE
AGES. Harvest Books.

Rubenstein, Richard. 1984. THE AGE OF TRIAGE Beacon Press.

Ryle, Gilbert Ryle. 2009. THE CONCEPT OF MIND, Sixtieth Anniversary Edition. Routledge. Original published 1949.

Saint John of the Cross. 2003. DARK NIGHT OF THE SOUL. Dover Thrift Editions. Original written in sixteenth century.

Saint Thomas Aquinas. 1981. SUMMA THEOLOGICA. Christian Classics. Original written in thirteenth century.

Schaefer, Jame. 2009. THEOLOGICAL FOUNDATIONS FOR ENVIRONMENTAL ETHICS: RECONSTRUCTING PATRISTIC & MEDIEVAL CONCEPTS. Georgetown University Press.

Schaupp, Joan. 1975. WOMAN IMAGE OF THE HOLY SPIRIT. Dimension Books.

Schuck, Michael. 1991. THAT THEY ALL MAY BE ONE: THE SOCIAL TEACHING OF THE PAPAL ENCYCLICALS 1740-1989. Georgetown University Press.

Seung, T.K. 1994. KANT'S PLATONIC REVOLUTION IN MORAL AND POLITICAL PHILOSOPHY. Johns Hopkins University Press.

Sheehan, Arthur. 1943. "Interview with Peter Maurin." CATHOLIC WORKER, July, May, June, and July-August.

Sibley, Angus. 2013. THE "POISONED SPRING" OF ECONOMIC LIBERTARIANISM: MENGER, MISES, HAYEK, ROTHBARD: A CRITIQUE FROM CATHOLIC SOCIAL TEACHING OF THE 'AUSTRIAN SCHOOL' OF ECONOMICS. Pax Romana.

Sibley, Angus. 2015. CATHOLIC ECONOMICS: ALTERNATIVES TO THE JUNGLE. Liturgical Press.

Smith, Christian, with Kari Christoffersen, Hilary Davidson, & Patricia Snell Herzog. 2011. LOST IN TRANSITION: THE DARK SIDE OF EMERGING ADULTHOOD. Oxford University Press.

Snyder, T. Richard. 2001. THE PROTESTANT ETHIC AND THE SPIRIT OF PUNISHMENT. W. B. Eerdmans.

Sorrell, Roger D. 1988. ST. FRANCIS OF ASSISI AND NATURE: TRADITION AND INNOVATION IN WESTERN CHRISTIAN ATTITUDES TOWARD THE ENVIRONMENT Oxford University Press.

Sperry, Earl Evelyn. 1905. AN OUTLINE OF THE HISTORY OF CLERICAL CELIBACY IN WESTERN EUROPE TO THE COUNCIL OF TRENT. Doctoral Dissertation for Columbia University.

Spretnak, Charlene. 2011. RELATIONAL REALITY: NEW DISCOVERIES OF RELATEDNESS THAT ARE TRANSFORMING THE MODERN WORLD. Green Horizon Books.

Spretnak, Charlene. RESURGENCE OF THE REAL: BODY, NATURE, AND PLACE IN A HYPER-MODERN WORLD. Routledge.

Spretnak, Charlene. STATES OF GRACE: THE RECOVERY OF MEANING IN A POST-MODERN AGE. Harper San Francisco.

Spretnak, Charlene. THE SPIRITUAL DIMENSION OF GREEN POLITICS. Bear & Company.

Sullivan, Rev. Patrick Sullivan.2014. FIVE GIANTS IN THE BISHOP'S SOCIAL ACTION DEPARTMENT AMONG MORE THAN FOUR HUNDRED U.S CATHOLIC LABOR PRIESTS. Volume One, CATHOLIC LABOR PRIESTS IN THE UNITED STATES: A 20TH CENTURY STORY OF SOLIDARITY. Pacem in Terris Press.

Teresa of Avila. 2007. THE INTERIOR CASTLE. Dover Thrift Edition. Original published in sixteenth century.

Toffler, Alvin. 1984. THE THIRD WAVE Bantam.

Tornelli, Andrea & Giacomo Galeazzi. 2015. THIS ECONOMY KILLS: POPE FRANCIS ON CAPITALISM AND SOCIAL JUSTICE. Liturgical Press.

Trevor, Meriol. 2000. POPE JOHN BLESSED JOHN XXII. Gracewing.

Tuana, Nancy. 1992. WOMAN AND THE HISTORY OF PHILOSOPHY. Paragon House.

Tucker, Mary Evelyn, & John Grimm, eds. 2016. LIVING COSMOLOGY: CHRISTIAN RESPONSES TO THE JOURNEY OF THE UNIVERSE. Orbis Books.

Vendler, Zeno.1989. "Descartes' Exercises," CANADIAN JOURNAL OF PHILOSOPHY. Volume 9, Number 2, pp. 193-224.

Weil, Simone. 1952. THE NEED FOR ROOTS: A DECLARATION OF DUTIES TOWARD MANKIND. Translated by Arthur Wills. Preface by T.S. Eliot. Routledge Kegan.

Weiss, Monica. 2016. THOMAS MERTON AND THE CELTS: A NEW WORLD OPENING UP. Pickwick.

Whitehead, Alfred North. 1926. SCIENCE AND THE MODERN WORLD. Cambridge University Press.

Wilson, Catherine. EPICUREANISM: A VERY BRIEF INTRODUCTION Oxford University Press, 2016.

Wilson, Edward O. 2007. THE CREATION: AN APPEAL TO SAVE LIFE ON EARTH. W.W. Norton.

Wojtyla, Karol. 1979. SIGN OF CONTRADICTION. Seabury.

OTHER BOOKS
FROM PACEM IN TERRIS PRESS

THOMAS BERRY IN ITALY
Reflections on Spirituality & Sustainability
Elisabeth M. Ferrero, Editor, 2016

PETER MAURIN'S
ECOLOGICAL LAY NEW MONASTICISM
*A Catholic Green Revolution Developing
Rural Ecovillages, Urban Houses of Hospitality,
& Eco-Universities for a New Civilization*
Joe Holland, 2015

PROTECTION OF RELIGIOUS MINORITIES
*A Symposium Organized by Pax Romana at the United Nations
and the United Nations Alliance of Civilizations*
Dean Elizabeth F. Defeis & Peter F. O'Connor, Editors, 2015

CATHOLIC LABOR PRIESTS
*Five Giants in the United States Catholic Bishops Social Action Department
Volume I of US Labor Priests During the 20th Century*
Patrick Sullivan, 2014

BOTTOM ELEPHANTS
*Catholic Sexual Ethics & Pastoral Practice in Africa:
The Challenge of Women Living within Patriarchy
& Threatened by HIV-Positive Husbands*
Daniel Ude Asue, 2014

CATHOLIC SOCIAL TEACHING & UNIONS
IN CATHOLIC PRIMARY & SECONDARY SCHOOLS
The Clash between Theory & Practice within the United States
Walter "Bob" Baker, 2014

SPIRITUAL PATHS TO
A GLOBAL & ECOLOGICAL CIVILIZATION
Reading the Signs of the Times with Buddhists, Christians, & Muslims
John Raymaker & Gerald Grudzen, with Joe Holland, 2013

PACEM IN TERRIS
*Its Continuing Relevance for the Twenty-First Century
(Papers from the 50th Anniversary Conference at the United Nations)*
Josef Klee & Francis Dubois, Editors, 2013

PACEM IN TERRIS
Summary & Commentary for the Famous Encyclical Letter
of Pope John XXIII on World Peace
Joe Holland, 2012

100 YEARS OF CATHOLIC SOCIAL TEACHING
DEFENDING WORKERS & THEIR UNIONS
Summaries & Commentaries for Five Landmark Papal Encyclicals
Joe Holland, 2012

HUMANITY'S AFRICAN ROOTS
Remembering the Ancestors' Wisdom
Joe Holland, 2012

THE "POISONED SPRING" OF ECONOMIC LIBERTARIANISM
Menger, Mises, Hayek, Rothbard: A Critique from
Catholic Social Teaching of the Austrian School of Economics
Pax Romana / Cmica-usa
Angus Sibley, 2011

BEYOND THE DEATH PENALTY
The Development in Catholic Social Teaching
Florida Council of Catholic Scholarship
D. Michael McCarron & Joe Holland, Editors, 2007

THE NEW DIALOGUE OF CIVILIZATIONS
A Contribution from Pax Romana
International Catholic Movement for Intellectual & Cultural Affairs
Pax Romana / Cmica-usa
Roza Pati & Joe Holland, Editors, 2002

Other Books By Joe Holland

In Addition to books published by Pacem in Terris Press

MODERN CATHOLIC SOCIAL TEACHING 1740-1958
The Popes Confront the Industrial Age
Paulist Press, 2003

"THE EARTH CHARTER"
A Study Book of Reflection for Action
Co-Author Elisabeth Ferrero
Redwoods Press, 2002
(also Italian & Portuguese versions)

VARIETIES OF POSTMODERN THEOLOGY
Co-Editors David Griffin & William Beardslee,
State University of New York Press, 1989

CREATIVE COMMUNION
Toward a Spirituality of Work
Paulist Press, 1989

AMERICAN AND CATHOLIC
The New Debate
Co-Editor Anne Barsanti
Pillar Books, 1988

VOCATION AND MISSION OF THE LAITY
Co-Author Robert Maxwell
Pillar Books, 1986

SOCIAL ANALYSIS
Linking Faith and Justice
Co-Author Peter J. Henriot SJ
Orbis Books, 1980 & 1983

THE AMERICAN JOURNEY
A Theology in the Americas Working Paper
IDOC, 1976

This book and other books from Pacem in Terris Press
are available at:

www.amazon.com/books

Made in the USA
Monee, IL
16 October 2020

45349113R00187